Praise for Grant R. Jeffrey's
Best-Selling Books

"Grant Jeffrey has written an extraordinary book, *The Signature of God*, that provides astonishing proof that the Bible was inspired by God. Grant is recognized as the leading researcher in Bible prophecy today."
> —HAL LINDSEY, Hal Lindsey Ministries

"*The Next World War* is a must-read for anyone who cares about what is next on God's prophetic calendar."
> —DR. TIM LAHAYE, coauthor of the best-selling Left
> Behind series

"*The Prophecy Study Bible* is a phenomenal publishing effort by one of America's premier prophecy experts. Comprehensive, understandable, and powerful. A great work!"
> —DR. ED HINDSON, distinguished professor of religion,
> Liberty University

"*The Prophecy Study Bible* is the most comprehensive, contemporary, and in-depth study of the most relevant prophecies in the Bible. A must addition to every serious student of the Word of God."
> —DR. CHUCK MISSLER, Koinonia House Ministries

"*Prince of Darkness* was written by acclaimed Bible prophecy teacher Grant R. Jeffrey. This unequaled masterpiece is the result of thirty years of intense research. It will stir you and inspire you as few books have.... It is extraordinarily researched and fascinatingly presented.... This is the best book I have ever read on this subject."
> —JACK VAN IMPE, president of Jack Van Impe Ministries
> International

Also by Grant R. Jeffrey

Apocalypse
Armageddon
By Dawn's Early Light
Countdown to the Apocalypse
Creation
Final Warning
Flee the Darkness
The Handwriting of God
Heaven
Jesus: The Great Debate
Journey into Eternity
Messiah
Millennium Meltdown
The Mysterious Bible Codes
The New Temple and the Second Coming
The Next World War
Prince of Darkness
Prophecy Marked Reference Study Bible
Shadow Government
Spear of Tyranny
Triumphant Return
Unveiling Mysteries of the Bible
War on Terror

The SIGNATURE of GOD

REVISED EDITION

Conclusive Proof That
EVERY TEACHING,
EVERY COMMAND,
EVERY PROMISE
in the Bible Is True

GRANT R. JEFFREY

WATERBROOK

THE SIGNATURE OF GOD

All Scripture quotations, unless otherwise indicated, are taken from the King James Version. Scripture quotations marked (AMP) are taken from The Amplified® Bible. Copyright © 1954, 1958, 1962, 1964, 1965, 1987 by The Lockman Foundation. Used by permission. (www.Lockman.org).

Italics in Scripture quotations reflect the author's added emphasis.

Trade Paperback ISBN 978-0-307-44484-4
eBook ISBN 978-0-307-45905-3

Published in the United States by WaterBrook, an imprint of the Crown Publishing Group, a division of Penguin Random House LLC, New York.

WATERBROOK® and its deer colophon are registered trademarks of Penguin Random House LLC.

Library of Congress Cataloging-in-Publication Data
Jeffrey, Grant R.
    The signature of God : conclusive proof that every teaching, every command, every promise in the Bible is true / Grant R. Jeffrey. — 3rd ed.
        p. cm.
    Includes bibliographical references.
    ISBN 978-0-307-44484-4 — ISBN 978-0-307-45905-3 (electronic)
    1. Apologetics. 2. Eschatology. 3. Bible science. I. Title.
    BS480.J44 2010

2020 — Third Edition

147842142

*The Bible is the greatest of all the books ever penned by men;
to study it diligently is the most worthy of all possible
pursuits; to clearly understand what the Lord is saying to us
through its pages is truly the most noble and the highest of
my goals. The application to my heart, mind, and spirit of
the truths of the Word of God through the Holy Spirit's gift
of understanding and my subsequent obedience to that
revelation is my supreme purpose and duty.*

—Author unknown. These words were found
in an inscription in an old Bible in England.

Contents

Preface

Is there a God? Does my life have any meaning, or does everything in the universe happen solely by random chance? How can I find the real truth about life and death? What will happen to me when I die? Is the Bible truly the "inspired" Word of God, or is it just the philosophical writings of a group of men in ancient times?

These questions occur to every one of us at some point in our lives. Our answers to these questions are vitally important because the answers will affect our goals, our relationships, our peace of mind, and, ultimately, our eternal destiny. The Bible claims to be the inspired Word of God and declares repeatedly that its message is absolutely true—without any error. Therefore, it is of utmost importance that each one of us determines for ourselves whether the Bible is truly the Word of God.

If the Bible is true and God does exist, then we will some-day stand before almighty God to be judged by Him as to our eternal destiny—either heaven or hell. The Scriptures tell us that, following death, we will give an account to God about how we responded to Jesus Christ's offer of salvation through His death on the cross. On the other hand, if the Bible is not true and God does not exist, then we are free to live as we please. If God does not exist, then we will experience the consequences of our choices solely in this world. The philosophy of "eat, drink, and be merry, for tomorrow we die" is a logical response if there is no God and the universe has no purpose. If there is no God, then we are free to live as we please.

However, the answer to the question "Is the Bible truly the Word of God?" is of the greatest possible importance to every person, whether we admit it or not. Our fundamental beliefs determine our decisions and the ultimate course of our lives. If we change our deeply held beliefs, we will inevitably change our actions, our decisions, and the direction of our lives. So if you question the truth and the inspiration of the Bible, it is well worth your time to examine that belief in light of the best evidence regarding the Scriptures. If you question whether the Bible is the authoritative, inspired, absolutely true Word of God, then by all means you need to consider all the evidence.

But is it really possible to determine the truth about God and the Bible? I believe it is, and I have good reason to hold that belief. This book, *The Signature of God*, will examine exceptional scientific, medical, historical, and prophetic discoveries that *prove* that the Bible is authoritative and inspired by God. Some people are content to follow a blind faith based on the religious convictions of others. However, many of us want to examine these matters for ourselves to determine the answers. I wrote *The Signature of God* so that all people—skeptics, new Christians, agnostics, those with serious doubts and questions, and committed Christians who want to learn the facts that back up their faith—can study the evidence that verifies the Bible's claims about its power, authority, and reliability.

How Would God Reveal Himself to Humanity?

Let's conduct an experiment to examine the question of how God would reveal Himself to humanity if He decided to make Himself known. After creating the universe and everything in it—including humanity—how would God introduce Himself to make Himself known and convey His instructions? He could choose to speak to every single one of the billions of humans living in every generation, but that would be impractical. On the other hand, God could choose a number of men living in various generations over a period of centuries and inspire those men to record in writing His instructions for the rest of humanity. Obviously, the second option is the most practical.

However, there is another problem that God would face in revealing His will and instructions to us. How would He prove that the Bible was His legitimate revelation? There are many religious texts that claim to convey the message of God. The challenge would be to find a method to differentiate the genuine, inspired Scriptures from other religious books produced by religious philosophers over the centuries. I believe the solution is obvious: God would authenticate His own revelation by writing His "signature" on the pages of His Scriptures. This unmistakable "signature of God" would consist of evidence, prophetic knowledge, and phenomena found in the text that no unaided human could possibly have written. In other words, the genuine Scriptures would contain supernatural evidence within its text that no one, apart from a divine intelligence, could possibly create.

I believe that God left no room for doubt regarding the truth and reliability of His written Word. In fact, the Scriptures contain a direct statement from God that He provided precisely this type of supernatural evidence. Twenty-five centuries ago, the prophet Isaiah recorded this amazing declaration from God: "Remember the former things of old: for I am God, and there is none else; I am God, and there is none like me, declaring the end from the beginning, and from ancient times the things that are not yet done, saying, My counsel shall stand, and I will do all my pleasure" (Isaiah 46:9–10).

In this passage God declared that fulfilled prophecy proves that the Scriptures are inspired by the Lord. It is impossible for any human, or even Satan, to predict future events with precise accuracy. (The writers of other religious books know they cannot accurately predict the future, so they refrain from exposing themselves to ridicule by avoiding detailed prophecies that will prove to be false. Instead, they issue vague predictions that can easily be recast and reinterpreted later on to fit whatever might happen in the world.) God is the only One who knows the future as well as the past.

My thesis in *The Signature of God* is that the Bible contains fascinating evidence that absolutely authenticates that the Scriptures are the inspired and authoritative Word of God. The evidence from hundreds of fulfilled prophecies regarding the life and death of Jesus Christ provides the strongest and most obvious proof of the Bible's divine inspiration. However, there are a number of other intriguing prophecies and undeniable facts that prove that only God could have inspired the ancient writers to record His message in the Scriptures. We will examine that evidence in the chapters that follow.

Evidence That the Bible Is a Genuine Revelation from God

How would God authenticate His message so that skeptical men and women could be assured that the Scriptures were not simply the speculations of religious philosophers? How would the Lord identify His presence, His divine nature, and His commands—and provide proof that this written communication was truly from Him? There are a number of ways He would confirm His message to us:

1. The written revelation of God's nature and commands was progressively revealed to a series of carefully chosen men over a period of sixteen centuries. The recipients were closely connected by race and faith to facilitate their gathering, assembling, preserving, and distributing God's written revelation. The Lord chose the Jewish people, a defined race that has maintained its identity over the centuries, as the faithful guardian of His written revelations.
2. Although God's divine communications were transmitted by inspiration to a variety of individuals, it was recorded in a permanent written form capable of being examined and read by the writers' contemporaries as well as all generations that would follow.
3. These divine communications were occasionally accompanied by miracles to authenticate their divine origin.
4. This written revelation from God contains *internal evidence* that proves that God is the ultimate Author. The

Bible includes information that could not have been written by limited humans. This includes scientific and medical knowledge that was not discovered or widely known until centuries following the time when the biblical writers recorded it in the Scriptures.

5. The Bible contains thousands of detailed prophecies concerning events that were precisely fulfilled many years after the predictions were made. Their fulfillment proves that God inspired the Bible. No one but God can accurately prophesy future events in such detail and never be wrong.

6. God inspired the biblical writers to record His profound wisdom and truth that transcend all human wisdom.

7. God's Holy Spirit supernaturally transforms the lives of millions who commit themselves to the Bible's revelation. There is undeniable supernatural power in the written Word of God.

8. The Bible's primary purpose is to reveal God's plan of salvation. However, whenever Scripture deals with history, archaeology, nature, medicine, or science, it reveals advanced knowledge that is true and verifiable. Such biblical statements were first recorded far in advance of the knowledge available during the time of the original human writer.

9. The Bible's wisdom, knowledge, and ethics proclaim its supernatural origin to anyone who is seeking answers to life's most profound questions. The wisest people of all cultures and times are committed to its truths.

10. The Scriptures contain advanced medical and sanitation knowledge that was thousands of years ahead of its time. This medical knowledge has saved countless lives. In addition, its lifesaving commands still prove their worth in our day.

11. A careful examination of the names and numbers in the Bible's text reveals special mathematical designs and codes that are so complex that even a supercomputer could not have produced these features. Many of the designs occur throughout a series of biblical

books recorded by different authors over a span of several centuries. There is no human explanation for this phenomenon except for the Bible's divine inspiration.

12. In the 1990s, Jewish computer scientists in Israel and the United States discovered a series of remarkable Hebrew words encoded at equally spaced intervals hidden within the Hebrew text of the first five books of the Bible, the Torah. Additional researchers later proved that this phenomenon, known as Equidistant Letter Sequence (ELS), existed throughout the Old Testament Hebrew text. (It is not limited to the Torah.) God inspired the biblical writers to unconsciously use specific words and letters to produce the most intriguing and incredibly complicated mathematical and letter codes ever found. These features were hidden from the eyes of everyone until the development of mathematical and supercomputer analysis. These complex patterns constitute a powerful argument for the divine inspiration of the Bible. And while these intricate patterns exist in the Hebrew text of the Old Testament, none of the apocryphal Hebrew texts, such as 1 Maccabees, displays this pattern. Further, researchers have never found clusters of complex codes in any other Hebrew religious or secular texts, such as the Talmud. This incredible phenomenon, referred to as the Bible Codes, provides compelling evidence that the Author of the inspired Scriptures was God.

13. In human literature, authors naturally try to present themselves in the best light possible. However, the Bible presents the major human figures in Scripture in both victory and defeat, in righteousness and sinfulness, and in obedience and rebellion. The Bible often portrays even the leading biblical heroes as weak, afraid, and lacking in wisdom. Additionally, biblical revelation contains many intricate details and unintended coincidences in its stories that, while easily overlooked, prove the overall truthfulness of the historical accounts.

14. Although written by forty-four men over a span of six-teen centuries, the complete text of the Bible reveals a coherent unity and progressive revelation from start to finish—from Genesis to Revelation. The story that is told in the Bible consistently reveals and develops God's plan of redemption for humanity. The books of the Old Testament continuously point to the coming of a Messiah-King to redeem His people. (We know that Messiah to be Jesus of Nazareth, God's Son.) The New Testament displays the fulfillment of these divine prophecies in the life, death, and resurrection of Jesus. The unity of theology and the focus on the message of redemption throughout the Bible argue strongly that a single Author created this text. How else would forty-four writers over sixteen centuries write sixty-six different books that all tell the same story?

Three thousand years ago King David, the great king of Israel, wrote these words revealing the nature of God's inspired Word:

> The law of the LORD is perfect, converting the soul: the testimony of the LORD is sure, making wise the simple. The statutes of the LORD are right, rejoicing the heart: the commandment of the LORD is pure, enlightening the eyes. The fear of the LORD is clean, enduring for ever: the judgments of the LORD are true and righteous altogether. More to be desired are they than gold, yea, than much fine gold: sweeter also than honey and the honeycomb. Moreover by them is thy servant warned: and in keeping of them there is great reward. (Psalm 19:7–11)

The Divine Inspiration of Scripture

The early Christians, Jewish scribes, and generations of Christian believers shared an unshakable conviction that the Scriptures contain the infallible, inspired, and authoritative words of God. The Bible itself claims that "all scripture is given by inspiration of God, and is profitable for doctrine, for reproof, for correction, for instruction in righteousness" (2 Timothy 3:16). The Greek word that is translated "inspired" literally means "God-breathed," indicating the Lord's direct supervision of the writing by the biblical writers. The Bible claims that its words were not written by men in an ordinary manner, such as one might write a history book, a news article, poetry, or a letter to a friend. But instead, God inspired men to record His direct words. Just as God created only one sun to provide light to our planet, He gave us only one book, the Bible, to enlighten our world spiritually. And as we will see in a later chapter, *each word* of Scripture is essential.

Tragically, during the twentieth century, many pastors, professors, and laypeople lost their faith and confidence that the Bible is the inspired and reliable Word of God. Dr. Kennedy, a Regius Professor of Greek at Cambridge University in the early decades of the twentieth century, warned of the battle that was about to begin over the authority of the Bible. "The inspiration of Scriptures will be the last battle ground between the Church and the world," he stated. Unfortunately, many in our churches and seminaries abandoned this battlefield and accepted defeat at the hands of skeptics who attacked the truth, authority, and reliability of the Scriptures. The widespread rejection of the truthfulness of the Bible reveals the folly of people who "have forsaken me [God] the fountain of living waters, and hewed them out cisterns, broken cisterns" of vain philosophy (Jeremiah 2:13). The prophet Jeremiah spoke those words twenty-five centuries ago, and his prophecy was fulfilled in the last century.

The Bible declares in numerous passages that it is the inspired Word of God. The prophet Jeremiah declared, "Then the LORD put forth his hand, and touched my mouth. And the LORD said unto me, Behold, I have put my words in thy mouth" (Jeremiah 1:9).

God confirmed that He directly inspired the prophets to record His words and instructions, not just in a general sense, but "word for word." In the New Testament, the apostle Peter declared, "Knowing this first, that no prophecy of the scripture is of any private interpretation. For the prophecy came not in old time by the will of man: but holy men of God spake as they were moved by the Holy Ghost" (2 Peter 1:20–21). One of the strongest statements found in the Bible records the inspired words of

Jesus, who declared, "The scripture cannot be broken" (John 10:35). God's Son, the promised Messiah, on a number of occasions assured us of the absolute truth and authority of the Bible.

In this book we will carefully examine the overwhelming historical, medical, scientific, archaeological, mathematical, and other evidence that proves the inspiration and authenticity of the Bible. The evidence will establish the credibility and authority of the Scriptures for both nonbelievers and Christians, so that we all can know that the Bible is the only reliable foundation for faith in God's revelation.

Here are the areas in which the Scriptures can be tested to prove that the Bible is the written Word of God:

1. Ancient inscriptions and manuscripts that prove the historical accuracy of the Scriptures.
2. Little-known archaeological discoveries that provide overwhelming confirmation of the accuracy of the biblical accounts, including such references as the Tower of Babel and the Exodus of the Hebrews from Egypt.
3. Accurate scientific statements in the Bible that cannot be explained apart from God's inspiration. It is impossible that these statements could have been made by accident or by random chance.
4. The precise fulfillment of ancient prophecies in our generation.
5. The staggering phenomenon of hidden codes and mathematical patterns found in the text of the Bible. These could not have happened by chance, and neither could they have been produced by human intelligence.
6. Biblical "coincidences" that confirm the divine inspiration of the Scriptures.
7. The phenomenon of the transformed character and lives of the writers of the Bible.
8. The unprecedented influence of the Bible on the lives of individuals, the culture, and history of the Western world.

While many of the topics we will explore in this book are fascinating in and of themselves, their true value lies in their ability to confirm and illustrate the events, personalities, and statements of the Word of God. Alexander Knox once wrote about the relationship between human and sacred knowledge: "If in the rills which trickle down amidst these intellectual Alps and Apennines, I could discern no connection with that river which maketh glad the city of God, I own that I should look upon them with as little interest as upon the rocky fragments through which they passed."[1]

As a researcher and writer I feel a tremendous responsibility to carefully check the accuracy of every statement because of the exceptional importance of prophecy and scriptural truths. Those who write about the truths of the Scriptures are like the scribes of ancient Israel. The Scriptures declare that "every scribe which is instructed unto the kingdom of heaven is like unto a man that is an householder, which bringeth forth out of his treasure things new and old" (Matthew 13:52). When we as researchers, students of Scripture, and writers seek to explore the wonderful truths of the Bible, we also "bring forth out of his treasure things new and old" in our attempt to reveal the deeper truths of the Word of God. I take my work very seriously.

The Undeniable Accuracy of the Bible Manuscripts

Over the last four thousand years, Jewish scribes and, later, Christian scribes were very careful to correctly copy and transmit the original manuscripts of sacred Scripture without any significant error. The Jewish scribes who copied by hand the manuscripts of the Old Testament were called "Masoretic," derived from the Hebrew word for "wall" or "fence." Their extreme care in counting the letters of the Bible created a "fence around the Law" to defend the accuracy of the biblical text. For example, out of the 78,064 Hebrew letters that make up the book of Genesis, the scribes and sages were so precise that they were able to pinpoint the middle verse of Genesis, which is "And by thy sword shalt thou live, and shalt serve thy brother; and it shall come to pass when thou shalt have the dominion, that thou shalt break his yoke from off thy neck" (27:40). When a scribe completed his copy of the Scriptures, a master examiner would count every letter to confirm that there were no errors in the newly copied manuscript. If an error was found, the corrupted copy was destroyed to prevent it from ever being used as a master copy in the future.

As proof of the accuracy of this transmission of the biblical text through the centuries, consider the Masoretic and Yemenite translations of the Torah. More than one thousand years ago, Yemenite Jews were separated from their brother Jews in the Middle East and Europe. Despite separate transmissions and copying of their Torah manuscripts, a thousand years later *only 9 Hebrew letters,* out of some 304,805 letters in the Yemenite Torah manuscript, differ from the accepted Hebrew Masoretic text. A variation of only 9 letters out of more than 300,000 Hebrew letters amounts to only 0.00295 or 1/339th of 1 percent![2] And it is important to note that none of these 9 variant letters changes the meaning of a significant word in the Torah. This proves how exceptionally careful, even over a thousand-year period, Jewish scribes were in copying the manuscripts.

God preserved the original text of His Scriptures throughout the last thirty-five hundred years, enabling us to have confidence that we still possess the accurate text of the inspired Word of God. The prophet Isaiah declared that the Word of God is eternal: "The grass withereth, the flower fadeth: but the word of our God shall stand for ever" (Isaiah 40:8). In the New Testament, Jesus confirmed the indestructibility of His Word: "For verily I say unto you, Till heaven and earth pass, one jot or one tittle shall in no wise pass from the law, till all be fulfilled" (Matthew 5:18).

In the eighteenth century the famous English critic and conversationalist Dr. Samuel Johnson made this valuable suggestion: "Keep your friendships in repair." This is excellent advice in human relationships as well as in regard to our relationship to the Bible. Our personal relationship with the Word of God needs to be cared for just as much as our human friendships. We need to respect God's Word and handle it with love and care. We can enjoy the unchanging companionship of God expressed through His divine Word even when we are separated from friends by distance or death. While our experiences, possessions, and relationships constantly undergo change, we can return again and again to the unchanging Word of God as a solid foundation for our faith. The Bible will always be there to speak to our hearts with God's words of wisdom, comfort, and love. Such is the gift we have in God's eternal Word.

Unexpected Discoveries: Evidence of God

Archaeologists discovered more than one thousand items of jewelry and pottery in nine burial caves across the Hinnom Valley opposite the southern walls of the Old City of Jerusalem. The treasures included two silver charms bearing remarkable biblical inscriptions. The cave where the charms were found is about nine hundred yards south of where Solomon's Temple stood three thousand years ago. The items of jewelry were composed of thin pieces of pure silver rolled up like tiny scrolls, designed to be worn as charms around the neck. While part of the text was lost, the remaining portion revealed that the charms contained the oldest biblical inscription ever found. The remaining text recorded the priestly blessing from the book of Numbers: "The LORD bless thee, and keep thee: the LORD make his face shine upon thee, and be gracious unto thee: the LORD lift up his countenance upon thee, and give thee peace" (6:24–26).

I had the privilege of examining this inscription in the Israel Museum. This biblical text was inscribed more than twenty-six hundred years ago, in the seventh century before Christ. It predates by *more than four hundred years* the writing of most of the Dead Sea Scrolls.

The Bible records only one statement made by God to atheists and agnostics. God declares that those who deny His existence are fools: "The fool hath said in his heart, There is no God" (Psalm 14:1; 53:1). When I attended school, I used to engage in debates with atheists and agnostics about the existence of God. However, as I analyzed the underlying attitude of the people I debated, I realized that debates of this kind were futile. Now when I get into a discussion with an atheist or an agnostic, I simply respond as follows: "I will not debate you about whether God exists for the same reason that I would not debate someone about whether the world is round. I believe that those who claim, 'There is no God,' in the face of overwhelming evidence found throughout nature are either fools or liars. Any person who honestly believes that all of the marvelous complexity of this universe simply happened by chance is a fool. If he is not a fool, yet still claims to believe that this incredibly complex universe is a result of random chance, then I must conclude that he is not being honest. In either case it is clearly a waste of time to argue the obvious."

The wonders of creation reveal God's awesome creative power to anyone whose eyes are open to see the truth. God's providence reveals His wisdom; God's Law revealed in the Old Testament shows us His great justice; the four Gospels reveal His overwhelming love for humanity through the person of Jesus Christ. God has made sure that wherever we look, we can find evidence of His existence—if we are seriously looking for it.

The Supreme Value of the Bible

Sir Walter Scott (1771–1832) was the brilliant poet and author of more than sixty popular books. When he was finally approaching the moment of death, Scott asked his son-in-law and biographer, John G. Lockhart, to bring "the book" from his library. When Lockhart asked, "Which book, Sir Walter?" Scott answered, "There is only one book," pointing to the Holy Bible. In his deathbed conversation, Scott correctly assessed the supreme value of the Scriptures far above the other great books in his library, which included his own classics.

The most important event in history is the life, death, and resurrection of Jesus Christ. The most important fact in the universe is the reality of God and His revelation to us through His Word. The most important decision in the life of any person is the choice he or she must make in regard to personal faith in Jesus Christ.

Another great man, President Abraham Lincoln, wrote the following regarding the Bible in a "Reply to Loyal Colored People of Baltimore upon Presentation of a Bible": "It is the best gift God has given to man. All the good the Saviour gave to the world was communicated through this book."[3]

The Pony Express Bible
The history of the pony express forms a fascinating chapter in the history of the American West. Dedicated and resourceful riders carried the mail from St. Joseph, Missouri, over more than

nineteen hundred miles through dangerous Indian country to Sacramento, California. The pony express acquired five hundred of the strongest and fastest horses the company could find. Forty brave men rode in relays, with each man riding fifty miles to the next station. Using four relays per day, the pony express traveled as far as two hundred miles per day. A letter could be delivered over the nineteen-hundred-mile distance in only ten days.

To cut down on any unnecessary weight, riders would use the lightest saddles made, with small, flat leather bags holding the mail. Riders carried no rifles, and letters were written on very thin paper. (The postage rate was five dollars per ounce, equal to two hundred dollars per letter in today's currency.)

The managers of the pony express believed that the Scriptures were so important that they presented a full-size pony express Bible to each rider when he joined this unusual company. Despite their concern for reducing the weight of a rider's equipment, every rider carried a Bible. Further, every pony express rider took the following oath: "I do hereby swear before the great and living God that during my engagement with Russell, Majors and Waddell [the pony express management], I will under no circumstances use profane language, that I will drink no intoxicating liquors, that I will not quarrel or fight with other employees of the firm, and that in every respect I will conduct myself honestly, be faithful in my duties, and so direct all my acts as to win the confidence of my employers. So help me God."[4]

Stanley and Livingstone

The famous missionary and explorer David Livingstone disappeared during his trip into previously unexplored regions of central Africa. News from his expedition reported that Livingstone was sick and without supplies, and that he had been deserted by his native guides. Many in Europe gave Livingstone up as lost after more than a year with no additional news. However, a small group of supporters in London and the United States funded a rescue mission to save "Scotland's finest son." In 1869 the *New York Herald* outfitted reporter and explorer Henry M. Stanley to mount an expedition to find Livingstone in Africa.

When he commenced his journey, Stanley carried baggage

that included several cases containing seventy-three hardbound books. However, as he and his African carriers began to succumb to fatigue, Stanley began to abandon (or burn for fuel) his precious books. As the group continued through the jungle, Stanley's library dwindled in size until there was only one book left, his precious Bible.

With God's assistance Stanley finally found Livingstone and greeted him with the famous words, "Dr. Livingstone, I presume?" The explorers shared their deep faith in Jesus Christ. Livingstone told Stanley about the wonderful conversions of many African tribes to faith in Christ, although these tribes previously had engaged in cannibalism. When he returned from his extraordinary journey, Stanley reported that he had read his Bible three times from Genesis through Revelation during his long and arduous journey.

As you read *The Signature of God*, I hope you will experience the same thrill of discovery and wonder that I have felt as the Lord led me to carefully research the evidence for the inspiration of the Scriptures. I hope this book will enable many readers to restore their confidence in the Bible as God's inspired Word. God provided abundant, convincing proof through the evidence of His signature, which appears throughout the Bible's pages. We will discover and read His signature again and again in the chapters that follow.

Notes

1. Alexander Knox, quoted in Charles Forster, *Sinai Photographed* (London: Richard Bentley, 1862).
2. Jeffrey Satinover, *Cracking the Bible Code* (New York: William Morrow, 1997), 51.
3. Abraham Lincoln, "Reply to Loyal Colored People of Baltimore upon Presentation of a Bible," in *The Collected Works of Abraham Lincoln*, ed. Roy P. Basler (New Brunswick, NJ: Rutgers University Press, 1953–55), 7:542.
4. The solemn oath of the pony express riders can be found at www.officialponyexpress.org/index_files/Page860.htm.

Introduction

The Battle for the Bible

The world has departed from the religious faith that governed the founding fathers of both the United States and Canada. Today it is almost impossible for the average citizen to recognize the gulf that exists between the beliefs of our current society and the beliefs of those who founded our nations. The colonists who came to North America were determined to escape religious oppression. They wanted to create a nation on this continent where men and women could worship God freely and without restriction. The founders of the United States determined to create an educational system based on Christianity and the Word of God. A close examination of the lives and the writings of the framers of the U.S. Constitution reveals that their intent was to create freedom for religious expression, not a freedom *from* religious expression.

Frederick Rudolph wrote in his book *The American College and University* that within a generation of their landing at Plymouth, the Puritan settlers laid the foundation of an educational system dedicated to training "a learned clergy and a lettered people." These Christians created Harvard College in 1636 as an institution dedicated to upholding the truths of the Bible. In fact, during the first century of Harvard University's existence, every one of its professors was a minister of the gospel.

The initial 1636 charter of Harvard College proclaimed the following essentials:

> Every one shall consider the main end of his life and studies to know God and Jesus Christ which is eternal life. Seeing the Lord giveth wisdom, every one shall seriously by prayer in secret seek wisdom of Him. Every one shall so exercise himself in reading the Scriptures twice a day that they be ready to give an account of their proficiency therein, both in theoretical observations of languages and logic, and in practical and spiritual truths.... Every one shall consider the main end of his life and studies to know Jesus Christ which is eternal life.[1]

It has been calculated that 87 percent of the first 119 colleges built in the United States were established by Christians to educate young people in their faith. This includes Harvard, Princeton, Yale, and Columbia. More than 25 percent of the 1855 graduating class of these universities became ministers. And although our society is increasingly agnostic, millions of people still seek the truth by studying God's Word. A Gallup survey reported that 14 percent of Americans belong to a Bible study group.[2]

The Attempt to Destroy the Bible

Throughout history there has been a relentless conflict between acceptance of God and an open rebellion against His authority and His rule of the affairs of humanity. This struggle can be correctly described as the ongoing war between the City of God and the City of Man. For two thousand years the battleground has revolved around the Bible. Satan hates the Word of God because it reveals the truth about Jesus Christ, our only hope of salvation, and the eternal destiny facing each one of us—either heaven or hell.

A close examination of the history of Christianity reveals that the greatest attacks that occurred during the first centuries following Christ came from pagans. However, during the last 150 years, the most effective enemies of the Cross arose from *within the Church*—false Christians who profess to follow Christ but deny the authority of the Bible and Jesus' identity as the Son of God. It is easy to spot pagans who actively oppose God and the truth of the gospel. But it is more difficult to identify false Christians.

The Roman emperors attempted to destroy the new faith of Christianity. As an example, in AD 303, Emperor Diocletian issued a command to kill Christians and burn their sacred books. Stanley L. Greenslade, one of the editors of *The Cambridge History of the Bible*, recorded the history of this persecution:

> An imperial letter was everywhere promulgated, ordering the razing of the churches to the ground and the destruction by fire of the Scriptures, and proclaiming that those who held high positions would lose all civil rights, while those in households, if they persisted in their profession of Christianity, would be deprived of their liberty.[3]

However, the dedication of Christians to the Scriptures in the first centuries following Christ motivated them to produce numerous manuscripts that were widely copied, distributed, and translated throughout the Roman Empire. Ignatius, the bishop of Antioch in AD 70, was responsible for several churches in Syria. In his writings he quoted extensively from the books that would become the New Testament. Clement, the bishop of Rome in AD 70 (mentioned by Paul in Philippians 4:3), also quoted extensively from these books only forty years after Christ's resurrection. The personal writings of early Church leaders helped spread the written Word of God.

According to Professor J. Harold Greenlee, the quotations from what would become the New Testament "are so extensive that the N. T. could virtually be reconstructed from them without the use of New Testament manuscripts."[4] Historians have recovered nearly one hundred thousand manuscripts and letters that were composed by Christian writers in the first few centuries of this era. Their love and devotion to the Scriptures was so overwhelming that these letters contain an enormous number of direct quotations from the New Testament books. This was the primary way that the truths of Scripture were transmitted throughout the Roman Empire, despite rampant persecution and the burning of the Scriptures by Roman authorities.

Even if the Roman government had succeeded in destroying every copy of the Scriptures throughout the vast empire, the written Word of God would still have been available in the many copies made by early Christians, including the one hundred thousand letters that have been recovered, containing an astonishing 98 percent of the New Testament text. The copies made by early Christians verify the integrity of the New Testament text as it exists today.

Despite the efforts of pagan emperors to burn every copy of the Scriptures during the first three centuries after Christ, Christianity became the official state religion of the Roman Empire following the conversion of Emperor Constantine in AD 325. Centuries later, however, the medieval Church fell into apostasy and compromised with the kings and aristocracy of Europe. After many centuries, laws were issued that made possession of the Bible illegal for all but the clergy. After 1199, during the centuries of the Inquisition in Europe, appalling punishments were carried out, including burning at the stake, against anyone found to possess a copy of the Scriptures. During the Dark Ages, even priests were usually unable to read the Latin manuscripts of the Bible for themselves. As a result of their ignorance of the Bible, both priests and laypeople were unable to compare the false doctrines of the medieval Church with the doctrines of the Word of God. Few Christians today realize that in Italy it was illegal to possess a Bible until 1870, due to the hatred of apostate church officials for the truth of the Scriptures.

John Lea reported in his book *The Greatest Book in the World* that a French king once proposed to his court that they should launch a new wave of persecution against the Christians within his realm. However, a wise counselor and general replied to the king's proposal with these words: "Sire, the Church of God is an anvil that has worn out many hammers."[5]

Enemies of the Bible have attacked the Scriptures without respite for almost two thousand years. However, the Bible still stands unshaken as the most widely read and published book in history, while the philosophies of the enemies of Scripture are buried with their spokesmen. The survival of the Scriptures against the attacks of Satan provides irrefutable evidence that the Bible is inspired by God.

The Truth of Scripture Leads to the Reformation

Finally, after almost one thousand years of virtual spiritual darkness, in 1520 the Protestant Reformation instigated by Martin Luther opened the floodgates of biblical truth to the European population. The Bible was translated and printed in contemporary languages such as German, French, and English. The new spiritual freedom surpassed anything ever seen in history.

One spiritual rallying cry of the Protestant Reformation was *sola scriptura*, meaning "solely Scripture." In opposition to the medieval Roman Church's position that church councils, traditions, and papal decrees could supersede the teaching of Scripture, the Reformers insisted that every doctrine must be drawn from the clear teaching of the Bible. This reliance on the actual words of the Word of God placed the Reformation on the strongest possible spiritual foundation. The stronghold of Scripture motivated the Reformers to preach the gospel of Jesus Christ everywhere, leading to the greatest influx of souls into the Kingdom of God in the history of the Church.

In past centuries, most people in the West accepted the truth of God's existence and His creation of the universe, but a growing number in the modern world deny the existence of God. Those who accept evolution as the authoritative explanation for how human life was formed have rejected the concept of a divine Creator. In addition, large numbers of people reject the inspiration and authority of the Scriptures in the false belief that the Bible has been proven to be full of errors and contradictions. The unrelenting attacks by agnostic scholars and the news media against the authority of the Bible is unprecedented in Western history.

Attacks on the accuracy and reliability of Scripture and the resurrection of Jesus Christ have come not only from academics outside the Church but also from pastors and theologians who have lost their faith in the authority of God's Word. Professor E. B. Pusey, in his brilliant defense of the authenticity of the book of Daniel, wrote about the continual attacks on the inspiration of Scripture:

> The faith can receive no real injury except from its defenders. Against its assailants, those who wish to be safe, God protects. If the faith shall be (God forbid!) destroyed in England, it will not be by open assailants, but by those who think that they defend it, while they have themselves lost it. So it was in Germany. Rationalism was the product, not of the attacks on the Gospel but of its weak defenders. Each generation, in its controversies with unbelief, conceded more of the faith, until at last it was difficult to see what difference there was between assailants and defenders. Theology was one great graveyard; and men were disputing over a corpse, as if it had life. The salt had "lost its savour." The life was fled.[6]

The Loss of Faith by Mainline Protestant Leaders

Few things are as pathetic and spiritually ineffective as a preacher or seminary professor who has lost faith in the authority and inspiration of Scripture yet continues to teach about the Bible. Sociologist Jeffrey Hadden completed a survey of the beliefs of ten thousand Protestant ministers and found that an alarming percentage lacked faith in the inspiration of the Bible.

Here are the answers to a few of the survey questions:

1. *Was Jesus born of a virgin?*

More than 50 percent of the ministers failed to reply "totally agree."

2. *Was Jesus the Son of God?*

More than 80 percent did not "totally agree" with this assertion.

3. *Is the Bible the inspired Word of God?*

Again, more than 80 percent did not "totally agree" to the inspiration of Scripture.

A majority of the pastors surveyed qualified their answers, ranging from partial agreement to complete disagreement. However, just one hundred years ago, the vast majority of clergy would have answered "totally agree" to all the questions.[7] When pastors and teachers lose their faith in the Word of God, they would be more honest if they left the Christian ministry rather than lead a generation of churchgoers to an eternity without Christ. It is difficult for many believers to discern between true Christians and false Christians. That is why these false teachers are so dangerous.

The widespread agnosticism and atheism in government, mass media, universities, and even theological schools has resulted in the moral collapse of our society. Philosopher Thomas Hobbes (1588–1679) described the inevitable effects of the growing agnosticism and the gradual abandonment of the authority of Scripture. Hobbes predicted the terrible results that would follow the widespread loss of faith in Christ in the United States: "No arts, no letters, no society, and which is worst of all, continual fear and danger of violent death, and the life of man solitary, poor, nasty, brutish and short."[8] Tragically, his prediction was accurate.

Within 325 years, America had abandoned the Bible as the moral anchor of society and education. It should surprise no one that, after decades of teaching children that there is no absolute right and wrong, we face an appalling breakdown in public morality and widespread corporate and government corruption, as well as growing fear of violent crime. President Andrew Jackson strongly believed in the central position of Scripture to the life of this nation. As he lay on his deathbed, he pointed to a Bible and said to his companion, "That Book, Sir, is the rock on which our Republic rests."[9]

The Authenticity of the Old Testament

Dr. Robert Dick Wilson was professor of Semitic philology at Princeton Seminary for many decades. He was an expert in forty-five languages and dialects, and he was considered the greatest expert on the Hebrew Old Testament. Wilson contributed numerous scholarly works confirming the accuracy of the Old Testament. His brilliant criticism of errors and weaknesses in the positions of the higher critical school were so powerful they were never answered. Liberal critics simply ignored his devastating arguments against their dismissal of the Bible's accuracy, rather than attempt to mount a credible rebuttal.

Wilson summarizes the situation as follows:

> We claim that the assaults upon the integrity and trustworthiness of the Old Testament along the line of language have utterly failed. The critics have not succeeded in a single line of attack in showing that the diction and style of any part of the Old Testament are not in harmony with the ideas and aims of writers who lived at, or near, the time when the events occurred that are recorded in the various documents.... We boldly challenge these Goliaths of ex-cathedra theories to come down into the field of ordinary concordances, dictionaries, and literature, and fight a fight to the finish on the level ground of the facts and the evidence.[10]

Over the years a series of authorities, including Robert Dick Wilson, James Orr, Oswald Allis, and Edward J. Young, refuted the anti-Bible claims of the higher critics.

Old Testament Statements Regarding Its Divine Inspiration

The Scriptures themselves repeatedly declare that the Bible is inspired by God. Moses closed his ministry with this command to the children of Israel, affirming the Scripture's divine inspiration: "Set your hearts unto all the words which I testify among you this day, which ye shall command your children to observe to do, all the words of this law" (Deuteronomy 32:46). The book of Proverbs also states, "Every word of God is pure: he is a shield unto them that put their trust in him. Add thou not unto his words, lest he reprove thee, and thou be found a liar" (30:5–6).

Jesus Confirmed the Authority of the Old Testament

One of the most important evidences that establishes the accuracy and divine inspiration of the Old Testament Scriptures is that both Jesus Christ and the apostles confirmed the authority and inspiration of these writings. Jesus declared that "the scripture cannot be broken" (John 10:35). In another passage He stated, "And it is easier for heaven and earth to pass, than one tittle of the law to fail" (Luke 16:17). In addition, the Lord confirmed that Moses was the writer of the first five books of the Law (see Luke 24:27; John 5:46–47). Christ also stated that Isaiah was the author of the book of Isaiah (see Matthew 13:14–15, citing Isaiah 6:9–10).

One of Jesus' most significant statements was His declaration that Daniel wrote the book of Daniel (see Matthew 24:15), contradicting critics who claim that the book of Daniel was written by someone pretending to prophesy in 165 BC. Jesus also spoke of Adam, Eve, and their son Abel as real personalities (see Matthew 19:4–5; 23:35). In Luke 17:26–28, Jesus referred to both Noah and Lot. According to John 8:56–58, the Lord confirmed the Bible's narrative about Abraham. Perhaps most important, Jesus confirmed the accuracy of the Genesis account about the creation of the world (see Mark 10:6–9) and the worldwide flood (see Matthew 24:37–39).

Christ affirmed His belief in the Old Testament miracles when He talked about God's supernatural judgment on Sodom and Gomorrah (see Luke 17:29), including the death of Lot's wife (see Luke 17:32). In other passages Jesus described the feeding of manna to the Israelites during the Exodus (see John 6:32) and the miraculous healing after the serpents' bites (see John 3:14).

The Gospels record Christ's confirmation of the miraculous events in the life of Elijah and Elisha (see Luke 4:25–27) and the miraculous swallowing of Jonah by a great fish (see Matthew 12:39–40). Jesus settled all doubts in His declaration: "For verily I say unto you, Till heaven and earth pass, one jot or one tittle shall in no wise pass from the law, till all be fulfilled" (Matthew 5:18).

Jesus Christ demonstrated and affirmed the power of Scripture when He rebuked Satan by quoting Deuteronomy 8:3: "Man doth not live by bread only, but by every word that proceedeth out of the mouth of the LORD doth man live" (quoted in Matthew 4:4; see also Luke 4:4). In His discussion with the Pharisees, Jesus won His argument based on the presence of a single word in the Scriptures. The Lord asked the Jewish scholars, "If David then call him Lord, how is he his son?" (Matthew 22:45).

In light of these confirmations by Jesus the Messiah of historical events and miraculous occurrences in the Old Testament, it is astonishing that some Christians would dare deny the truthfulness of these biblical events. Those who accept Jesus Christ as God should find it quite easy to accept His divine verdict that the Old Testament is absolutely truthful and inspired directly by God. If I accept Jesus as my God and Savior, then I will accept His confirmation that I can trust in the authority of the Old Testament. For Christians, this should stand as the highest and most trustworthy evidence of the Bible's accuracy, authority, and divine inspiration.

Statements from the Apostles

The apostles affirmed the verbal inspiration of the Bible. Paul described the Scriptures as the "oracles of God" (see Romans 3:2; also note Hebrews 5:12). Also, in Galatians 3:16, Paul said, "Now to Abraham and his seed were the promises made. He saith not, And to seeds, as of many; but as of one, And to thy seed, which is Christ." Notice that Paul based his argument on the presence of a *single word* in Scripture and noted the fact that the word was the singular *seed* and not the plural *seeds*. Paul's doctrine regarding the divine inspiration of Scripture is absolutely clear: "All scripture is given by inspiration of God, and is profitable for doctrine, for reproof, for correction, for instruction in righteousness: that the man of God may be perfect, thoroughly furnished unto all good works" (2 Timothy 3:16–17).

The Early Date of the Writing of the New Testament

It is now acknowledged, even by many liberal scholars, that the New Testament Gospels and Epistles were written and widely circulated at a very early date—within fifty years of the events they describe. This fact is of overwhelming importance in verifying the historical accuracy of these sacred documents. Thousands of people who personally witnessed the events of Jesus Christ's life, teaching, death, and resurrection were still alive when the disciples composed and distributed the documents that became the books of the New Testament. These carefully copied manuscripts were read in hundreds of Christian assemblies by millions of Gentile and Jewish believers, from the northern shores of Britain to the deserts of Syria and North Africa.

In addition to Christian testimony about the enormous number of new believers, even the enemies of Christ, such as the Roman historians Tacitus and Pliny, acknowledged that there were vast multitudes of Christians throughout the Roman Empire.[11] If the New Testament documents had contained factual errors regarding the events of Christ's life, His teaching, or the miracles He performed, there would have been an enormous split within the early Church. Those who witnessed the actual historical events described in the Scriptures would have contested any inaccurate records if they had existed.

A Greek Manuscript of the New Testament

Although Christians were subjected to the most brutal and terrifying forms of torture and martyrdom, there is no record that any Christian ever declared that the gospel accounts of Jesus Christ were in error. If they had denied the reality of the life, death, and resurrection of Jesus, Roman judges would have set them free. Obviously, if any believer had known that the biblical documents were false or in error, he or she would have made that known rather than suffer the violence of torture and death.

And if any believers had made such allegations against the Bible's reliability, it is certain that the Roman authorities would have widely published such denials of the truth of the gospel accounts. Biblical statements about Christ's death and resurrection, if called into question by His followers, would have been broadcast widely throughout the empire. However, despite the fact that a large number of official Roman records and a much larger number of Christian writings have survived until today, we cannot find evidence of a single eyewitness to the events described in the Gospels who ever denied their truthfulness. This fact is of outstanding importance in assessing the reliability and truthfulness of the gospel records. Those who were eyewitnesses to the events portrayed in the Gospels went to their death rather than deny the accuracy of the biblical accounts.

The early Church had many enemies, and during the second and third centuries, some pagans and Gnostics infiltrated the Church. In response to the warnings of our Lord and the apostle Paul about false teachers and "teachers, having itching ears" (2 Timothy 4:3), church leaders were vigilant in detecting and rejecting any spurious writings that counterfeited the genuine New Testament writings. As just one example, two important early church writers, Tertullian and Jerome, tell us that a presbyter from Asia (modern-day Turkey) published a counterfeit epistle that he claimed Paul had written. Church leaders instantly held an ecclesiastical trial to examine this claim. They subsequently convicted the counterfeiter and repudiated his spurious forgery. Their rejection of this forgery was widely published to other churches throughout the empire, so that no believers would be led astray by the counterfeit.

Considering the vigilance of the leaders of the early Church, it is not plausible that they would have blindly accepted the New Testament record of Christ's miracles and His resurrection unless they possessed overwhelming proof of its truthfulness. When you consider that millions of Christian converts willingly suffered torture and died as martyrs rather than deny their Lord, it stands to reason that they were convinced of the truth of Scripture. They believed with all their minds, souls, and spirits that the four Gospels spoke the truth about Jesus Christ as the Son of God.

The Universal Distribution of the New Testament
Scholars acknowledge that the New Testament was widely copied and translated into many languages during the first few decades following the resurrection of Jesus Christ. Numerous ancient manuscripts of the New Testament have survived to this day in a number of different languages. These manuscripts confirm that, even when comparing biblical texts translated into a variety of languages, there were no differences in the text regarding doctrine or factual matters. The libraries of Europe and North America contain many ancient copies and translations of the Greek New Testament, including the Syriac, Egyptian, Arabic, Ethiopian, Armenian, Persian, Gothic, Slavonic, and Latin translations.

The widespread copying and translation of the Scriptures made it impossible for anyone to corrupt the legitimate text of the New Testament by introducing a false doctrine or an invented story of a miracle. Any alteration would have been instantly detected and denounced throughout the hundreds of churches. Once the original Greek manuscript was translated into other languages between AD 60–70, it would have been impossible for anyone, even a corrupt church official, to impose a counterfeit text on the Christians of that era.

These documents were treasured by the churches and read in their Sunday worship services. The profound love of the ancient saints for the New Testament assures us that they were vigilant in their defense and preservation of the integrity of the Scriptures. Their vigilance assures us that the Bible we have today is faithful to the original inspired text.

The Survival of the Bible

The famous French writer Voltaire, a skeptic, often expressed his contempt for the Bible and Christianity. He had an intense hatred of the Word of God, probably because it reminded him that he would someday stand before the Great White Throne to be judged by almighty God. More than two centuries ago, Voltaire wrote a prediction about the future of the Bible: "I will go through the forest of the Scriptures and girdle all the trees, so that in one hundred years Christianity will be but a vanishing memory."[12] Despite Voltaire's prediction, there are more Christians alive today than at any other time in human history. Every day, more than 115,000 people accept Christ as their personal Savior. Despite Voltaire's confident prediction about the death of Christianity, his library, in which he wrote his false prediction, was acquired years later by the British and Foreign Bible Society. The library of this famous skeptic was soon filled from floor to ceiling with thousands of copies of the Bible he hated but could not destroy.

Despite the opposition of Satan and his followers to the Scriptures, the Bible remains the most widely read, published, and influential book in history. Its truth has changed the lives and destiny of untold billions. The Scriptures have profoundly influenced the course of history for nations and empires. When an ambassador of an African prince was introduced to Queen Victoria, he asked her the question his monarch had requested he present to her: "What is the secret of your country's power and success throughout the world?" Queen Victoria picked up a Bible and answered, "Tell your prince that this book is the secret of England's greatness."

Notes

1. Taken from the Harvard College Rules and Precepts, the school's original 1636 charter. See "How Christians Started the Ivy League," *Forerunner,* April 2008, www .forerunner.com/forerunner/X0101_Christians_Started_I .html (accessed October 22, 2009).

2. Alec Gallup and Wendy W. Simmons, "Six in Ten Americans Read Bible at Least Occasionally: Percentage of Frequent Readers Has Decreased over the Last Decade," Gallup, October 20, 2000, www.gallup.com/poll/2416/ six-ten-americans-read-bible-least-occasionally.aspx (accessed February 2, 2010).

3. Stanley L. Greenslade and others, eds., *The Cambridge History of the Bible,* 3 vols. (Cambridge: Cambridge University Press, 1963).

4. J. Harold Greenlee, *Introduction to New Testament Textual Criticism* (Grand Rapids: Eerdmans, 1964).

5. John Lea, *The Greatest Book in the World* (Philadelphia: J. W. Lea, 1929).

6. E. B. Pusey, *The Prophet Daniel* (Plymouth, England: Devonport Society, 1864), xxv–xxvi.

7. The results of Jeffrey Hadden's research were reported in *Christ for the Nations,* May 1982, http://giftsforhim .speedyweb.com/templepublishing/Chapter%20One .htm (site now discontinued).

8. Found at www.rjgeib.com/thoughts/nature/hobbes-bio .html (site now discontinued).

9. Andrew Jackson, quoted in Paul Lee Tan, ed., *Encyclopedia of 7700 Illustrations* (Hong Kong: Bible Communications, 1991), 192.

10. Robert Dick Wilson, *A Scientific Investigation of the Old Testament* (Chicago: Moody, 1959), 130.

11. See, for example, Tacitus *Annals* 15.44.

12. Voltaire, quoted in David John Donnan, ed., *Treasury of the Christian World* (New York: Harper Brothers, 1953).

1

Historical Documents Verify the Accuracy of the Old Testament

Although the Bible is attacked relentlessly, it still stands as the most accurate and authoritative book ever written. Evidence from historical inscriptions and manuscripts discovered in the last century proves that the Bible is divinely inspired. Although we will never be able to verify every one of the thousands of historical personalities, events, and places recorded in the Bible, the evidence that is detailed in this chapter will assure you of the credibility of the greatest book ever written.

My library contains hundreds of books that record the accounts of historians from the ancient world, including Herodotus, the so-called Father of History. But despite this accolade, another historian labeled Herodotus "the Father of Lies" in recognition of the factual inaccuracy of his fanciful accounts of the past. Any examination of these secular histories reveals gross errors involving dates, locations, the people who were involved in major events, and the sequence and duration of these events. To say that ancient secular historians were casual in their approach to accuracy is an understatement. An example of this surfaces in Herodotus's own history, where he wrote, "My business is to record what people say. But I am by no means bound to believe it—and that may be taken to apply to this book as a whole."[1]

Historical references in the Bible stand in stark contrast to this tradition. The biblical writers are extremely careful and accurate in their recording of historical facts. We know this because, again and again, historical references in the Bible are confirmed by independent sources. Archaeological discoveries during the last century, for example, reveal ancient references to forty-one kings of Israel and the surrounding nations who are identified in the Old Testament. In fact, the entire body of ancient literature, as well as the historical records, document the accuracy of Scripture to a far greater extent than they verify the reliability of secular documents from the same eras.

In the last 150 years, many biblical critics upheld the so-called Documentary Hypothesis, which denied that Moses wrote the book of Genesis and the rest of the Torah. The critics claimed that the different names for God that appear in Genesis (including Elohim, Jehovah, and Adonai) indicate the work of five different authors. The critics argued that an editor later compiled the work of the five authors into one book, approximately six hundred years before the time of Christ.

This theory is absurd when you consider the history of the Jewish people. Remember that in a court of law a judge and jury place great weight on evidence that is acknowledged to be factual by both sides. When the prosecution and defense both acknowledge the same facts, it's clear that neither side has an ulterior motive for asserting the accuracy of the issue. Under these circumstances, it is extremely likely that the matter in question is true.

If you are familiar with Jewish tradition and culture, you know the importance of widespread agreement on the same matter. The Jewish people are known for their willingness to debate at great length any issue involving their religion and history. In light of this, would the Jews willingly adopt the complicated religious regulations of Passover, Pentecost, and the Feast of Tabernacles unless their forefathers had begun celebrating these feasts to commemorate the miraculous events of the Exodus? Such national festivals were passed down from generation to generation through the ages. How could this happen if the miraculous deliverance from Egypt had never occurred?

Moses, the great lawgiver of Israel, reminded the Hebrews in the Sinai wilderness that they had witnessed God's supernatural acts in freeing them from slavery.

> And know ye this day: for I speak not with your children which have not known, and which have not seen the chastisement of the LORD your God, his greatness, his mighty hand, and his stretched out arm, and his miracles, and his acts, which he did in the midst of Egypt unto Pharaoh the king of Egypt, and unto all his land; and what he did unto the army of Egypt, unto their horses, and to their chariots; how he made the water of the Red sea to overflow them as they pursued after you, and how the LORD hath destroyed them unto this day; and what he did unto you in the wilderness, until ye came into this place;…but your eyes have seen all the great acts of the LORD which he did. (Deuteronomy 11:2–5, 7)

If an anonymous "editor" had compiled the writings of various authors into the five books of the Torah one thousand years after they were written, how could that individual have convinced the Jewish people to accept these books as the work of Moses? At that time the Jews were scattered from Iran to Spain. How could the editor have suddenly talked them into observing the festivals of Passover, Pentecost, and the Feast of Tabernacles? If the Jews had not already been observing these festivals, they surely would not have accepted the word of the editor. Such a person would have had no credibility whatsoever.

At the very least, if such an editor had appeared with a cobbled-together Torah, the rabbis and Jewish sages would have conducted long debates to oppose the introduction of a book that no one had seen before. However, there is no record that such debates ever occurred. The biblical critics' theory of an unknown editor creating the Torah is absurd.

Evidence from the Samaritan Pentateuch

The Samaritans were a group of colonists imported into what is today the West Bank of Israel. Around 700 BC the Assyrians brought in these immigrants to repopulate the area after they took the Israelites of the ten northern tribes in chains back to Assyria (modern-day Iraq and Iran). One of the oldest manuscripts in the world is the Samaritan Pentateuch, an ancient copy of the first five books of the Law, which contains virtually every word found in the Hebrew text of the Torah. From the moment the Samaritan colonists moved into the center of Israel, they found themselves in opposition to the Jews who returned from the Babylonian captivity, which continued into the time of Christ's ministry. Although the Samaritans accepted the five books of the Torah as genuine, their own version was jealously guarded and preserved for thousands of years. Why would the Samaritans, who hated the Jews, accept the historical accuracy and authority of the Torah if they knew the five books were not authoritative and true? The fact that the Samaritans agree with the Jews in accepting the genuineness of the five books of Moses further verifies that we have in today's version of the Torah the original, unaltered writings of Moses.

Critics have also suggested that Moses could not have written his account in the fifteenth century before Christ because, they claim, writing had not yet been invented. However, the discovery of numerous ancient written inscriptions, including the famous black stele containing the laws of Hammurabi written before 2000 BC, prove that writing was widespread for many centuries *before* the time of Moses.

The Greek historian Herodotus discussed the Exodus from Egypt in his book *Polymnia:* "This people [the Israelites], by their own account, inhabited the coasts of the Red Sea, but migrated thence to the maritime parts of Syria, all which district, as far as Egypt, is denominated Palestine."[2] It is interesting to note that Strabo, a pagan historian and geographer born in 64 BC, also confirmed the history of the Jews and their escape from Egypt. He wrote, "Among many things believed respecting the temple and inhabitants of Jerusalem, the report most credited is that the Egyptians were the ancestors of the present Jews. An Egyptian priest named Moses, who possessed a portion of the country called lower Egypt, being dissatisfied with the institutions there, left it and came to Judea with a large body of people who worshipped the Divinity."[3]

Food and Water in Sinai

Critics of the reliability of Scripture have suggested that a desert area as barren as the Sinai could never have supported the huge flocks of sheep of the Israelites, as recorded in the book of Exodus. However, research conducted in the nineteenth century disputes such an assumption. In 1860, F. W. Holland explored most of the Sinai Peninsula. Despite the area's current desolate and dry condition, Holland found that some areas would still support large flocks of sheep. And if the average temperature or annual level of rainfall were only slightly changed, the amount of available pasturage would have been much greater than today's conditions would indicate.

In "Recent Explorations in the Peninsula of Sinai," Holland wrote:

Large tracts of the northern portion of the plateau of the Tih, which are now desert, were evidently formerly under cultivation. The Gulf of Suez (probably by means of an artificial canal connecting it with the Bitter Lakes) once extended nearly fifty miles further north than it does at present, and the mountains of Palestine were well clothed with trees. Thus there formerly existed a rain-making area of considerable extent, which must have added largely to the dews and rains of Sinai. Probably, also, the peninsula itself was formerly much more thickly wooded. The amount of vegetation and herbage in the Peninsula, even at the present time, has been very much underrated; and a slight increase in the present rainfall would produce an enormous addition to the amount of pasturage. I have several times seen the whole face of the country, especially the wadies, marvelously changed in appearance by a single shower.[4]

And then there are the discoveries of references to biblical figures that have been found outside the biblical texts. Numerous biblical personalities (including Nebuchadnezzar, Belshazzar, and Darius), who were repudiated by higher critics in past decades, have been reliably verified by recent historical and archaeological discoveries. In the past, critics of the Bible rejected the story of the defeat of the confederation of five kings from the east by the small army of Abraham (see Genesis 14). The critics claimed that there was no evidence to support this biblical account and therefore denied the story. However, archaeological research has uncovered ample evidence proving that the story is credible in all its particular details.

Dr. Nelson Glueck, considered by many to be the leading Palestinian archaeologist of the twentieth century, was president of Hebrew Union College. Reporting on the newly discovered evidence about this invasion, Glueck wrote the following in his book *Rivers in the Desert:*

> Centuries earlier, another civilization of high achievement had flourished between the 21st and 19th centuries BC, till it was savagely liquidated by the Kings of the East. According to the Biblical statements, which have been borne out by the archaeological evidence, they gutted every city and village at the end of that period from Ashtaroth Karnaim, in southern Syria through all of Trans-Jordan and the Negev to Kadesh-Barnea in Sinai (Genesis 14:1–7).[5]

Glueck spent many years exploring the land of Israel in his search for archaeological records. As a result of his discoveries, he concluded that the Bible was totally reliable in every area for which he could examine the evidence.[6]

With each new archaeological discovery, we find exciting confirmations of the most remarkable statements from the Word of God. In this chapter we will look at a few of the most fascinating discoveries and their implications for the authority of the Bible.

Nebuchadnezzar's Inscription About the Tower of Babel

From the time of Adam and Eve, "the whole earth was of one language, and of one speech" (Genesis 11:1), prior to the dispersion of the population following God's supernatural act of causing the confusion of languages at the Tower of Babel. God confounded the language of all people on earth so they could not understand the speech of their neighbors (see Genesis 11:9). He did this to force them to disperse throughout the earth.

The people had gathered in sinful pride and in defiance of God in an attempt to build a tower that would reach to the heavens. Moses recorded God's subsequent judgment and destruction of the tower and the city of Babylon. The remains of the Tower of Babel are vitrified (melted to form a kind of rough glass), which indicates that God used a huge amount of heat to destroy it.

Philologists—scientists who study the origin of languages—have concluded that it is probable that the thousands of dialects and languages throughout the planet can be traced back to an original shared language. Professor Alfredo Trombetti claims that he can prove the common origin of all languages. Max Mueller, one of the greatest Oriental language scholars in modern times, declared that all languages can be traced back to a single original language.[7]

The French government sent Professor Julius Oppert to report on the cuneiform inscriptions found in the ruins of Babylon. Oppert translated a long inscription by King Nebuchadnezzar in which the king referred to the tower in the Chaldean language as *Barzippa,* which means "tongue-tower." The Greeks used the word *Borsippa,* with the same meaning of tongue-tower, to describe the ruins of the Tower of Babel. Nebuchadnezzar's inscription identified the original tower of Borsippa with the Tower of Babel described by Moses in Genesis.

King Nebuchadnezzar later rebuilt the city of Babylon in great magnificence and then decided to rebuild the lowest platform of the Tower of Babel in honor of the Chaldean gods. During the millennium since God had destroyed it, the tower had been reduced to just its huge base (measuring 460 feet by 690 feet). Today the remaining ruins stand about 150 feet above the plain, with a circumference of 2,300 feet.

Nebuchadnezzar resurfaced the base of the tower with gold, silver, cedar, and fir atop a hard surface of baked clay bricks. These bricks were engraved with the seal of Nebuchadnezzar.

In an inscription found on the base of the ruins of the Tower of Babel, Nebuchadnezzar speaks in his own words from thousands of years ago to confirm one of the most interesting events of the ancient past.

King Nebuchadnezzar's Inscription

The tower, the eternal house, which I founded and built.

I have completed its magnificence with silver, gold, other metals, stone, enameled bricks, fir and pine.

The first which is the house of the earth's base, the most ancient monument of Babylon; I built and finished it.

I have highly exalted its head with bricks covered with copper.

We say for the other, that is, this edifice, the house of the seven lights of the earth, the most ancient monument of Borsippa.

A former king built it, [they reckon forty-two ages] *but he did not complete its head.*

Since a remote time, people had abandoned it, without order expressing their words.

Since that time the earthquake and the thunder had dispersed the sun-dried clay.

The bricks of the casing had been split, and the earth of the interior had been scattered in heaps. Merodach, the great god, excited my mind to repair this building.

I did not change the site nor did I take away the foundation.

In a fortunate month, in an auspicious day, I undertook to build porticoes around the crude brick masses, and the casing of burnt bricks.

I adapted the circuits, I put the inscription of my name in the Kitir of the portico.

I set my hand to finish it. And to exalt its head.

As it had been in ancient days, so I exalted its summit.[8]

Professor Oppert initially translated the king's inscription. Later, William Kennett Loftus translated the inscription and included it in his book *Travels and Researches in Chaldea and Sinai.* The ancient words confirm the accuracy of one of the most fascinating stories in the book of Genesis. The pagan king Nebuchadnezzar provided the details that "a former king built it, but he did not complete its [the tower's] head." Thus, Nebuchadnezzar confirmed the truthfulness of the Genesis account that God stopped the original builders from completing the top of the tower.

In the book of Genesis, we read the biblical description of this event:

> And it came to pass, as they journeyed from the east, that they found a plain in the land of Shinar; and they dwelt there. And they said one to another, Go to, let us make brick, and burn them thoroughly. And they had brick for stone, and slime had they for morter. And they said, Go to, let us build us a city and a tower, whose top may reach unto heaven; and let us make us a name, lest we be scattered abroad upon the face of the whole earth. And the LORD came down to see the city and the tower, which the children of men builded. And the LORD said, Behold, the people is one, and they have all one language; and this they begin to do: and now nothing that will be restrained from them, which they have imagined to do. Go to, let us go down, and there confound their language, that they may not understand one another's speech. So the LORD scattered them abroad from thence upon the face of all the earth: and they left off to build the city. Therefore is the name of it called Babel; because the LORD did there confound the language of all the earth: and from thence did the LORD scatter them abroad upon the face of all the earth. (11:2–9)

Compare the biblical statement with the words engraved on the ancient inscription of King Nebuchadnezzar: "A former king built it, but he did not complete its head. Since a remote time, people had abandoned it." The words of Moses in Genesis 11:8 declare, "So the LORD scattered them abroad from thence upon the face of all the earth: and they left off to build the city." Even more startling is the phrase of the pagan king where he declared that the reason they could not complete the top of the tongue-tower was that the "people abandoned it, without order express-ing their words." This expression by Nebuchadnezzar confirms the remarkable historical event recorded in Genesis 11, when God "did there confound the language of all the earth" and "scat-ter them abroad upon the face of all the earth" (verse 9).

Joseph and the Seven Years of Famine

An intriguing inscription confirms the Bible's account of the "seven years of great plenty" followed by the "seven years of famine" when Joseph served Pharaoh in Egypt (see Genesis 41:29–30). This inscription was discovered during the nineteenth century in southern Saudi Arabia. The inscription was found on a marble tablet in a ruined fortress on the seashore of Ha-dhramaut in present-day Yemen. An examination of the writing suggests that it was written approximately eighteen hundred years before the birth of Christ, a time that corresponds with the biblical narrative about Jacob and his twelve sons. This inscrip-tion was first rendered in Arabic by Professor Hendrik Albert Schultens and was later translated into English by Rev. Charles Forster:

> We dwelt at ease in this castle a long tract of time; nor had we a desire but for the region-lord of the vineyard.
>
> Hundreds of camels returned to us each day at evening, their eye pleasant to behold in their resting-places.
>
> And twice the number of our camels were our sheep, in comeliness like white does, and also the slow moving kine.
>
> *We dwelt in this castle seven years of good life*—how difficult for memory its description!
>
> *Then came years barren and burnt up: when one evil year had passed away, then came another to succeed it.*

And we became as though we had never seen a glimpse of good.

They died and neither foot nor hoof remained.

Thus fares it with him who renders not thanks to God:

His footsteps fail not to be blotted out from his dwelling.[9]

This ancient poem records the devastation of the years of famine and barrenness that followed the seven years of plenty. The language of the poem implies that the famine also lasted seven years. This account from ancient Arabia provides independent evidence confirming the accuracy of the biblical account of the seven years of plenty in the Middle East followed by seven years of famine that occurred during the rule of Joseph as prime minister of Egypt.

Moses recorded the history of the Egyptian famine and the wise preparations that Joseph made to gather surplus grain during the seven years of plenty to provide food during the coming years of famine.

> And he [Joseph] gathered up all the food of the seven years, which were in the land of Egypt, and laid up the food in the cities: the food of the field, which was round about every city, laid he up in the same. (Genesis 41:48)

Again, Moses recorded:

> And the seven years of plenteousness, that was in the land of Egypt, were ended. And the seven years of dearth began to come, according as Joseph had said: and the dearth was in all lands; but in all the land of Egypt there was bread.... And the famine was over all the face of the earth: and Joseph opened all the storehouses, and sold unto the Egyptians; and the famine waxed sore in the land of Egypt. And all countries came into Egypt to Joseph for to buy corn; because that the famine was so sore in all lands. (Genesis 41:53–54, 56–57)

Explorers during the last century discovered a number of other interesting inscriptions in the Middle East that confirm facts recorded in the Scriptures. Ebn Hesham, an Arab from Yemen, showed the English explorer Mr. Cruttenden the tomb of a wealthy Yemenite woman who died during the time of the Egyptian famine recorded in Genesis 41. This tomb was discovered around 1850 after being exposed by a flood that uncovered the grave site.[10] The tomb contained the body of a noblewoman who was covered in jewels. Seven collars of pearls surrounded her neck; her hands and feet were covered with seven bracelets, armlets, rings, and ankle rings displaying costly jewels. In addition, her tomb contained a coffer filled with treasure.

However, the greatest treasure of all was an engraved stone tablet bearing the woman's final inscription, which appears to confirm the biblical account of Joseph's careful management of food reserves during the seven years of famine in Egypt. The original engraving was photographed and appeared in Professor Carsten Niebuhr's *Voyage en Arabie* (plate 59). The Yemenite inscription reads as follows:

> In thy name O God, the God of Hamyar, I Tajah, the daughter of Dzu Shefar, *sent my steward to Joseph,*
>
> And he delaying to return to me, I sent my hand maid
>
> With a measure of silver, to bring me back a measure of flour:
>
> And not being able to procure it, I sent her with a measure of gold:
>
> And not being able to procure it, I sent her with a measure of pearls:
>
> And not being able to procure it, I commanded them to be ground:
>
> And finding no profit in them, I am shut up here.
>
> Whosoever may hear of it, let him commiserate me;
>
> And should any woman adorn herself with an ornament
>
> From my ornaments, may she die with no other than my death.[11]

This inscription reveals a Yemenite Arab noblewoman's complaint that she could not purchase Egypt's grain with her gold. The tragic history of famines often recorded the bartering of the most valuable jewels and precious metals in trade for the smallest amount of food available.

Ancient Histories Confirm the Exodus

> And the children of Israel journeyed from Rameses to Succoth, about six hundred thousand on foot that were men, beside children. And a mixed multitude went up also with them; and flocks, and herds, even very much cattle. (Exodus 12:37–38)

Few Christians are aware that numerous historical records and ancient inscriptions confirm the miracles involved in God's deliverance of the Jews from slavery in Egypt. The Jewish historian Flavius Josephus reported that two Egyptian priest-scholars, Manetho and Cheremon, named Joseph and Moses as leaders of the Jews in their history of Egypt.[12] Josephus recorded that the Egyptians remembered a tradition of a mass exodus from their nation by the Jews, whom they hated because they believed the Israelites were unclean. Manetho wrote that the Jews "went out of that country afterward, and settled in that country which is now called Judea, and there built Jerusalem and its temple."[13]

Manetho and Cheremon also stated that the Jews rejected Egyptian customs, including the worship of Egyptian gods. Manetho declared that Osarsiph "Moses" became the lawgiver and leader of the Jewish slaves, and that he "made this law for them, that they should neither worship the Egyptian gods, nor should they abstain from any one of those sacred animals which they have in the high esteem, but kill and destroy them all.... [He] had made such laws as these, and many more such as were mainly opposite to the customs of the Egyptians."[14]

Most important, the pagan historians acknowledged that the Jews killed the animals that the Egyptians held as sacred, indicating the Israelites' practice of sacrificing lambs on that first Passover. The historians also confirmed that the Israelites immigrated into the area of "southern Syria," which was the Egyptian name for ancient Palestine. Perhaps the most important confirmation is found in the statement by Manetho that the sudden Exodus from Egypt occurred in the reign of "Amenophis, son of Rameses, and father of Sethos, who reigned toward the close of the 18th dynasty."[15] This reference places the Exodus between 1500 and 1400 BC, which confirms the chronological data found in the Old Testament that suggests the Exodus occurred approximately in 1491 BC.

Several years ago, after much searching, I was able to locate a complete set of volumes containing the forty books in the library of Diodorus Siculus, a Greek historian from Agyrium in Sicily. He lived from 80 BC until approximately twenty years before the birth of Jesus. Diodorus traveled extensively throughout the Middle East acquiring a vast knowledge of ancient events. He compiled records from various peoples, which in many instances contain fascinating historical details that would otherwise have been lost forever.

In his book, Diodorus reported:

In ancient times there happened a great plague in Egypt, and many ascribed the cause of it to God, who was offended with them because there were many strangers in the land, by whom foreign rites and ceremonies were employed in their worship of the deity. The Egyptians concluded; therefore, that unless all strangers were driven out of the country, they should never be freed from their miseries. Upon this, as some writers tell us, the most eminent and enterprising of those foreigners who were in Egypt, and obliged to leave the country…who retired into the province now called Judea, which was not far from Egypt, and in those times uninhabited. These emigrants were led by Moses, who was superior to all in wisdom and prowess. He gave them laws, and ordained that they should have no images of the gods, because there was only one deity, the heaven, which surrounds all things, and is Lord of the whole.[16]

The historical records and inscriptions described in this chapter don't begin to scratch the surface of the many outside sources that confirm the accuracy of the Old Testament accounts. However, these discoveries provide ample evidence that we can trust the Old Testament writers as accurate historians, even when they describe miraculous developments. When we read the biblical accounts of such events as the destruction of the Tower of Babel, the seven-year famine in Egypt, and God's deliverance of the Jews from bondage in Egypt, we can trust that these things really happened just as they were recorded.

Notes

1. Herodotus, quoted in Alma E. Guinness, ed., *Mysteries of the Bible* (New York: Reader's Digest Association, 1988).

2. Herodotus, *Polymnia* sec. C.89.

3. Strabo, *Geography* lib. 16.c2.

4. F. W. Holland, "Recent Explorations in the Peninsula of Sinai," *Proceedings of the Royal Geographical Society* 13 (1868–69).

5. Nelson Glueck, *Rivers in the Desert: A History of the Negev* (New York: Farrar, Straus and Cudahy, 1959), 11.

6. Glueck, *Rivers in the Desert*, 31.

7. See Joseph Free, *Archeology and Bible History* (Wheaton, IL: Scripture Press, 1969).

8. King Nebuchadnezzar's inscription is reproduced in William Kennett Loftus, *Travels and Researches in Chaldea and Sinai* (London: James Nisbet, 1857), 29. Italics added for emphasis.

9. The inscription found on a marble tablet in a ruined fortress on the seashore of Hadhramaut is reproduced in Charles Forster, *Sinai Photographed* (London: Richard Bentley, 1862). Italics added for emphasis. See also William Harris Rule and J. Corbet Anderson, *Biblical Monuments*, 4 vols. (Croydon: Werteimer, Lea and Co., 1871–73).

10. See Rule and Anderson, *Biblical Monuments*, 1:9.

11. The inscription by an ancient Yemenite noblewoman is reproduced in Rule and Anderson, *Biblical Monuments*, 9. Italics added for emphasis.

12. Flavius Josephus, *Josephus Against Apion*, trans. William Whiston (Grand Rapids: Kregel, 1960), 1.26–27, 32.

13. Josephus, *Josephus Against Apion*, 1.26.

14. Josephus, *Josephus Against Apion*, 1.26.

15. Josephus, *Josephus Against Apion*, 1.26.

16. Diodorus Siculus, *Library of History*, Books 1–2.34, trans. Charles H. Oldfather, Loeb Classical Library (Cambridge, MA: Harvard University Press, 1993).

2

Startling Archaeological Discoveries

Can we trust the Bible? The answer is an overwhelming *yes!* For the past 150 years, scholars have conducted detailed archaeological examinations at thousands of sites throughout the Middle East. Their discoveries prove that the Bible is reliable and accurate in every area in which its statements can be tested. As you will see, archaeological discoveries show that the Bible is an accurate record of events in ancient Israel.

The field of biblical archaeology exploded in the last century and a half. The discoveries provide tremendous insight into the life, culture, and history of the biblical world. Most important, these discoveries confirm thousands of biblical statements as true. Throughout most of the last two thousand years, the majority of people living in the Western world accepted the statements of the Scriptures as genuine. Respected biblical scholars, including Rev. David Brown, Rev. Adam Clarke, Rev. Robert Jamieson, and Rev. A. R. Faussett, among many others, wrote Bible commentaries in the early part of the nineteenth century. However, despite their best efforts, their knowledge of the history and archaeology of the ancient world was limited solely to the Bible and excerpts from classical works from Greek and Latin writers. Unfortunately, most writers of the classics either exaggerated or failed to differentiate between mythology and historical events. As a result, most Bible commentators in past centuries were unable to add much additional knowledge to confirm the Bible's accounts of events.

Beginning in the nineteenth century, with the higher critical school of biblical critics in Germany and England, European seminaries gradually abandoned the earlier commitment to the authority of Scripture. However, even as late as the 1960s, most North American seminaries still accepted the basic records of the Old and New Testaments as being historically true. But since that time, we have witnessed a wholesale abandonment of belief in the historical accuracy of the Bible. Many critics now completely reject God's inspiration of the Scriptures and deny all supernatural events, such as miracles and biblical prophecy. To these unbelieving critics, the presence of a miracle or prophecy in a biblical text was proof that the account was *not* genuine. Ironically, critics rejected the possibility of divine inspiration, miracles, and prophecy *before* they examined the evidence.

At the same time, archaeologists working at sites throughout the Middle East continued to discover extraordinary artifacts that contradicted the assertions of the skeptics. Dr. Nelson Glueck, the most outstanding Jewish archaeologist of the last century, wrote in his book *Rivers in the Desert:*

> It may be stated categorically that no archaeological discovery has ever controverted a Biblical reference. Scores of archaeological findings have been made which confirm in clear outline or in exact detail historical statements in the Bible. And by the same token, proper evaluation of Biblical descriptions has often led to amazing discoveries. They form tesserae in the vast mosaic of the Bible's almost incredibly correct historical memory.[1]

Another respected scholar, Dr. J. O. Kinnaman, declared:

Of the hundreds of thousands of artifacts found by the archeologists, not one has ever been discovered that contradicts or denies one word, phrase, clause, or sentence of the Bible, but always confirms and verifies the facts of the biblical record.[2]

Well-known language scholar Dr. Robert Dick Wilson, formerly professor of Semitic philology at Princeton Theological Seminary, made the following statement:

After forty-five years of scholarly research in biblical textual studies and in language study, I have come now to the conviction that no man knows enough to assail the truthfulness of the Old Testament. When there is sufficient documentary evidence to make an investigation, the statement of the Bible, in the original text, has stood the test.[3]

Comparing the Bible's Claims to the Outside Evidence

The Bible claims that it is the inspired and accurate Word of God. Therefore, it is vital that we compare the scriptural records against archaeological discoveries uncovered at the sites where many of the thrilling events of the Bible occurred. The results of these investigations are available for anyone to examine. Scholars have not found one confirmed archaeological discovery that absolutely disproves a statement of the Scriptures. No one should expect that archaeology will provide detailed confirmation of personal events recorded in Scripture, such as the sacrifice of Isaac by Abraham. (By their personal nature, the vast majority of events in our lives, although they definitely occurred, would never be confirmed archaeologically. Most personal events recorded in the Bible would have left little or no evidence that could be discovered thousands of years after the event.) However, whenever the Bible deals with major events, such as the rise and fall of cities, rulers, or kingdoms, the spade of the archaeologist has often been able to discover wonderful confirmation of the truth of the account.

Only fifty years ago many disbelieving scholars totally rejected the historical accuracy of the Bible because they claimed the Scriptures made reference to kings and other individuals whose identities could not be confirmed from other historical or archaeological records. Recent discoveries, however, have shown that the skeptics should not have rejected the Bible's authenticity so easily. If they had only trusted in the truthfulness of the Bible or waited a little longer, they would have been rewarded with archaeological discoveries that confirm many biblical details, events, and personalities.

For example, many scholars and textbooks reject any statements in the Scriptures about Solomon or King David. They argue that David is only a mythical creation or a literary fiction. Examples of this critical approach include the books *In Search of Ancient Israel* by Philip R. Davis and *Early History of the Israelite People* by Thomas L. Thompson. Thompson wrote, "The existence of the Bible's 'United Monarchy' during the tenth-century [BC] is...impossible."[4]

The so-called minimalist scholars accept only the minimum of information found in the Bible, rejecting a statement unless it can be established by nonbiblical evidence. Professor Anson Rainey of the Tel Aviv Institute wrote a significant article in the well-respected magazine *Biblical Archaeology Review,* denouncing the minimalist school as "a circle of dilettantes." He claimed their ideas were a "figment of their vain imaginations" while concluding that the archaeological discoveries, including the inscription about the "house of David" at Dan in northern Israel, should announce the "death knell to their conceit" in rejecting the existence of David, Solomon, and numerous other biblical figures.

The minimalist approach that discounts all biblical statements unless supported by nonbiblical sources would be rejected out of hand in any other area of study. Imagine a student of Plato's philosophy who automatically rejected outright any statement made by Plato himself, his followers, or any Greek writer in later years who quoted Plato favorably. This is an absurd way to approach the study of any subject, let alone the Bible, which has been supported by a greater number of archaeological discoveries than any other ancient book.

The rational way to study ancient history is to carefully examine every bit of evidence regarding a personality or event, considering the evidence both from those who support and those who oppose the particular subject. The true scholar will then weigh the evidence of all sources and come to a balanced conclusion based on the facts. Yet many biblical scholars continue to adhere to the minimalist approach.

Independent Confirmation of Biblical References

Archaeological investigations have demolished the position of those who rejected the biblical account of Israel's kings, including King David. In 1993, archaeologists digging at Tel Dan in northern Israel found a fragment of a stone inscription that clearly refers to the "House of David" and identifies David as the "king of Israel." This is the first inscription outside the Bible that confirms that David was the king of Israel in the ninth century before Christ. Many Bible critics who had rejected David as an actual historical figure were upset to discover their position could no longer be defended. Some critics suggested that the fragment was a fake. But the following summer two additional fragments of the original inscription were found. When assembled, the fragments provided scholars with the entire inscription, confirming that it referred to David as king of Israel.

Another scholar, Professor André Lemaire from the Collège de France, discovered another ninth-century BC stone inscription created by King Mesha of Moab. That inscription also referred to "the House of David." These important inscriptions, recorded a century after King David's death, confirm that David was the king of Israel at the time the Bible stated and that he established a royal dynasty, the "House of David," as the Scriptures report.[5]

Evidence of Abraham

Dr. Millar Burrows, a professor at Yale University, studied the evidence that indicates the historicity of Abraham and the other patriarchs of Israel. "Everything indicates that here we have an historical individual.... [He] is not mentioned in any known archaeological source, but his name appears in Babylonia as a personal name in the very period to which he belongs."[6]

Burrows discussed the underlying reason most scholars reject the authority of the Bible: "The excessive skepticism of many liberal theologians stems not from a careful evaluation of the available data, but from an enormous predisposition against the supernatural.... On the whole, however, archaeological work has unquestionably strengthened confidence in the reliability of the scriptural record."[7]

The Merneptah Stele's Reference to Israel

A stone inscription found in Egypt confirms that the children of Israel were a people known to the Egyptians many centuries before the reign of King David, as the Bible claims. The Merneptah Stele is a seven-and-one-half-foot-high stone inscription discovered in 1895 in the temple of Pharaoh Merneptah at Thebes in Egypt. Scholars believed that Pharaoh Merneptah launched an invasion into the area of the modern-day West Bank, in ancient Canaan, and defeated the Jewish inhabitants of the land. The second line from the bottom of this inscription refers to Israel. The pharaoh's inscription boasts: "Israel is laid waste; his seed is not."[8]

Many scholars have assumed that this inscription referred to a military victory over the nation of Israel after the Israelites had conquered the people inhabiting Canaan. However, recent work by archaeologist Professor David Rohl suggests that the Merneptah Stele's inscription actually refers to the pharaoh's terrible oppression of the Israelite slaves, the descendants of Jacob (who was renamed Israel). The phrase "his seed is not" probably refers to the genocide of the male Jewish children as recorded in Exodus 1:22: "And Pharaoh charged all his people, saying, Every son that is born ye shall cast into the river, and every daughter ye shall save alive."

Many scholars have wondered if the Bible's account of the Jewish captivity in Egypt could be true, since no other inscriptions referring to the Exodus have been discovered. However, there is a simple explanation for this. Ample evidence shows that Egyptian rulers were averse to recording either their defeats or the victories of their enemies. The pharaohs also often altered monuments erected by their predecessors by engraving their own inscriptions on the same stones. So it is not surprising that Egyptian records of their devastating defeat at the hands of Israel's God have not been uncovered.

Merneptah—the Pharaoh Who Drowned

Egyptian archaeologists discovered the mummified body of Pharaoh Merneptah more than a century ago but didn't complete a medical examination until 1975. His body had been removed from its burial chamber thousands of years earlier following a grave robbery. The priests repaired the damage and reburied Merneptah's mummy in a small room in the new royal tomb of Pharaoh Amenhotep II in approximately 1000 BC. Fortunately the priests included Merneptah's name in the outermost wrappings of the repaired mummy. The mummified body was first discovered, but not identified, by French archaeologist Victor Loret in 1898.

A detailed medical examination of Merneptah's body was completed in 1974–75 with the aid of x-rays and modern forensic techniques. Professor Michel Durigon of the Paris Police Forensic Laboratory examined the pharaoh's tissue under a microscope and discovered the body had been in water for a short time. Dr. Maurice Bucaille, the former chief of the surgical clinic at the University of Paris, participated in the examination and included the following statement in his book *The Hebrews in Egypt:*

> [The] conservation of the transversal striations of muscular fibrillae gave evidence of the impossibility for the body to have remained more than a short time in the water, for, otherwise, these striations would not have appeared in the microscopic examination.[9]

Although the internal organs had been removed during the initial mummification process, scientists were amazed to discover that massive injuries had been inflicted on this body. The pharaoh's body had suffered extreme violence from external blows that caused massive loss of tissue and bone in three areas: the abdomen, the thorax, and the cranium (skull). The back also was severely damaged from a massive blow. The remarkable violence inflicted on the pharaoh's body was unusual because most

Egyptian pharaohs died peacefully or by poison. Yet the forensic evidence proved that this particular pharaoh had died during an incredibly violent incident, probably in water.

This raises the obvious question: what could account for these injuries? If Pharaoh Merneptah died in an onrushing of seawater, and he had been trampled by panicking horses or crushed by overturned chariots, that could account for the injuries. As the Egyptian army pursued the escaping Hebrew slaves between walls of water in the Red Sea, the horses would have panicked as the sea suddenly rushed together again. Certainly the soldiers and Pharaoh would have sustained terrible injuries as they drowned.

The book of Exodus records that the pharaoh led his army to pursue the departing Jews and was killed with his army and their horses in the onrushing waters: "And the LORD hardened the heart of Pharaoh king of Egypt, and he pursued after the children of Israel: and the children of Israel went out with an high hand" (Exodus 14:8). In Psalms we read of the death of Pharaoh and his army: "To him which divided the Red sea into parts: for his mercy endureth for ever: and made Israel to pass through the midst of it: for his mercy endureth for ever: but overthrew Pharaoh and his host in the Red sea: for his mercy endureth for ever" (136:13–15).

Sir Flinders Petrie, one of the greatest Egyptologists, concluded that Pharaoh Merneptah was the pharaoh of the Exodus. Professor Karl-Richard Lepsius also identified Merneptah with the Exodus account.[10] Professor Gaston Maspero cited an Alexandrian legend that names Merneptah as the pharaoh of the Exodus "who is said to have perished in the Red Sea."[11]

The Kings of Israel

The Bible claims that the Holy Spirit inspired the biblical writers to correctly record the events of history. The Bible is extremely accurate as to events, chronology, the sequence of events, and the persons involved. In addition to archaeological evidence for King David, we also have confirmation of other kings of Israel. The name of Omri, a king of Israel, is recorded on an inscription known as the Stele of King Mesha of Moab. In addition, Omri's name appears on the rock inscriptions of three kings of Assyria, the annals of both Tiglath-Pileser III and Sargon II, and the Black Obelisk of King Shalmaneser III, who wrote, "I conquered…all of the Land of Omri (Israel)."

Other Assyrian inscriptions found in Nineveh confirm the Bible's records about these additional kings of Israel: Ahab, Jehu, Joash, Menehem, Pekah, and Hoshea. In addition, the names of many of the kings of the southern kingdom of Judah are recorded on inscriptions of nations that fought against the Jews. Inscriptions discovered by archaeologists working in the Middle East confirm the names of these kings of Judah: Ahaziah, Uzziah, Ahaz, Hezekiah, Manasseh, and Jehoiachin. Scholars found ration records of the army of Nebuchadnezzar, king of Babylon (606–562 BC), that state, "ten sila of oil to Jehoiachin, king of Judah." The fact that foreign nations listed the kings of Israel and Judah provides the strongest evidence confirming the accuracy of the Word of God.

In 1846, explorer Austen Henry Layard discovered an incredible black obelisk in the ruins of Nimrud (present-day Iraq), the ancient capital of the Assyrian Empire that conquered the northern kingdom of Israel. This six-and-one-half-foot-high black obelisk, bearing a four-sided inscription in stone, recorded the conquest of the Assyrian king Shalmaneser III over numerous foreign kings and kingdoms, including King Jehu of Israel (approximately 841–814 BC). A detailed examination of the obelisk reveals King Jehu bowing down in obedience to the Assyrian king. The obelisk refers to Jehu as the "son of Omri," indicating an awareness that his dynasty traced back to Omri, as stated in the book of 1 Kings.[12]

The Walls of Jericho

During excavations of Jericho conducted between 1930 and 1936, Professor John Garstang found one of the most incredible confirmations of the biblical record about the conquest of the Promised Land. He took the precaution of preparing a written declaration of the archaeological discovery, signed by himself and two members of his team: "As to the main fact, then, there remains no doubt: the walls fell *outwards* so completely that the attackers would be able to clamber up and over their ruins into the city."[13]

This fact is important because the evidence from all other archaeological digs around ancient cities in the Middle East reveals that walls of cities always fall *inward* as invading armies pushed their way into a city. However, in the account in Joshua 6:20, we read, "The wall fell down flat, so that the people went up into the city, every man straight before him, and they took the city." The biblical description matches the evidence uncovered by Professor Garstang in ancient Jericho. Only the supernatural power of God could have caused the city's walls to fall outward, just as it is described in Joshua's account.

Incredible Discoveries in Jerusalem

Following the fall of East Jerusalem to the Jordanians during Israel's 1948 war of independence, the Jordanian army dynamited synagogues and other buildings in the Jewish Quarter of Jerusalem. The wanton destruction over a twenty-year period, until Jerusalem was liberated during the Six-Day War, created a unique archaeological opportunity. When the Jews recaptured the Jewish Quarter in 1967, they had to rebuild because of the Jordanian destruction. However, the rebuilding process made it possible for Israeli archaeologists to remove rubble that had built up over the last two thousand years. As a result, they were able to explore the ancient bedrock of this fascinating city.

Scholars under the leadership of Nahman Avigad of Hebrew University found the remains of the wall of King Hezekiah, built when the Assyrian army attacked Israel in 701 BC. The Bible tells us that King Hezekiah built the walls of Jerusalem to resist the Assyrian armies:

> And when Hezekiah saw that Sennacherib was come, and that he was purposed to fight against Jerusalem, he took counsel with his princes...and they did help him.... Also he strengthened himself, and built up all the wall that was broken, and raised it up to the towers, and another wall without. (2 Chronicles 32:2–3, 5)

Israeli archaeologists found that portions of the wall actually cut through walls of houses that were standing at the time, indicating the urgency of the defensive actions and the authority of the king. This is confirmed in the Bible's account: "And ye have numbered the houses of Jerusalem, and the houses have ye broken down to fortify the wall" (Isaiah 22:10).

The Seals of Biblical Personalities

One of the most fascinating discoveries in Jerusalem concerns two bullae, or official clay seals, that bear the impression of the seal used by the biblical personality Baruch, the scribe who recorded the inspired messages of Jeremiah the prophet, including the book of Jeremiah (circa 606 BC). Baruch, the son of Neriah, was Jeremiah's friend and scribe during the dangerous years of the prophet's imprisonment. (The Lord promised the scribe Baruch that he would be spared when the city of Jerusalem was destroyed by the Babylonian army: "Behold, I will bring evil upon all flesh, saith the LORD: but thy life will I give unto thee for a prey in all places whither thou goest" [Jeremiah 45:5].)

Both of the bullae bear the inscription, "Belonging to Berekhyahu, son of Neriyahu, the Scribe." The second bulla was found in Jerusalem and purchased by a Jewish collector, Shlomo Moussaieff of London, who owns the greatest private collection of ancient Jewish inscriptions in the world. This second clay seal, bearing the same inscription, also reveals a fingerprint that probably belonged to Baruch.

In 1903 another intriguing seal was discovered in the ruins of Megiddo in northern Israel that bore an inscription of a beautiful lion and the words "Belonging to Shema servant of Jeroboam." This indicates that the seal belonged to an official of King Jeroboam of Israel. Other seals have been discovered confirming the biblical records about King Uzziah (777–736 BC) and King Hezekiah (726–697 BC).[14]

Another important seal discovered in Jerusalem dates from the seventh century before Christ and is inscribed as follows: "Belonging to Abdi Servant of Hoshea." This seal, made of orange chalcedony and used to authenticate royal documents for security purposes, belonged to Abdi, a high official of King Hosea, the last king of the northern kingdom of Israel before it was conquered by the Assyrian Empire in 721 BC.[15]

Yet another large seal, this one on red limestone, was found bearing the inscription "Belonging to Asayahu, servant of the king" together with a galloping horse. The name Asaiah is a short form of the name Asayahu. This name occurs twice in the Old Testament in connection with the title "servant of the king." In 2 Chronicles 34:20 we read of "Asaiah a servant of the king's" and in 2 Kings 22:12 of "Asahiah a servant of the king's." It is possible that this seal was owned by a high court official who was sent by King Josiah to examine the scroll of the lost book of Deuteronomy that was found in the Temple by the high priest Hilkiah in approximately 622 BC.

The Decree of King Cyrus

Explorers in Iraq in the nineteenth century found the inscribed clay cylinder bearing the decree of King Cyrus of Persia allowing the various captured natives of many different nations to return freely to their homelands. It was the government policy of the preceding Babylonian Empire of King Nebuchadnezzar to displace entire people groups, such as the Jews, and resettle them in the far reaches of the Babylonian Empire. However, King Cyrus of Persia, a moderate and God-fearing monarch, reversed the policy. Immediately after conquering the Babylonian Empire, King Cyrus issued a decree allowing the Jews to return to Israel, ending their seventy-year captivity.

The decree began with these words: "I am Cyrus, king of the world, great king." After describing his conquests and deeds, the cylinder inscription reads, "I gathered all their former inhabitants and returned to them their habitations."

In the incredible discovery of this clay cylinder we find confirmation of one of the most astonishing events in Scripture. The story is found in the book of Ezra:

> Now in the first year of Cyrus king of Persia, that the word of the LORD by the mouth of Jeremiah might be fulfilled, the LORD stirred up the spirit of Cyrus king of Persia, that he made a proclamation throughout all his kingdom, and put it also in writing, saying, Thus saith Cyrus king of Persia, The LORD God of heaven hath given me all the kingdoms of

the earth; and he hath charged me to build him an house at Jerusalem, which is in Judah. Who is there among you of all his people? his God be with him, and let him go up to Jerusalem, which is in Judah, and build the house of the LORD God of Israel, (he is the God,) which is in Jerusalem. (1:1–3)

Dr. Henry M. Morris concluded his study of the archaeological evidence concerning the Bible with these words: "Problems still exist, of course, in the complete harmonization of archaeological material with the Bible, but none so serious as not to bear real promise of imminent solution through further investigation. It must be extremely significant that, in view of the great mass of corroborative evidence regarding the Biblical history of these periods, there exists today not one unquestionable find of archaeology that proves the Bible to be in error at any point."[16]

Archaeological Evidence of the New Testament

The entire basis for the faith and hope of Christians depends on the truthfulness of the historical records of the New Testament. Our hope for heaven and eternal salvation depends on the accuracy of the words of Jesus and the apostles as recorded in the New Testament. Those who hate the Bible understand that if they can cause people to doubt the New Testament, then their faith will be immeasurably weakened. Fortunately, archaeological discoveries continue to provide new evidence that confirms the reliability of the written documents that form the foundation of the Christian faith.

English scholar William Ramsay traveled as a young man to Asia Minor with the sole purpose of disproving the Bible's history as described by Luke in his gospel and in the book of Acts. Ramsay and his professors believed that Luke could not be correct in his history of Christ or in his account about the growth of the Church during the first decades following Christ. Ramsay began to dig in the ruins of sites throughout Greece and Asia Minor, searching for ancient names, boundary markers, and other archaeological finds that would prove that Luke had invented his history of Christ and the Church. To his amazement, however, Ramsay discovered that the statements of the New Testament scriptures were accurate in the smallest detail.

As a result, Dr. Ramsay accepted Jesus Christ as his Savior. He became both a Christian and a great biblical scholar. As a result of his conversion, William Ramsay's books became classics in the study of the history of the New Testament.

Another great scholar, A. N. Sherwin-White, was a classical history scholar at Oxford University who studied evidence for and against the historical accuracy of the book of Acts. Sherwin-White wrote his conclusion after studying the evidence: "For Acts the confirmation of historicity is overwhelming... Any attempt to reject its basic historicity even in matters of detail must now appear absurd."[17]

Dr. William F. Albright, one of the world's most brilliant biblical archaeologists, wrote in 1955: "We can already say emphatically that there is no longer any solid basis for dating any book of the New Testament after circa AD 80."[18] However, additional discoveries over the next decade convinced Albright that all the books in the New Testament were written "probably sometime between circa AD 50 and 75." Significantly, he concluded that the writing of the New Testament within a few years of the events it described made it almost impossible that errors or exaggeration could have entered the text. He wrote that the duration between the events of Christ's life and the writing was "too slight to permit any appreciable corruption of the essential center and even of the specific wording of the sayings of Jesus."[19] In other words, one of the greatest minds in the field of archaeology and ancient texts concluded that the New Testament records the truth about Jesus Christ and His statements.

Dr. John A. T. Robinson was a distinguished lecturer at Trinity College, Cambridge. He accepted the academic consensus held since 1900, which denied that the apostle Paul and the disciples of Jesus wrote most of the New Testament. He concluded that the New Testament books actually were written up to one hundred years after Christ. However, an article in *Time* magazine reported that Robinson decided to personally investigate the arguments behind this scholarly consensus. He was shocked to discover that much of the past scholarship that was critical of the New Testament text was untenable because it was based on a "tyranny of unexamined assumptions" and what he felt must have been an "almost willful blindness."

To the amazement of his university colleagues, Robinson concluded that the apostles must have been the genuine writers of the New Testament books at an early date—in the years prior to AD 64. He challenged other scholars to complete the original research necessary to fully examine the question without introducing bias and faulty assumptions. As a result of such a new analysis, Robinson believed it would necessitate "the rewriting of many introductions to—and ultimately, theologies of the New Testament." Robinson's book *Redating the New Testament* suggests that Matthew's gospel, for example, was written as early as AD 40, within eight years of Christ's death and resurrection.[20]

Ancient Egyptian Coins Bearing the Image of Joseph

Recent research conducted on previously overlooked Egyptian coins confirms the biblical story of Joseph and his role in government service in ancient Egypt. In 2009, archaeological authorities from the Egyptian National Museum announced that a cache of ancient coins had been "rediscovered." Initially discovered almost a century earlier, the coins had been in storage. They were uncovered in the vast storage vaults of the national museum and the Antiquities Authority. Cairo's *Al Ahram* newspaper reported that the coins bear the name and image of the biblical Joseph.[21]

The cache of more than five hundred coins had been set aside decades earlier in the belief that they were miscellaneous objects of worship and likely of no significance. However, scientists re-examined the coins using recently developed technology and discovered that a number of them dated to the time of ancient Egypt. Most of the coins were engraved with the year they were minted and their monetary value and the effigies or images of the pharaohs ruling Egypt when the coins were minted. Researchers concluded that the "Joseph coins" originated in the period when Joseph served as Pharaoh's treasurer—during the seven years of plenty and seven years of famine (see Genesis 41:41–45). Biblical history suggests a date for Joseph's high position in the Egyptian government that coincides with the date of the minting of the coins in the cache (approximately 2000 BC). Amazingly, some of the coins bear both Joseph's name and image.[22]

On its Web site Israel National News reported that the Egyptian archaeologists "discovered many charms from various eras before and after the period of Joseph, including one that bore his effigy as the minister of the treasury in the Egyptian pharaoh's court."[23]

Archaeologists had previously believed that the Egyptians of Joseph's day did not use coins but rather used barter to trade. However, Dr. Sa'id Muhammad Thabet, head of the research team, found several Koranic verses that speak of coins being used in ancient Egypt. He concluded that the coins were genuine and that their stated date of minting was accurate. He confirmed that the dates agreed with both biblical and historical chronology.

Thabet's team described the "Joseph coins" as having

> two faces: one with an inscription, called the inscribed face, and one with an image, called the engraved face—just like the coins we use today.... Some of the coins are from the time when Joseph lived in Egypt.... [T]here was one coin that had an inscription on it, and an image of a cow symbolizing Pharaoh's dream about the seven fat cows and seven lean cows, and the seven green stalks of grain and seven dry stalks of grain.

> Joseph's name appears twice on this coin, written in hieroglyphs: once the original name, Joseph, and once his Egyptian name, Saba Sabani, which was given to him by Pharaoh when he became treasurer. There is also an image of Joseph, who was part of the Egyptian administration at the time.[24]

Anyone who carefully examines the ancient, extrabiblical historical records with an open mind cannot honestly hold on to the belief that the Bible is nothing more than a collection of legends, fables, and myths. The figures mentioned in Scripture—both the heroic and the ordinary—are not fanciful characters in a work of fiction. They were actual people who did and said what the Bible recounts of their lives. All of this confirms that the Scriptures were divinely inspired. The writers of the books of the Bible were not writing down what they had decided we need to hear but exactly what God commanded them to record.

It is reasonable to assume that if the Bible is accurate in its claims, descriptions, and accounts of events, then many of those facts would be verified by outside sources. And as we have seen from the evidence produced by recent archaeological discoveries, the biblical facts are confirmed again and again. Ancient government officials, historians, and citizens left behind seals, decrees, proclamations, and inscriptions that continue to be uncovered in the Middle East. A multitude of independent sources have verified the truth of the Scriptures.

For now, let's continue our investigation by examining the historical evidence that confirms the life and work of Jesus Christ during His thirty-three years on earth.

Notes

1. Nelson Glueck, *Rivers in the Desert: A History of the Negev* (New York: Farrar, Straus and Cudahy, 1959), 31.
2. Quotation from J. O. Kinnaman found at www .geocities.com/Heartland/7234/quotes.html (accessed October 26, 2009).
3. Quotation from Robert Dick Wilson found at www .geocities.com/Heartland/7234/quotes.html (accessed October 26, 2009).
4. Thomas L. Thompson, *Early History of the Israelite People: From the Written and Archaeological Sources* (Leiden, Netherlands: Brill, 1992).
5. *U.S. News & World Report*, October 25, 1999.
6. Millar Burrows, *What Mean These Stones? The Significance of Archeology for Biblical Studies* (New York: Meridian Books, 1956), 258–59.
7. Burrows, *What Mean These Stones?*
8. As translated by Professor John Wilson and recounted in *Ancient Near East Texts* (1969): 376.
9. Maurice Bucaille, *The Hebrews in Egypt* (Tokyo: NTT Mediascope, 1994).
10. Karl-Richard Lepsius, *Die Chronologie der Aegypter Bearbeitet* (Berlin: Nicolaische Buchhandlung, 1849), 388.
11. Gaston Maspero, *Guide to the Visitor of Cairo Museum* (Cairo).
12. Austen H. Layard, *Discoveries Among Nineveh and Babylon* (New York: Harper & Brothers, 1853), 523.
13. John Garstang, *The Foundations of Bible History: Joshua, Judges* (London: Constable, 1931). Italics added for emphasis.
14. Found at www.biblehistory.net/Chap20.htm (site now discontinued).
15. Andre Lemaire, "Royal Signature: Name of Israel's Last King Surfaces in a Private Collection," *Biblical Archaeology Review* 21, no. 6 (June 1995): 48–52.
16. Henry M. Morris, *The Bible and Modern Science* (Chicago: Moody, 1956).

17. A. N. Sherwin-White, quoted in Rubel Shelley, *Prepare to Answer* (Grand Rapids: Baker Books, 1990).
18. William F. Albright, *Recent Discoveries in Biblical Lands* (New York: Funk and Wagnalls, 1955), 136.
19. Albright, *Recent Discoveries in Biblical Lands.*
20. Reported in *Time,* March 21, 1977, quoted at http://members.christhost.com/ResourceCentre/history.htm (site now discontinued). For more on this research, see also John A. T. Robinson, *Redating the New Testament* (Philadelphia: Westminster, 1976).
21. Wajih Al-Saqqar, "Archeologists Find 'Joseph-Era' Coins in Egypt," *Al Ahram*, September 22, 2009. Found at www.jpost.com/servlet/Satellite?pagename=JPost%2FJPArticle%2FShowFull&cid=1253820674074 (accessed September 25, 2009).
22. Al-Saqqar, "Archeologists Find 'Joseph-Era' Coins."
23. Hillel Fendel, "Top Egyptian Daily: Joseph's Era Coins Found in Egypt," Arutz Sheva Israel National News .com, September 25, 2009, www.israelnationalnews.com/News/News.aspx/133601 (accessed September 25, 2009).
24. Al-Saqqar, "Archeologists Find 'Joseph-Era' Coins in Egypt." The Arabic-to-English translations of the information regarding the Joseph-era coins are courtesy of MEMRI (Middle East Media Research Institute), a not-for-profit organization. For more information on MEMRI, visit the Web site www.memri.org.

3

The Historical Evidence About Jesus Christ

Many modern scholars reject the Gospels' accounts of the life, death, and resurrection of Jesus Christ. The Jesus Seminar, a group of liberal New Testament scholars, meets semiannually to determine whether any of the Gospels' quotations of Jesus' words meet with their approval. Incredibly, members of the group examine individual sayings of Jesus, and each academic votes to accept or reject the statement. Working on a case-by-case basis, they set themselves up as authorities and pass judgment on Jesus.

Arthur Dewey of Xavier University is a member of the Jesus Seminar. He has stated that, while the group rejects most of Christ's words, they believe Jesus was occasionally humorous. "There is more of David Letterman in the historical Jesus than Pat Robertson," he is quoted as saying.[1] The Jesus Seminar is sponsored by the Westar Institute, a private California study center founded by Robert Funk, a liberal New Testament scholar. The group has decided that its members are particularly qualified to determine whether any biblical statement is "genuine."

Obviously, these scholars are contemptuous in their rejection of the authority of the Bible. However, they represent only the tip of the iceberg of academic scholarship that rejects, in whole or in part, most of Scripture as being the inspired Word of God. It is virtually the universal opinion among secular academics that the Bible is without historical accuracy and cannot be relied upon.

Members of the Jesus Seminar use a system of colored beads to indicate their vote or determination of the validity of particular statements that Jesus made. If they think Jesus would "certainly" have made such a statement, they vote by dropping a red bead into a box. If they believe Jesus "might" have made a statement close to what the gospel writer recorded, they vote by dropping in a pink bead. When they believe the statement may be close to what Jesus thought but not what He actually stated, they drop a gray bead into the box. Finally, when they reject a statement in the Gospels as something they believe Jesus would never have said, the scholars drop a black bead into the box.

Incredibly, this group has chosen to publish a new version of the Gospels that displays what they have determined to be the "words of Jesus," using various colors of ink to reflect their verdicts on the validity of His words. It won't surprise you to learn that very little of their final text reveals Christ's words printed in red, indicating that few of these scholars voted with red beads. Their overall approach was to question or reject outright most of Christ's statements. When they examined the text of the Lord's Prayer, for example, they rejected every word as spurious except for two words: "Our Father."

The Built-In Bias of Biblical Critics

In reality, these liberal scholars declare by their votes whether they would have made these gospel statements if they were Jesus! The cable channel Cinemax 2 ran a program in 1996 called *The Gospel According to Jesus.* The program showed people reading from a new version of the Bible created by author Stephen Mitchell. In this astonishing version, Mitchell eliminated almost all the statements as well as most of the miracles of Jesus as recorded in the Gospels.

During a meeting held in Santa Rosa, California, the scholars decided that the gospels of Matthew, Mark, Luke, and John were "notoriously unreliable: the [Jesus Seminar] judges...had to throw out the Evangelists' testimony on the Nativity, the Resurrection, the Sermon on the Mount." An article published in *Time* magazine went on to repeat a determination, announced by the seventy-five-member "self-appointed Seminar three years ago, that close historical analysis of the Gospels exposes most of them as inauthentic."[2] The criteria used by the scholars to judge the gospel records reveals why they reject almost everything that Christians have believed during the last two thousand years. Their criteria holds suspect any prophetic statements, statements Jesus made on the cross, descriptions of His trial, accounts of the Resurrection, and any claims Jesus made to be the Messiah or the Son of God. Their bottom-line rule: "When in sufficient doubt, leave it out."[3]

However, if members of the Jesus Seminar are correct that almost nothing definite can be known about the life of Jesus, the basis for all Christian belief is destroyed.

Evangelical scholar Michael Green of Regent College rejects the analysis of the Jesus Seminar. He has stated that the Gospels are the most thoroughly authenticated of all documents originating from that era. "We have copies...going back to well within the century of their composition," Green said, "which is fantastic compared with the classic authors of the period. And in striking contrast to the two or three manuscripts we have attesting the text of these secular writers, we have hundreds of the New Testament. They give us the text of the New Testament with astonishing uniformity." He also noted, "The artless, unplanned harmony in their accounts is impressive and convincing."

Many people see Jesus as a wonderful moral teacher but reject the Bible's claims of His deity and that He died on the cross for our salvation. However, this view is contradicted by historical evidence and logic. C. S. Lewis presented his famous trilemma argument along these lines:

Any person who did the miracles and spoke the messages ascribed to Jesus could not be a mere human teacher or an uninspired prophet, no matter how enlightened or exalted.

Anyone who performed the miracles ascribed to Jesus and made the statements Jesus made about His nature and powers must be the Son of God as He claimed. And if He is not, then He is either a liar or a lunatic.

You cannot regard Jesus as simply a great moral teacher. Anyone who claimed the things that Jesus said must be either a liar, a lunatic, or the Lord.[4]

When you examine the evidence from history and the overwhelming evidence found in the gospel records, it is not difficult to conclude that Jesus Christ could not possibly have been a liar or a lunatic. This analysis leaves us with the final remaining possibility: that Jesus of Nazareth was precisely who He claimed He was, namely, the Son of God. He is the Lord of the universe and the Savior of humanity. We can trust that He did and said exactly what the gospel writers recorded.

Historical Documents About Jesus

As we have noted already, a growing number of documents and ancient inscriptions confirm the historical accuracy of the gospel accounts. In this chapter I can touch only on the highlights, but the evidence will provide ample proof that the gospel statements regarding Jesus of Nazareth can be relied on. A tremendous amount of historical evidence exists both within and outside the Bible that confirms the details of the life, ministry, death, and resurrection of Jesus.

Skeptics reject out of hand the historical evidence that has survived from the first century, which confirms many of the facts about Jesus that are recounted in the Gospels. One of the strongest pieces of evidence comes from Jewish historian Flavius Josephus, who lived at the time of the apostle Paul. Josephus mentions Jesus twice in his exhaustive history, *The Antiquities of the Jews*. One of these references, known as the Testimonium Flavianum Passage, confirms a number of facts regarding the life, death, and resurrection of Jesus.[5] The historian's written testimony will be examined later in this chapter.

After conducting a detailed analysis of the historical evidence for the life and resurrection of Jesus Christ, Professor Simon

Greenleaf, the greatest Western authority on the matter of legal evidence, concluded that the evidence for Jesus was overwhelming.[6] Even in a court of law, the evidence would stand up to close scrutiny.

Sir William Ramsay began his scholarly career as a complete skeptic regarding the historical evidence about Jesus of Nazareth. Possibly the greatest of all New Testament archaeologists, Ramsay completed the most in-depth studies ever done on the book of Acts. He wrote, "Luke is a historian of the first rank; not merely are his statements of fact trustworthy; he is possessed of the true historic sense.... In short this author should be placed along with the very greatest of historians."[7] Professor Merrill F. Unger concurred, stating, "The Acts of the Apostles is now generally agreed in scholarly circles to be the work of Luke, to belong to the first century and to involve the labors of a careful historian who was substantially accurate in his use of sources."[8]

Luke, of course, is also the writer of the gospel account that bears his name. Of the four gospel writers, Luke recorded the greatest number of details about Christ's virgin birth, career, death, and resurrection. If Luke's writing is reliable in the book of Acts, as Ramsay attested, then he is also a worthy historian regarding the details of Christ's life and resurrection recorded in the accounts of the gospel of Luke.

Daniel Webster, one of the greatest lawyers of his age, declared, "I believe the Scriptures of the Old and New Testaments to be the will and word of God, and I believe Jesus Christ to be the son of God." President Abraham Lincoln was an agnostic until he reached the age of forty. Then he read Dr. James Smith's brilliant examination *The Christian's Defence* (1843), which proved the historical reality of the events in Christ's life. The evidence brought to light in that book convinced Lincoln, resulting in his conversion. The president is quoted as saying, "My doubts scattered to the winds and my reason became convinced by the arguments in support of the inspired and infallible authority of the Old and New Testaments."[9]

To any unbiased observer who is willing to evaluate the evidence without prejudice, the accumulated evidence that confirms the record of the four Gospels is overwhelming. Scholar

Otto Betz stated, "No serious scholar has ventured to postulate the non-historicity of Jesus."[10]

Some writers have suggested that there is little historical evidence that confirms the biblical accounts of the life of Jesus. For example, Solomon Zeitlin wrote, "Even Paul's epistles have awakened the question, Does he speak of a real historical personage or of an ideal? The main sources for the historicity of Jesus, therefore, are the Gospels." However, Zeitlin dismissed the historical accounts in the Gospels and concluded, "So we are right to assume that even the Gospels have no value as witnesses of the historicity of Jesus. The question therefore remains: Are there any historical proofs that Jesus of Nazareth ever existed?"[11]

Scholars such as Zeitlin dismiss the strong historical evidence that validates the gospel accounts about Jesus because it contradicts the critics' antisupernatural bias. If liberal scholars applied the same arbitrary rejection of historical evidence to other ancient personages, such as Julius Caesar or Alexander the Great, they would be forced to reject all history as myth.

However, an unbiased analysis of the historical sources will convince most fair-minded readers that Jesus of Nazareth is the Messiah of both history and prophecy. Historian F. F. Bruce wrote, "The historicity of Christ is as axiomatic for an unbiased historian as the historicity of Julius Caesar."[12]

Scholars Have Confirmed the Reliability of the New Testament

During the earlier years of the twentieth century, many liberal scholars questioned the historical accuracy of the Gospels because they believed they were written almost one hundred years after the events they described. The scholars concluded that the gospel documents were based on hearsay and oral traditions rather than on eyewitness accounts.

However, the Gospels and the Epistles declare that they are direct eyewitness accounts of the life of Christ. Luke declared that he wrote these truths "even as they delivered them unto us, which from the beginning were eyewitnesses, and ministers of the word" (Luke 1:2). Later, in the book of Acts, Luke confirmed that his reports as written to the Roman officer Theophilus contained "infallible proofs," the strongest historical and legal proofs possible. Luke stated that Jesus "showed himself alive after his passion by many infallible proofs, being seen of them forty days" (Acts 1:3).

Fortunately, advances in historical research and biblical archaeology have convinced most scholars in the last two decades that the Gospels and Epistles were written within thirty-five years or less of the events they describe. The late William F. Albright, the greatest biblical archaeologist of his day, declared: "In my opinion, every book of the New Testament was written by a baptized Jew between the forties and eighties of the first century AD."[13] It would have been impossible to widely distribute a blatantly false story about Christ while thousands of His followers and eyewitness observers were still alive to dispute any falsehoods.

One of the chief followers of Christ, the apostle John, remained the bishop in charge of seven churches in Asia Minor (present-day Turkey) until the first few years of the second century (AD 105). Obviously John would have detected and denounced as heretical any counterfeit passages that might have been inserted into the biblical manuscripts. The writings of the early Church confirm that John read the gospels composed by Matthew, Mark, and Luke and confirmed their accuracy. Then he wrote the gospel of John to cover the activities of Jesus' first year of ministry that had not been covered by the other gospel writers.

Sir Frederic G. Kenyon, director of the British Museum, was possibly the most respected New Testament textual scholar in the twentieth century. He sided with the overwhelming evidence that the Gospels were composed shortly after the events of Christ's life and that the early Church distributed them widely within a relatively short period of time. Kenyon wrote:

> The interval, then, between the dates of original composition and the earliest extant evidence becomes so small as to be in fact negligible, and the last foundation for any doubt that the Scriptures have come down to us substantially as they were written has now been removed. Both the authenticity and the general integrity of the books of the New Testament may be regarded as finally established.[14]

Kenyon went on to state: "It is reassuring at the end to find that the general result of all these discoveries and all this study is to strengthen the proof of the authenticity of the Scriptures, and our conviction that we have in our hands, in substantial integrity, the veritable Word of God."[15]

Commenting on the sustained attacks on the authority of the Bible, biblical scholar Bernard Ramm noted that the attacks failed to make a serious dent in the popularity and influence of the Scriptures: "A thousand times over, the death knell of the Bible has been sounded, the funeral procession formed, the inscription cut on the tombstone, and committal read. But somehow the corpse never stays put."[16]

Early Biblical Manuscripts

Modern scholars possess more than five thousand manuscript copies of portions of the New Testament in the Greek language. There are an additional fifteen thousand manuscripts in other languages from the first few centuries of this era. In stark contrast, no other important text—either historical or religious—has more than a few dozen early copies that have survived until our generation. The twenty thousand surviving manuscripts of the New Testament reveal numerous very minor differences, such as individual differences in spelling. However, this unprecedented number of manuscripts provides the strongest evidence possible that the Bible we have today is true to the original manuscripts. Scholars are able to trace the origin of the various readings to ascertain with certainty the original text. The minor variations and discrepancies leave no doubt regarding the intent of the wording. Not one of the small differences affects a single important fact or doctrine of the Bible.

To put this in perspective, imagine that in the 1990s a writer wanted to create a false story about President John Kennedy performing miracles and being raised from the dead after his assassination in November 1963. To succeed with his fraud, the writer would have to accomplish two impossible things.

First, he would have to simultaneously acquire every one of the millions of books and newspaper reports about the president and insert the writer's counterfeit passages into all of this material. Further, he would have to do this without being detected by a single reader.

Second, he would have to simultaneously convince millions of people to accept his forgeries as true, despite the fact that many of these people were alive when Kennedy served as president. They would each have their own independent recollections that contradict the writer's invented story. They might remember John F. Kennedy as an admired president, or they might have supported his opponent. But either way, they would be certain that Kennedy had performed no miracles or any other acts after his assassination in Dallas. The lies would be obvious to these readers.

This is a hypothetical situation, of course, but it is not as far-fetched as you might think. Liberal scholars who suggest that the gospel records were altered to introduce new doctrines and statements about Christ's virgin birth and resurrection are proposing something that is just as implausible as the example I gave about a fraudulent account of the life and death of John F. Kennedy. The only reason these scholars have been able to convince anyone to accept their theory is that there is a great desire in the minds of many people to reject the truth of the Bible. If they accept the reality of the Bible's accuracy, they must admit in their own minds that they will someday have to give God an account of their lives. Their inability to face this reality forces them to reject the possibility that the gospel records are true. As long as they hold onto doubts about the truth of the Scriptures, they can tell themselves that the biblical teachings about God's final judgment are probably in error as well.

However, the evidence is convincing for anyone who will openly examine it. The combined testimony of thousands of early manuscripts and manuscript fragments agrees on one thing: the text of the Bible has remained unchanged in all essential details for thousands of years.

Beyond the study and comparison of early biblical manuscripts, another highly convincing proof is a simple one. If you track the pervasive influence that Jesus Christ has exerted on the entire world for two millenniums, you have to ask and answer two questions:

1. How did this one individual, who was penniless and without political power and living in an obscure part of the ancient world, gain so much influence over the world's population?
2. Why has His influence continued, without diminishing, for two thousand years?

I invite you to study the multitude of ways that Jesus Christ's life and teachings have affected philosophy, theology, religion, ethics, political theory, and a great variety of other ideas, commitments, and practices. These are things that touch our lives every day. The effect that Christ has over people and how they live—including people who don't even believe in Him—serves as evidence of the supernatural nature of Christ's life.

Biblical scholar Bernard Ramm described this incredible influence:

> From the Apostolic Fathers dating from AD 95 to the modern times is one great literary river inspired by the Bible—Bible dictionaries, Bible encyclopedias, Bible lexicons, Bible atlases, and Bible geographies. These may be taken as a starter. Then at random, we may mention the vast bibliographies around theology, religious education, hymnology, missions, the biblical languages, church history, religious biography, devotional works, commentaries, philosophy of religion, evidences, apologetics, and on and on. There seems to be an endless number.[17]

Confirmation from Non-Christian Sources

Large numbers of Roman and pagan historical manuscripts from the early centuries of the Christian era document the life, death, and resurrection of Jesus Christ and the spiritual influence He exerted far beyond the area where He lived and taught.

Cornelius Tacitus—Governor of Asia

Cornelius Tacitus was a Roman historian and governor of Asia (present-day Turkey) in AD 112. He referred to Jesus as he wrote about the persecution of Christians following Emperor Nero's false accusation that the Christians had burned Rome: "Christus [Christ], the founder of the name, was put to death by Pontius Pilate, procurator of Judea in the reign of Tiberius: but the pernicious superstition, repressed for a time, broke out again, not only through Judea, where the mischief originated, but through the city of Rome also."[18] Tacitus, as a careful historian with access to the government archives of Rome, recorded details that confirmed many accounts in the Gospels, Acts, and Romans.

Suetonius — Roman Historian

Suetonius was the official historian of Rome in AD 125. In his *Life of Claudius* (25.4), he referred to the Christians as causing disturbances in Rome, which led to their being banished from the city. He identified the sect of Christians as being derived from "the instigation of Chrestus," which was his spelling of the name Christ.[19]

Pliny the Younger

Plinius Secundus, known as Pliny the Younger, declared that the Christians were "in the habit of meeting on a certain fixed day before it was light, when they sang in alternate verse a hymn to Christ as to a God, and bound themselves to a solemn oath, not to any wicked deeds, but never to commit any fraud, theft, adultery, never to falsify their word, not to deny a trust when they should be called upon to deliver it up."[20]

Pliny was governor of the Roman province of Bithynia (present-day Turkey) in AD 112. He wrote to the emperor, requesting instructions about the interrogation of the Christians whom he was persecuting. In his epistles, he states that these believers would not worship Emperor Trajan and would not curse their leader, Jesus Christ, even when enduring the suffering of extreme torture. Pliny described the Christians as people who loved the truth at any cost. As we consider the testimony of these early believers, it is impossible to believe that they would willingly suffer and die for something they knew to be a lie. Their martyrdom was based on the fact that they knew the truth of the statements in the Gospels about Jesus.

Lucian of Samosata

Lucian lived in Samosata a century after Christ. In his book *The Passing Peregrinus,* he declared that Jesus was worshiped by His followers and was "the man who was crucified in Palestine because he introduced this new cult into the world."

Flavius Josephus

Jewish historian Flavius Josephus, a contemporary of the apostle Paul, recorded the following:

> Now there was about this time Jesus, a wise man, if it be lawful to call him a man, for he was a doer of wonderful works, a teacher of such men as receive the truth with pleasure. He drew over to him both many of the Jews, and many of the Gentiles. He was [the] Christ, and when Pilate, at the suggestion of the principal men among us, had condemned him to the cross, those that loved him at the first did not forsake him: for he appeared to them alive again the third day: as the divine prophets had foretold these and ten thousand other wonderful things concerning him. And the tribe of Christians so named from him are not extinct at this day.[21]

Josephus was a Pharisee and a Jewish priest living in Jerusalem. Born in AD 37, he witnessed firsthand the events leading up to the destruction of Jerusalem in AD 70. He fought as a general of the Jewish rebel forces in Galilee in the war against Rome. Josephus was captured by the Romans at the fall of the city of Jotapata and befriended the Roman general Vespasian. As a historian, with access to both Roman and Jewish governmental records, he described the events in Israel during the turbulent decades of the first century.

In AD 94, Josephus published in Rome his definitive study of the history of the Jewish people, titled *Antiquities of the Jews.* One of the most fascinating passages in this history concerns the events in the life, death, and resurrection of Jesus Christ. As expected, numerous liberal scholars have declared that Josephus's reference to Jesus Christ and another reference to James and John the Baptist must be interpolations or forgeries added later by unnamed Christian editors. An assertion of forgery requires significant proof, but none of the scholars can produce an ancient copy of *Antiquities of the Jews* that does not contain the quoted passage on Jesus. Philip Schaff has declared that all ancient copies of Josephus's book, including the early Slavonic (Russian) and Arabic-language versions, do in fact contain the disputed passage about the life of Jesus Christ.[22]

Every copy of *Antiquities of the Jews* from the fourth and fifth centuries AD, in several different languages, contains these passages. If the events recorded in the Gospels actually occurred, it is only natural that Josephus would mention them in his narrative. In fact, it would be astonishing if Josephus had failed to mention anything about the ministry and resurrection of Jesus.

Biblical scholar Craig Blomberg wrote that "many recent studies of Josephus, however, agree that much of the passage closely resembles Josephus' style of writing elsewhere…. [M]ost of the passage seems to be authentic and is certainly the most important ancient non-Christian testimony to the life of Jesus which has been preserved." Blomberg concluded with this statement: "The gospels may therefore be trusted as historically reliable."[23]

In addition, R. C. Stone, in his article titled "Josephus," wrote the following: "The passage concerning Jesus has been regarded by some as a Christian interpolation; but the bulk of the evidence, both external and internal, marks it as genuine. Josephus must have known the main facts about the life and death of Jesus, and his historian's curiosity certainly would lead him to investigate the movement which was gaining adherents even in high circles. Arnold Toynbee rates him among the five greatest Hellenic historians."[24]

Evidence About James, the Brother of Jesus

In another passage in Flavius Josephus's *Antiquities of the Jews,* he described the death of James, the brother of Jesus: "As therefore Ananus (the High Priest) was of such a disposition, he thought he had now a good opportunity, as Festus (the Roman Procurator) was now dead, and Albinus (the new Procurator) was still on the road; so he assembled a council of judges, and brought before it the brother of Jesus the so-called Christ, whose name was James, together with some others, and having accused them as law-breakers, he delivered them over to be stoned." While many liberal scholars reject the historicity of passages regarding Jesus Christ, most modern scholars accept the authenticity of the passage about James "the brother of Jesus the so-called Christ."[25]

Evidence About John the Baptist

Josephus described the death of John the Baptist as follows:

> Now, some of the Jews thought that the destruction of Herod's army came from God, and that very justly, as a punishment of what he did against John, that was called the Baptist; for Herod slew him, who was a good man, and commanded the Jews to exercise virtue, both as to righteousness towards one another, and piety towards God, and so to come to baptism; for that the washing [with water] would be acceptable to him, if they made use of it, not in order to the putting away, [or the remission] of some sins [only] but for the purification of the body: supposing still that the soul was thoroughly purified beforehand by righteousness. Now, when [many] there came to crowd about him, for they were greatly moved [or pleased] by hearing his words, Herod, who feared lest the great influence John had over the people might put it into his power and inclination to raise a rebellion [for they seemed ready to do anything he should advise], thought it best, by putting him to death, to prevent any mischief he might cause, and not bring himself into difficulties, by sparing a man who might make him repent of it when it should be too late. Accordingly he was sent a prisoner, out of Herod's suspicious temper, to Macherus (Masada), the castle I before mentioned, and was there put to death.[26]

These historical descriptions by Josephus, together with the other sources mentioned earlier, provide ample evidence that Jesus of Nazareth lived in the first century of this era.

Further Confirmation from Julius Africanus and Thallus

Julius Africanus was a North African Christian teacher writing in AD 215. He recorded the writing of a pagan historian named

Thallus, who lived in AD 52, shortly after the resurrection of Christ. Thallus recorded in his history that there was a miraculous darkness covering the face of the earth at the Passover in AD 32. Julius Africanus records, "Thallus, in the third book of his histories, explains away this darkness as an eclipse of the sun—unreasonably, as it seems to me."[27] Africanus explained that Thallus's theory was unreasonable because a solar eclipse could not occur at the same time as the full moon, and it was at the season of the Paschal full moon that Christ died.

This historical reference by the pagan historian Thallus confirmed the gospel account regarding the darkness that covered the earth when Jesus was dying on the cross. Modern astronomers confirm that Julius Africanus was right in his conclusion that a normal eclipse could not occur at the time of a full moon, which was the time of Passover. The high priest carefully calculated the position of the full moon because the Jewish liturgical calendar, especially Passover, depended on following the lunar position exactly.

It is interesting to note that the ancient Jewish Targums, or paraphrases of the Old Testament, contain additional evidence that the Jews expected the Messiah to be born in Bethlehem, as prophesied in Micah 5:2. Seventy-two of the Targums contain information about the coming Messiah, although the biblical passage being cited did not contain the name Messiah. Two of the Targums clearly indicate that the Messiah would be born at or near Bethlehem. For example, the Targum on Genesis 35:21 talks about Israel pitching its tents "beyond the tower of Eder." The Targum of Jonathan adds detail about this location, calling it "the place where shall be revealed the King Messias in the end of days."[28]

In 1875, Charles R. Condor noted in his submission to the *Palestine Exploration Fund Report* that "Migdol Eder, or 'the Tower of the Flock' was known in AD 700 as about 1,000 paces from Bethlehem," which is the location of the ruins of the Monastery of the Holy Shepherds. Another Targum, commenting on Exodus 12:42, makes a fascinating reference to the area of Nazareth where Jesus was raised by His mother and Joseph. This Targum states that "Moses cometh forth from the desert and Messias goeth forth from Roma." Roma was a village near the town of Nazareth.[29]

Historian Philip Schaff outlined in his book *The Person of Christ* the overwhelming influence that the life of Jesus Christ has had on the subsequent history and culture of the Western world.

> This Jesus of Nazareth, without money and arms, con-quered more millions than Alexander, Caesar, Mohammed, and Napoleon; without science and learning, He shed more light on things human and divine than all philosophers and scholars combined; without the eloquence of schools, He spoke such words of life as were never spoken before or since, and produced effects which lie beyond the reach of orator or poet; without writing a single line, He set more pens in motion, and furnished themes for more sermons, orations, discussions, learned volumes, works of art, and songs of praise than the whole army of great men of ancient and modern times.[30]

While historical records provide overwhelming evidence to prove the absolute reliability of the New Testament records about Jesus Christ, we have not yet witnessed His awesome glory that will be revealed when He returns at the Second Coming. The Puritan writer John Owen discussed the glory of Christ in these words:

> Should the Lord Jesus appear now to any of us in His majesty and glory, it would not be to our edification nor consolation. For we are not meet nor able, by the power of any light or grace that we have received, or can receive, to bear the immediate appearance and representation of them. His beloved apostle John had leaned on His bosom prob-ably many a time in His life, in the intimate familiarities of love; but when He afterward appeared to Him in His glory, "he fell at His feet as dead."

When Christ finally appears in His revealed glory as almighty God at the great Day of the Lord, "then shall all the tribes of the earth mourn, and they shall see the Son of man coming in the clouds of heaven with power and great glory" (Matthew 24:30).

Extraordinary Evidence About Jesus in the Dead Sea Scrolls

If someone had asked a minister in 1947 to prove that the original Hebrew Scriptures were copied without error throughout the last two thousand years, he might have had some difficulty providing an answer. The oldest Old Testament manuscript used by the King James translators was dated approximately AD 1100. Obviously, that was a copy of a copy of a copy. How could we be sure that the text in the AD 1100 manuscript was identical to the original text as given to the writers by God? However, an extraordinary discovery occurred in 1947, the turbulent year before Israel became a nation. In Qumran near the Dead Sea, a Bedouin found a cave that ultimately yielded more than one thousand priceless manuscripts dating back before AD 68, when the Roman legions destroyed the Qumran village during the Jewish war against Rome.

An Arab shepherd boy discovered the greatest archaeological find in history. When the Hebrew scrolls from these caves were examined, scholars found that the Qumran site contained a library with hundreds of texts of both biblical and secular manuscripts that dated to before the destruction of the Second Temple and the death of Jesus. The most incredible discovery was the immense library of biblical manuscripts in Cave Four at Qumran, which contained every book of the Old Testament with the exception of the book of Esther. Multiple copies of some biblical texts, including Genesis, Deuteronomy, and Isaiah, were found in Cave Four.

Scholars discovered that the manuscript copies of the most authoritative Hebrew text, Textus Receptus, used by the King James translators in 1611, were virtually identical to the ancient Dead Sea Scrolls. Aside from a tiny number of spelling variations, not a single important word was altered from the original scrolls found in the caves. How could the Bible have been copied so accurately and faithfully over the many centuries without human error entering into the text? The answer is found in the overwhelming respect and fear of God that motivated Jewish and Christian scholars whose job was to faithfully copy the text of the Bible.

The Essenes were a Jewish community of ascetics that lived primarily in three communities: Qumran at the Dead Sea, the Essene Quarter of Jerusalem (Mount Zion), and Damascus. They appear to have existed from approximately 200 BC until the destruction of their communities in Jerusalem and Qumran by the Roman armies in AD 68. During the first century there were also three significant Jewish religious communities: the Pharisees, the Sadducees, and the Essenes. In their love for the Word of God, the Essenes faithfully copied each Old Testament scroll in their scriptorium in the village of Qumran. New evidence suggests that these men of God were aware of the new religious leader in Israel known as Jesus of Nazareth and the group of writings about Him known as the New Testament. The Christian historian Eusebius, who wrote around AD 300, believed that the Essenes were influenced in their beliefs by Christianity.

Quotes from the New Testament in the Dead Sea Scrolls

When the Dead Sea Scrolls were discovered, many Christian scholars wondered if they might contain evidence about the new faith of Christianity in the first century. For almost fifty years, the hopes of Christian scholars were frustrated by the decision of the small group of original scroll scholars to withhold publication and release of a significant number of the precious scrolls. Some scholars speculated publicly that there might be evidence about Christ in the unpublished scrolls, but the scroll scholars denied these claims. After forty-five years the original team responsible for the huge number of scrolls discovered in Cave Four had published only 20 percent of the five hundred Dead Sea Scrolls they had in their possession.

Finally, after a public relations campaign led by *Biblical Archaeology Review* magazine, the unpublished scrolls were released to the academic world. Scholars then found that the scrolls contain definite references to the New Testament and, most important, to Jesus. One of the most extraordinary of these scrolls appears to refer directly to the crucifixion of Jesus Christ.

The Crucified Messiah Scroll

A scroll fragment includes intriguing references to a Messiah who suffered crucifixion for the sins of humanity. The scroll was translated by Dr. Robert Eisenman, professor of Middle East religions at California State University–Long Beach. He declared, "The text is of the most far-reaching significance because it shows that whatever group was responsible for these writings was operating in the same general scriptural and Messianic framework of early Christianity."[31] Although the original scroll scholars still claimed there was no evidence about early Christianity in the unpublished scrolls, this single scroll contradicted their assertions.

This five-line scroll contains information about the death of the Messiah. It refers to "the Prophet Isaiah" and his Messianic prophecy (see Isaiah 53) that identified the Messiah as One who will suffer for the sins of His people. This scroll provides an amazing parallel to the New Testament revelation that the Messiah would first suffer death before He would ultimately rule the nations. Many scholars believed that the Jews during the first century of our era believed that, when He finally came, the Messiah would rule forever without dying. The Essene writer of this scroll understood the dual role of the Messiah, as Savior and King, just as the early Christians did. This scroll identified the Messiah as the "Shoot of Jesse" (King David's father) and the "Branch of David" and declared that he was "pierced" and "wounded." The word *pierced* reminds us of the Messianic prophecy in Psalm 22:16: "They pierced my hands and my feet."

The scroll also describes the Messiah as a "leader of the community" who was "put to death." This reference points clearly to the historical Jesus of Nazareth. Jesus is the only one who ever claimed to be the Messiah who would be crucified. The genealogies recorded in both Matthew's and Luke's gospels reveal that Jesus was the only one who could prove by the genealogical records kept in the Temple that He was of the lineage of King David. Additionally, the scroll identified the Messiah as "the sceptre," which probably refers to the Genesis 49:10 prophecy: "The sceptre shall not depart from Judah, nor a lawgiver from between his feet, until Shiloh come; and unto him shall the gathering of the people be." This scroll confirms the historical truthfulness of the New Testament record about Jesus and His crucifixion. The evidence from the scroll suggests that the Essene writer acknowledged that Jesus of Nazareth was the "suffering Messiah" who died for the sins of His people.

The Son of God Scroll Fragment

Another curious scroll fragment discovered in Cave Four, known as 4Q246, refers to the hope of a future Messiah figure. This is another of the scrolls that remained unpublished for fifty years. Amazingly, the text in this scroll refers to the Messiah as "the son of God" and the "son of the Most High." These words are an exact parallel to the wording recorded in the gospel of Luke (1:32, 35).

Scroll 4Q246, the Son of God scroll, contains these words: "He shall be called the son of God, and they shall designate [call] him son of the Most High."[32] Compare the words in scroll 4Q246 to the divinely inspired words found in Luke 1:32, 35: "He shall be great, and shall be called the Son of the Highest: and the Lord God shall give unto him the throne of his father David.... And the angel answered and said unto her [Mary], The Holy Ghost shall come upon thee, and the power of the Highest shall over-shadow thee: therefore also that holy thing which shall be born of thee shall be called the Son of God."

Anyone comparing these two first-century texts would be intrigued by the similarity of concept and wording describing the Messianic leader. One of the great differences between Christian and Jewish conceptions of the promised Messiah revolves around His relationship to God. While the Jews believe the Messiah will be a great man, such as Moses, with a divine mission, Christians believe the Bible teaches that the Messiah is uniquely "the Son of God." The Jewish view usually held that the concept of a "son of God" violated the primary truth of monotheism found in Deuteronomy 6:4: "Hear, O Israel: The LORD our God is one LORD."

Christians believe that Jesus' claim to be the Son of God is not a violation of Deuteronomy 6:4. Rather, Christians believe in the Trinity, the doctrine that the Father, the Son, and the Holy Spirit are one God revealed in three personalities. The presence of these statements in the Dead Sea Scrolls suggests the possibility that some of the Essenes either accepted the Messianic claims of Jesus Christ or anticipated this concept based on Old Testament prophecies.

Another possibility is this: could scroll 4Q246 contain a direct quote from an Essene writer who had heard the words of the gospel of Luke, which was being circulated at the time? The wording "the Son of God" is identical to that used in Luke 1:35. This stands as a tremendous witness to the early existence and transmission of the gospel records. If the Gospels were written and distributed within thirty-five years of the events of the life of Jesus, which corresponds with the date of scroll 4Q246, then they stand as the best eyewitness historical records we could hope to possess.

Other New Testament Quotes Identified in the Dead Sea Scrolls

In 1971, a biblical scholar named José O'Callaghan studied some of the small fragments of scrolls discovered in Cave Seven at Qumran. He was looking at fragments that contained small portions of a verse. In some cases only three or four lines remained from an original scroll.

O'Callaghan examined several fragments captured in a photo in *The Discoveries of the Judean Desert of Jordan.* He noticed that several of them, listed as "fragments not identified," did not fit any Old Testament text. However, these Greek-language fragments bore an uncanny resemblance to several verses in the New Testament. He read the Greek words *beget* and a word that could be *Gennesaret,* a word for the Sea of Galilee. The fragment containing *Gennesaret* appeared to be a quotation of the passage describing the events just after the feeding of the five thousand and Jesus walking on the water, found in Mark 6:52–53: "For they considered not the miracle of the loaves: for their heart was hardened. And when they [Jesus and the disciples] had passed over, they came into the land of Gennesaret, and drew to the shore."

If the scroll fragments contained portions of the gospel of Mark, they would certainly be the earliest New Testament texts ever discovered—*dating to only a few years after Christ's death.*

O'Callaghan identified eight fragments from Cave Seven that appear to be quotes from the following verses:

"For the earth bringeth forth fruit of herself." (Mark 4:28)

"And he saw them toiling in rowing." (Mark 6:48)

"And Jesus answering said unto them, Render to Caesar." (Mark 12:17)

"And when they had eaten enough, they lightened the ship." (Acts 27:38)

"And not only so, but we also joy in God through our Lord Jesus Christ." (Romans 5:11)

"And without controversy great is the mystery of godliness." (1 Timothy 3:16)

"For if any be a hearer of the word, and not a doer." (James 1:23)

As one example of O'Callaghan's study, he examined a small fragment known as 7Q5 that contained twenty Greek letters on five lines of text. Another scroll scholar, Carsten Thiede, agrees with O'Callaghan's conclusion that portions of the Mark 6:52–53 passage appear in this scroll fragment. While other scholars disagree with the identification of this fragment as a verse from the New Testament, they do admit that almost all the scrolls found in Cave Seven were written in the period between 50 BC and AD 50, which is consistent with the time of the writing of the gospel of Mark.[33]

At this stage we cannot be certain that O'Callaghan's conclusion is correct. However, the parallel in the wording of Scroll 4Q246 and Luke 1:32, 35 provides strong support for the possibility that these fragments are related to New Testament passages.

When we consider the total amount of evidence that confirms the biblical record about Jesus of Nazareth, we can have confidence that we know more about the life, death, and resurrection of Christ than we know about any other person in the ancient world. God has not left us in darkness concerning the truthfulness of the miracles, prophecies, and teaching of His Son.

Notes

1. Arthur Dewey, quoted in *Time,* April 1994.
2. Quotes taken from an article about the Jesus Seminar meeting in Santa Rosa, California, published in *Time,* April 6, 1996.
3. Found at www.songtime.com/sbcsearch.htm (site now discontinued).
4. For more on this argument, see C. S. Lewis, *Mere Christianity* (New York: Macmillan, 1952), especially *What Christians Believe,* chapter 3.
5. For more on this, see Flavius Josephus, *Antiquities of the Jews,* trans. William Whiston (Grand Rapids: Kregel, 1960).
6. For more on this, see Simon Greenleaf, *The Testimony of the Evangelists Examined by the Rules of Evidence Administered in Courts of Justice* (1846; repr., Grand Rapids: Baker, 1956).
7. William Ramsay, *The Bearing of Recent Discovery on the Trustworthiness of the New Testament* (1915; repr., Grand Rapids: Baker, 1953), 80.
8. Merrill F. Unger, *Archeology and the New Testament* (Grand Rapids: Zondervan, 1962).
9. Abraham Lincoln, quoted in Lionel Luckhoo, *Evidence Irrefutable Which Can Change Your Lives* (Dallas: Luckhoo Ministries, n.d.).
10. Otto Betz, *What Do We Know About Jesus?* (Philadelphia: Westminster, 1968).
11. Solomon Zeitlin, "The Halaka in the Gospels and Its Relation to the Jewish Law at the Time of Jesus," *Hebrew Union College Annual* 1 (1924): 372–73.
12. Frederick F. Bruce, *The New Testament Documents: Are They Reliable?* (Downers Grove, IL: InterVarsity, 1967).
13. William F. Albright, writing in *Christianity Today,* January 18, 1963. For more on this, see also William F. Albright, *Recent Discoveries in Bible Lands* (New York: Funk and Wagnalls, 1955).

14. Frederic G. Kenyon quotation found at www.geocities .com/Athens/Parthenon/2104/biblioNT.html (site now discontinued).
15. Frederic G. Kenyon, *The Story of the Bible* (Grand Rapids: Eerdmans, 1967), 133.
16. Bernard Ramm, *Protestant Christian Evidences: A Textbook of the Evidences of the Truthfulness of the Christian Faith for Conservative Protestants* (Chicago: Moody, 1953), 239.
17. Ramm, *Protestant Christian Evidences*, 239.
18. Tacitus *Annals* 15.44 (AD 112).
19. Suetonius *Life of Claudius* 25.4 (AD 125).
20. Pliny the Younger *Epistle X* 96 (AD 112).
21. Flavius Josephus, *Antiquities of the Jews*, trans. William Whiston (Grand Rapids: Kregel, 1960), 18.3.3.
22. Philip Schaff, *History of the Christian Church* (Oak Harbor, WA: Logos Research Systems, 1997).
23. Craig L. Blomberg, *The Historical Reliability of the Gospels* (Downers Grove, IL: InterVarsity, 1987).
24. R. C. Stone, writing on Josephus and Arnold Toynbee, *Zondervan Pictorial Encyclopedia of the Bible* 3:697.
25. Josephus, *Antiquities of the Jews*, 20.9.1.
26. Josephus, *Antiquities of the Jews*, 18.5.2.
27. Julius Africanus, *Post Nicene Fathers*, Ante-Nicene Fathers, 10 vols. (Grand Rapids: Eerdmans, 1987).
28. Charles R. Condor, *Palestine Exploration Fund Report*, Quarterly Report, April 1875.
29. Charles R. Condor, *Palestine Exploration Fund Report*, Quarterly Report, January 1875, 98.
30. Philip Schaff, *The Person of Christ: His Perfect Humanity a Proof of His Divinity*, rev. ed. (New York: American Tract Society, 1913).
31. Robert Eisenman and Michael Wise, eds., *The Dead Sea Scrolls Uncovered: The First Complete Translation and Interpretation of 50 Key Documents Withheld for over 35 Years* (New York: Penguin, 1993).

32. Geza Vermes, ed., *The Dead Sea Scrolls in English*, 3rd ed. (London: Penguin, 1987).

33. The scholarly magazine *Bible Review* ran a fascinating article on Dr. José O'Callaghan's research on the scroll fragments and their possible connection to the New Testament. See Graham Stanton, "A Gospel Among the Scrolls?" *Bible Review* 11 (December 1995): 36–42.

4

Scientific Evidence That the Bible Is Accurate

The greatest evidence that the Scriptures are inspired by God is that they reveal an astonishing amount of advanced scientific knowledge that cannot be explained unless a supernatural Being inspired the writing of the Scriptures. The Bible is not a scientific book; however, when it does make scientific statements, they are stunning in their accuracy.

David wrote, "That I may publish with the voice of thanksgiving, and tell of all thy wondrous works" (Psalm 26:7). As you consider God's wondrous works and the astonishing level of scientific knowledge revealed in the Bible, ask yourself a question: how could the writers of the Scriptures possibly know these facts unless these men were supernaturally inspired by God?

The book of Genesis describes the creation of humanity with these words: "And the LORD God formed man of the dust of the ground, and breathed into his nostrils the breath of life; and man became a living soul" (2:7). For many years scientists laughed at the simplicity of the account that God used "the dust of the ground" to construct the elements and complex molecules that make up a human being. However, after a century of scientific research, scientists were startled to discover that clay and earth contain every element found in the human body. Researchers at NASA's Ames Research Center confirmed the Bible's account from Genesis 2. The scientists concluded, "We are just beginning to learn. The biblical scenario for the creation of life turns out to be not far off the mark."[1]

Many of the greatest scientific minds of past centuries were Bible-believing Christians who accepted the scientific accuracy of the Word of God. Sir Isaac Newton, perhaps the greatest scientific mind in history, accepted the Word of God and the truth of creation. Other strong believers in God who changed the face of scientific knowledge include Lord Kelvin, the founder of the science of thermodynamics; Louis Pasteur, who made great advances in germ theory; Johann Kepler, who created modern astronomy; and Robert Boyle, the greatest chemist of his age.

The Creation of the Universe

The book of Genesis begins with the words "In the beginning God created the heaven and the earth" (1:1). Until 1950, most scientists believed in some variation of the steady state theory, which suggested that the universe has always existed as we observe it today. This theory contradicted the Word of God, which affirms that God had created the universe at a definite point in time. New discoveries in astronomy and astrophysics then forced the scientific world to change its theory. Today, virtually all scientists accept some variation of the big bang theory, which suggests the universe came into existence at a particular point in time, when an incredibly dense mass of matter exploded, forming all the galaxies and planets.

Dr. Paul Dirac, a Nobel Prize winner from Cambridge University, wrote, "It seems certain that there was a definite time of creation." Until quite recently, the word *creation* was never written or spoken approvingly by scientists. Then Dr. Alexander Vilenkin wrote a scientific article titled "Creation of the Universe from Nothing." In it, Vilenkin noted that scientists claim the creation of the universe is "outside the scope of presently known laws of physics."[2]

The Bible is explicit about the creation of the universe. It tells us that "God created the heaven and the earth." However, in opposition to the theoretical explosion of the big bang, the Bible affirms that God created everything from nothing with absolute purpose. The evidence from nature and recent scientific discoveries reveal the meticulous design of the supernatural intelligence and power of God.

The Lord challenged Abraham to count the stars, because God wanted to demonstrate the awesome number of heavenly bodies that He had created. "And he [God] brought him [Abraham] forth abroad, and said, Look now toward heaven, and tell the stars, if thou be able to number them: and he said unto him, So shall thy seed be" (Genesis 15:5). The unaided human eye can see about 1,029 stars. With a pair of binoculars or an inexpensive telescope you can see more than 3,300 stars. In the last few years, advanced telescopes have allowed us to view more than *two hundred million* stars, and that is just in the Milky Way galaxy.

Exploring the Boundaries of the Universe

As late as 1915 astronomers believed that our galaxy comprised the entire universe. Then in 1925 the great astronomer Edwin Hubble used his new one-hundred-inch mirror telescope on Mount Wilson to view new galaxies of stars that were more than six million trillion miles from Earth. Hubble proved that the universe contained as many galaxies outside our galaxy as there were stars inside our galaxy. During the last century, ever-more powerful telescopes revealed that the known universe contained more than ten billion galaxies. But that was just a start. A series of new discoveries, of a magnitude that taxes our imagination, was soon to come.

The Hubble Space Telescope, launched into orbit in 1990, focused on a tiny point in distant space so small that it is equivalent to focusing your eye on a grain of sand held at arm's length. After examining this very small area of space, astronomers determined that it contained an additional fifteen hundred galaxies, each one the size of the Milky Way. The universe is more than five times larger than astronomers previously believed. The known universe contains *more than fifty billion galaxies,* with each galaxy containing more than two hundred million stars.

To get some sense of the vastness of the universe, try this exercise. Draw two circles on a sheet of paper, with a small circle at the top of the page representing the sun. Using the scale of one inch to represent ten million miles, draw a much smaller circle nine inches below the sun, to represent Earth. Now draw a third small circle to represent the nearest neighboring star, Alpha Centauri. You would need to draw the circle representing Alpha Centauri more than forty miles distant from your sheet of paper to correctly represent the distance between Earth and the closest star other than the sun.

Light travels through space at the speed of 186,282 miles per second, or nearly six trillion miles every year. A ray of light leaving Alpha Centauri at this moment would take four years to reach Earth as it crosses twenty-four trillion miles of space.

Who Established the Boundaries?

In the Bible, the psalmist wrote, "By the word of the LORD were the heavens made; and all the host of them by the breath of his mouth.... For he spake, and it was done; he commanded, and it stood fast" (Psalm 33:6, 9). Scientists have failed to develop a credible theory to account for the existence of the universe.

In 1980, astronomer Herman Bondi declared the total failure of science to account for the universe: "As an erstwhile cosmologist, I speak with feeling of the fact that theories of the origin of the universe have been disproved by present day empirical evidence as have various theories of the origin of the solar system."[3] Another great astronomer, Harold Jeffreys, wrote, "To sum up, I think that all suggested accounts of the origin of the solar system are subject to serious objections. The conclusion in the present state of the subject would be that the system cannot exist."[4] In other words, Jeffreys admitted that none of the atheistic theories could account for the universe as we know it to exist.

The Bible declares that God separated the waters below from the waters that were above in the heavens: "And God said, Let there be a firmament in the midst of the waters, and let it divide the waters from the waters. And God made the firmament, and divided the waters which were under the firmament from the waters which were above the firmament: and it was so" (Genesis 1:6–7). God created a large amount of water that He placed in the heavens, or outer space. The existence of water in space seemed improbable, to say the least. However, astronomical discoveries have proven conclusively that massive amounts of water do exist in space, just as the Bible claimed. Naturally, because of extreme temperatures, the waters in space are frozen into permanent ice. Satellites have discovered ice on Mars as well as in the rings of Saturn. Further, the comets that travel through our solar system are composed of massive amounts of ice. And in 1998, NASA announced that the *Lunar Prospector* spacecraft had detected evidence of massive amounts of ice beneath the surface of the moon.[5]

A massive block of ice from space collided with the Earth at the beginning of the twentieth century at a point in northern Russia:

> In the morning of 30 June 1908, a fantastic explosion occurred in central Siberia.... Witnesses described an enormous meteoric bolide visible in the sky for a few seconds. Other witnesses from a distance of 60 kilometers [36 miles] from the point of impact were knocked over.... Seismic shocks were registered over the whole world... [T]his event was due to the collision with the earth of a block of ice weighing 30,000 tons which...released energy equivalent to that of a thermonuclear bomb of 12 megatons.[6]

The Siberian explosion was caused by a fragment of Encke's comet that broke away during its passage through the solar system.

Massive amounts of ice also exist at the outer edge of our solar system. The Oort Cloud is a vast region of space that is estimated to hold as many as one trillion large comets composed of ice and rock. Each comet is calculated to contain as much as one trillion tons of ice. The vast amount of water in our oceans is less than a fraction of the quantities of water that exist in the "firmament above," in the heavens, as reported in the book of Genesis. A passage in Job also refers to the ice and frost in the heavens: "Hath the rain a father? or who hath begotten the drops of dew? Out of whose womb came the ice? and the hoary frost of heaven, who hath gendered it? The waters are hid as with a stone, and the face of the deep is frozen. Canst thou bind the sweet influences of Pleiades, or loose the bands of Orion?" (38:28–31).

Not only is science discovering that the universe is much larger and much more complex than was assumed in the past, science also is beginning to confront the big questions for which scientists have no answers. However, the scientific community continues to resist answers to these questions that draw from the scientific truth found in the Bible.

The Laws of Thermodynamics

The laws of thermodynamics are among the most fundamental laws of science. These laws were developed to explain the processes and forces that govern the operations of the universe. No exceptions have ever been detected. Yet surprisingly, the ancient text of the Bible contains statements regarding these fundamental laws of science.

The Law of Conservation of Energy

After exhaustive experiments, modern scientists have developed two fundamental laws of the science of thermodynamics that describe the nature of our known universe. The first is the law of conservation of energy, which reveals that "energy can be neither created nor destroyed." This law describes the present state of the universe after its initial creation by God.

The law of conservation of energy was explained by the science writer Isaac Asimov as follows: "Energy can be transferred from one place to another, or transformed from one form to another, but it can be neither created nor destroyed." In other words, the combined amount of energy that exists throughout the universe can never increase or diminish. For example, when a nuclear device is detonated, the uranium 235 and plutonium within the warhead are not annihilated. The matter is simply transformed into a staggering release of heat and light energy.

Every experiment has confirmed the law of conservation of energy as the most basic fundamental understanding of the way the universe works.

Although this fundamental law of the universe was discovered and proven scientifically only during the last century, the Word of God recorded this principle thousands of years ago. Moses wrote in Genesis, "And on the seventh day God ended his work which he had made; and he rested on the seventh day from all his work which he had made. And God blessed the seventh day, and sanctified it: because that in it he had rested from all his work which God created and made" (2:2–3).

This inspired passage clearly declares that when God completed the creation of man and woman on the sixth day, He "rested from all his work which God...made." After the sixth day, God's work was complete, which accounts for the law of conservation of energy. The Scriptures reveal why nothing can now be totally annihilated, because Jesus Christ, who created all things, is "upholding all things by the word of his power" (Hebrews 1:3). In another passage the writer of the book of Hebrews declared that Jesus, the Creator of the universe, had finished His acts of creation: "For he that is entered into his rest, he also hath ceased from his own works, as God did from his" (4:10).

The Law of Entropy

In three key passages the Scriptures reveal another powerful law that governs our universe, the law of entropy. The prophet Isaiah wrote, "Lift up your eyes to the heavens, and look upon the earth beneath: for the heavens shall vanish away like smoke, and the earth shall wax old like a garment, and they that dwell therein shall die in like manner: but my salvation shall be for ever, and my righteousness shall not be abolished" (Isaiah 51:6).

The psalmist also expressed this law as follows: "Of old hast thou laid the foundation of the earth: and the heavens are the work of thy hands. They shall perish, but thou shalt endure: yea, all of them shall wax old like a garment; as a vesture shalt thou change them, and they shall be changed" (Psalm 102:25–26). The words in this verse exactly describe in simple, accurate language the law of entropy.

Finally, the book of Hebrews declares, "They shall perish; but thou remainest; and they all shall wax old as doth a garment" (1:11).

The second law of thermodynamics (the law of entropy) states that, in all physical processes, every ordered system becomes more disordered over time. In effect, everything in our universe is running down and wearing out as energy becomes less and less available for use. The universe will eventually run down to the extent that there will be a heat death. There will be no more usable energy available. Scientists discovered this fundamental law in the last century, but long before the law was discovered the Bible described it in concise terms.

If you give careful thought to this universal principle, you quickly see that it is impossible for the theory of evolution to be true. Evolution suggests that all simple systems and elements become increasingly more organized and complex through a process of random chance. However, scientific observation has shown that all systems and elements disintegrate over time to something less organized. In fact, the second law of thermodynamics, the law of entropy, absolutely proves the theory of evolution is nonsense.

The Implications of These Laws

Consider the implications. The law of conservation of energy proves that the universe could not have created itself. It had to be created by a supernatural force outside the universe. The law states that the combined amount of energy that exists in the universe is constant. It cannot be increased or decreased.

However, the law of entropy shows that the whole universe is running down as it decays. The universe is moving from a higher level of order and complexity to more and more disorder. At the same time, the universe has a lower order of available, usable energy. This reveals that the universe must have been created at a point in the past and has been running down like a clock ever since. The sun burns nuclear fuel at the rate of two hundred thousand nuclear explosions every second to flood our solar system with heat and light. However, since it is burning up its store of fuel, logic declares that there must have been a point in time when the sun was created and began this process.

The evolutionary theory that postulates a universe that appeared on its own, with no supernatural intelligence behind its creation, is contradicted by the known laws of science.

The Shape of the Earth

Critics of the Bible have falsely suggested that the Bible stated Earth was flat because of the biblical expression "the four corners of the earth" (see Isaiah 11:12; Revelation 7:1), as if the writers actually believed in a flat Earth. However, this phrase was simply a colloquial expression. It is still used today to indicate either the whole Earth or the four extremities of the globe from a central position. God inspired the prophet Isaiah to reveal that our planet was a sphere, knowledge that was far in advance of what was known about the Earth's shape: "It is he that sitteth upon the circle of the earth, and the inhabitants thereof are as grasshoppers; that stretcheth out the heavens as a curtain, and spreadeth them out as a tent to dwell in" (Isaiah 40:22). The expression "the circle of the earth" clearly describes the Earth as a globe.

This scientific knowledge was not limited to Isaiah. The gospel writer Luke described the coming of Christ in the daytime as follows: "Even thus shall it be *in the day* when the Son of man is revealed" (Luke 17:30). However, several verses later, Luke described the same event by declaring that Christ will come in the night: "I tell you, *in that night* there shall be two men in one bed; the one shall be taken, and the other shall be left" (verse 34). How could a single event, the coming of the Messiah, occur simultaneously "in the day" and "in that night"?

These statements must have appeared impossible and contradictory at any time from the first century until recently. However, we now understand that, on whatever day Christ returns, it will be a daytime event for those on one side of the globe while the event will occur during the night for those living on the other side of the planet. How could Luke have known this scientific fact two thousand years ago?

David wrote a wonderful song of praise to God in recognition of the awesome glory of the heavens: "Their line has gone out through all the earth, and their words to the end of the world. In them he hath set a tabernacle for the sun, which is as a bridegroom coming out of his chamber, and rejoiceth as a strong man to run a race. His going forth is from the end of heaven, and his circuit unto the ends of it: and there is nothing hid from the heat thereof" (Psalm 19:4–6). David declared that the sun traveled in "his circuit unto the ends of it [heaven]."

During the last few centuries many Bible critics denounced this statement as inaccurate because they falsely claimed that the Bible's statement declared that the sun moved in an orbit around the Earth. However, the Bible never made that claim. The Scriptures declare that the sun moved in "his circuit unto the ends of it [heaven]." Discoveries by the Hubble Space Telescope confirmed the accuracy of Scripture when astronomers proved that the sun moves through space in a circuit covering an orbit that lasts more than 260 million years.

The ancient book of Job tells us that "he [God] stretcheth out the north over the empty place, and hangeth the earth upon nothing" (26:7). This was an astonishingly advanced and accurate scientific statement. The ancient pagans, who were contemporary with Job, believed that the Earth was balanced on the back of an elephant that rested on the back of a turtle. Other pagans believed that the mythological hero Atlas carried the Earth on his shoulders. However, four thousand years ago, Job was inspired by God to reveal the truth that God "hangeth the earth upon nothing." Only a century ago scientists believed that the Earth and stars were supported by some kind of ether. Yet Job accurately stated that our planet moves in its orbit through empty outer space.

Astronomers discovered that the area to the north of the axis of our Earth, toward the polar star, is almost empty of stars. This stands in contrast to the heavenly bodies that appear in all other directions. There are far more stars in every other direction from our Earth than in the area to the far north. As Job reported, "He stretcheth out the north over the empty place" (Job 26:7). Mitchell Waldrop wrote the following in an article in *Science* magazine.

> The recently announced "hole in space," a 300 million-light-year gap in the distribution of galaxies, has taken cosmologists by surprise…. But three very deep core samples in the

Northern Hemisphere, lying in the general direction of the constellation Bootes, showed striking gaps in the red shift distribution.[7]

Scientists have proven that Job was correct.

The Bible is rich with unexpected scientific revelations. And bear in mind that God put this scientific data in Scripture thousands of years before modern science stumbled upon the same information. Scholars in Israel calculated that the Torah describes the exact duration of time that passes between the appearances of new moons. The time lapse is precisely twenty-nine days, twelve hours, forty-four minutes, and five seconds, or 29.53059 days. With billions of dollars of research and observations through sophisticated telescopes, NASA calculated that a new moon appears every 29.530588 days!

The Earth Was Created for Human Life

As recorded in Genesis, God created the Earth and everything in the universe with a clear purpose in mind: "And God blessed them, and God said unto them, Be fruitful, and multiply, and replenish the earth, and subdue it: and have dominion over the fish of the sea, and over the fowl of the air, and over every living thing that moveth upon the earth" (Genesis 1:28).

Scientists have declared that the solar system is "anthropic." This means that the Earth bears evidence that it was designed to support human life. An astonishing number of scientific variables fit within very narrow ranges that allow human life to flourish on a planet. If the Earth orbited much farther away from the sun, we would freeze. If it was much closer to the sun, we would burn up. If the magnetic forces within our planet were stronger or weaker, life could not exist. If our Earth did not rotate frequently, then one-half of the planet would be in extended darkness, with no vegetation. The other side of the planet would be an uninhabitable desert, baked by overwhelming heat.

If our Earth was not tilted on an axis of slightly more than twenty-three degrees, we would not have the seasonal variation that produces the abundance of crops that feed humanity. Without the twenty-three-degree tilt, less than half of the present land used for the cultivation of crops would be suitable to grow vegetables. The moon produces the tides that replenish the oceans with oxygen, allowing fish to breathe.

If our planet were twice as large, the effect of the increased gravity would make everything on the Earth's surface weigh eight times what it weighs today. This increased weight would destroy many forms of life. If the Earth were significantly smaller, the lessened gravity would be incapable of holding the atmosphere that is essential for breathing. A much thinner atmosphere would provide no protection from the twenty-five thousand meteors that burn up in the atmosphere over the Earth every day. In addition, a thinner atmosphere would be incapable of retaining the higher temperatures required for human and animal life to exist.

Professor Robert Jastrow, director of NASA's Goddard Institute for Space Studies for twenty years, stated:

> The smallest change in any of the circumstances of the natural world, such as the relative strengths of the forces of nature, or the properties of the elementary particles, would have led to a universe in which there could be no life and no man. For example, if nuclear forces were decreased by a few percent, the particles of the universe would not have come together in nuclear reactions to make the ingredients, such as carbon atoms, of which life must be constructed.[8]

In other words, if the universe were changed in the slightest way, human life could not exist. Our universe, solar system, and especially our Earth were all constructed with a definite purpose by a powerful Intelligence within very narrow parameters to allow human life to flourish. Nehemiah wrote the following words centuries before the birth of Jesus Christ: "Thou, even thou, art LORD alone; thou hast made heaven, the heaven of heavens, with all their host, the earth, and all things that are therein, the seas, and all that is therein, and thou preservest them all; and the host of heaven worshippeth thee" (Nehemiah 9:6).

The Hydrological Cycle

People living in past centuries did not have a clear understanding of the climatic patterns that control our planet's environment.

However, the books of Job, Ecclesiastes, Isaiah, and Jeremiah all provide details about the complexity of the weather system. The complete hydrological cycle governing evaporation, cloud formation, thunder, lightning, and rain is explained in surprising detail in the Old Testament. For example, the book of Ecclesiastes states, "If the clouds be full of rain, they empty themselves upon the earth" (11:3). Ecclesiastes confirms that most clouds are formed by evaporation from the oceans: "All the rivers run into the sea; yet the sea is not full; unto the place from whence the rivers come, thither they return again" (1:7). Most of the water that forms into clouds comes from the evaporation of the oceans that cover more than 70 percent of the Earth's surface.

The book of Job asks the question, "Dost thou know the balancings of the clouds, the wondrous works of him which is perfect in knowledge?" (37:16). When you consider the weight of water compared to air, it is astonishing that enormous quantities of water are raised from the oceans and lakes and lifted thousands of feet in the air, where they remain suspended for long periods. Air cools as it rises upward, supporting the water vapor in the clouds until the drops become heavy enough to fall to Earth as rain. The answer to the question in Job 37:16 is also found in Job: "For he [God] maketh small the drops of water: they pour down rain according to the vapour thereof; which the clouds do drop and distil upon man abundantly. Also can any understand the spreadings of the clouds, or the noise of his tabernacle?" (36:27–29). This incredible biblical passage reveals the complete hydrological cycle of evaporation, cloud formation, and precipitation.

The Complexity of Weather Patterns

King Solomon described the circular wind patterns that determine the weather around the globe: "The wind goeth toward the south, and turneth about unto the north; it whirleth about continually, and the wind returneth again according to his circuits" (Ecclesiastes 1:6). How could Solomon have known three thousand years ago that the planetary winds follow a circular pattern from south to north and south again? Job added even more detail: "For he looketh to the ends of the earth, and seeth under the whole heaven; to make the weight for the winds; and he weigheth the waters by measure. When he made a decree for the rain, and a way for the lightning of the thunder" (Job 28:24–26). Job's words reveal that the winds are governed by their weight, a fact that scientists determined only in the last century. How could Job have known that the air and the wind patterns are governed by their weight? Meteorologists have found that the relative weights of wind and water have a great deal to do with determining weather patterns.

There also is a connection between lightning, thunder, and the triggering of rainfall. Apparently, a slight change in the electrical charge within a cloud is one of the key factors that cause microscopic water droplets in clouds to join with other droplets until they are heavy enough to fall as rain. In addition, a powerful electrical charge—as high as three hundred million volts—in a cloud sends a leader stroke down through the air toward the ground. Only one-fiftieth of a second later, a second and more powerful return stroke travels back to the cloud, following the path opened by the leader stroke. Thunder occurs because the air within this path has been vaporized by superheating it to fifty thousand degrees. Superheated air expands outward at supersonic speed, creating the noise of thunder. Job's description, "he made a decree for the rain, and a way for the lightning of the thunder" (Job 28:26), is startling in its accuracy. No human could have known this in ancient times without the divine revelation of God.

Paths in the Sea

God asked Job about the deep springs of water at the bottom of the ocean: "Hast thou entered into the springs of the sea? or hast thou walked in the search of the depth?" (Job 38:16). King David also made reference to such springs: "The fowl of the air, and the fish of the sea, and whatsoever passeth through the paths of the seas" (Psalm 8:8).

Matthew Maury (1806–73) is considered the father of oceanography. Maury took note of King David's expression "paths of the seas" and decided to find them. Science is indebted to him for his remarkable discovery of the warm and cold continental currents, such as the Gulf Stream, which helps moderate the climates of the British Isles, continental Europe, and Scandinavia.

Fountains and Springs in the Oceans

A number of biblical passages refer to fountains and springs in the depths of the oceans, containing vast amounts of water beneath the seabed. In Genesis, Moses spoke about these springs in connection with the Flood: "In the six hundredth year of Noah's life...were all the fountains [springs] of the great deep broken up" (Genesis 7:11). The writer of Proverbs also wrote, "He [God] strengthened the fountains of the deep" (8:28).

However, until the last century there was no scientific confirmation of these biblical statements. In 1977, marine scientists discovered springs in the ocean off the coast of Ecuador at a depth of 1.5 miles.[9] The superheated water in these ocean springs registered approximately 450 degrees Fahrenheit, and as such are referred to as the Hot Springs. Researchers found six other ocean springs only sixty miles apart. Many other ocean springs have been discovered since 1977, including enormous springs in the Arctic Ocean, beneath the polar ice cap.

Critics of the Bible have claimed that the biblical account of the Flood is not credible because there is not enough water in the oceans to cover the Earth's surface to the height mentioned in Genesis—fifteen cubits, or twenty-two and a half feet (see Genesis 7:20). However, deep ocean valleys such as the Mariana Trench (more than six miles deep) contain vast amounts of water. If the topography of the pre-Flood world was largely flat, without mountains or deep valleys, ocean valleys would contain much of the water needed to flood the entire Earth. Further, the Earth's pre-Flood atmosphere likely contained significantly more water vapor than today's atmosphere holds. And add to this the discovery of huge quantities of water in the Earth's crust. Marine geologist and geophysicist Peter Rona suggested, "There is probably as much water circulating under the sea floor as there is in the oceans above."[10]

In addition, the reluctant prophet Jonah wrote in the Old Testament that there are mountains on the bottom of the ocean floor: "The waters compassed me about, even to the soul: the depth closed me round about, the weeds were wrapped about my head. I went down to the bottoms of the mountains; the earth with her bars was about me for ever" (Jonah 2:5–6). In the last century, marine scientists discovered towering mountains and deep trenches in the seabed. Some undersea mountains rise 12,000 feet above the ocean floor. (The Hawaiian Islands are in fact the tops of several undersea mountains formed from erupting volcanoes.) The majority of the ridges peak at about 8,000 feet, and the undersea mountain ranges can stretch out for up to 1,500 miles. Numerous ocean trenches run parallel to both continents and island chains. Eighteen trenches were found in the Pacific, with only three in the Atlantic Ocean. Several of the major trenches are up to 18,000 feet deep. The Challenger Deep in the Mariana Trench is 36,201 feet deep! That is more than 1.3 miles deeper than Mount Everest is high.

The book of Job contains other questions that suggest a level of knowledge that would be impossible for a human writer living in the Middle East during ancient times. For example, God asks Job about the deep oceans whose surface waters are frozen hard like a stone: "Out of whose womb came the ice? and the hoary frost of heaven, who hath gendered it? The waters are hid as with a stone, and the face of the deep is frozen" (Job 38:29–30). How could a man such as Job, living in ancient times in a desert area of present-day Saudi Arabia, have known about the polar ice caps without receiving that revelation from God?

Evolution or Creation?

The theory of evolution has destroyed the faith of countless people, causing untold numbers to refuse to seriously consider the claims of the Bible regarding personal salvation—because they wrongly believe the Bible is full of errors. The theory of evolution holds that there is no God and that everything in the universe, including the complexities of biological life, developed by random chance over a period of billions of years.

However, the theory is falling apart today in the face of a lack of evidence to support its hypothesis. Very few scientists still subscribe to the original theory of evolution as proposed by Charles Darwin. Many of them accept the evidence of mathematical odds, which show that it is impossible for life to form by random chance. As one example, Dr. Harold Urey, a Nobel Prize winner for his research in chemistry, wrote about the impossibility of evolution but still admitted he believed in the theory! "All of us who study the origin of life find that the more we look into it, the more we feel that it is too complex to have evolved anywhere." Incredibly, he added these words: *"We believe as an article of faith that life evolved from dead matter on this planet.* It is just that its complexity is so great, it is hard for us to imagine that it did" (emphasis added). He was admitting that his acceptance of evolution was not based on logic or evidence, but on blind faith. Bear in mind that scientists often ridicule Christians for accepting the truth of Scripture as a matter of faith, while holding to their own secular beliefs that cannot be proven by the scientific method.

At the Alpbach Symposium conference, which dealt with the growing problems with the theory of evolution, one speaker admitted that the reason evolution was still supported by intellectuals, the education establishment, and the media had nothing to do with whether the theory was true or false. The speaker stated, "I think that the fact that a theory so vague, so insufficiently verifiable and so far from the criteria otherwise applied in 'hard' science has become a dogma can be explained only on sociological grounds."[11] Here is the plain truth about the continuing popularity and acceptance of the theory of evolution: it has survived despite a lack of evidence because people want to believe it's true.

Charles Darwin admitted that millions of "missing links," that is, the absence of transitional life forms, would have to be discovered in the fossil record to prove the accuracy of his theory. Evolution holds that all species gradually evolved by chance mutation into new species. In spite of the intensive search for fossils worldwide, spanning more than a century, scientists have failed to locate a single one of the missing links out of the millions that must exist if the theory of evolution is to be vindicated. It is significant that the various educational groups supporting evolutionary teaching have encouraged their members to refuse to enter debates about evolution with creation science supporters. The evolution supporters found to their dismay that the audiences almost always believed in evolution before the debate began, but audience members accepted the evidence for divine creation by the end of the debate.

Evidence That Disproves Evolution

It is not my purpose to fully explore the errors of evolution, nor to fully present the overwhelming evidence for God's creation of the universe. Many excellent scholars have written books that demolish the theory of evolution. In the bibliography at the end of this book, I list several excellent books that I recommend to anyone who wishes to study this subject in depth. However, I will present some of the compelling evidence that proves that evolution is impossible. As we explore this topic we will encounter overwhelming evidence proving the inspiration of the Scriptures.

If the theory of evolution is rejected, then people have no other credible alternative than the Bible's account of the creation of the universe by a personal God. This alternative is unacceptable to many people because they dread the thought of having to face God after they die. They would like to evade this issue by avoiding the evidence that disproves evolution. The greatest obstacle to seeing the truth about God's role in creation is often our own prejudices. But if we will carefully examine the evidence, the truth about creation as well as our need for a relationship with God will become evident.

The mathematical odds against life evolving by chance are absolutely staggering. It is impossible to believe that the awesome complexity involved in the simplest living cell could have occurred as a result of chance, even if the process occurred gradually over billions of years. More than twenty different amino acids are required to produce the proteins that exist in the smallest living cell. In experiments where scientists tried to create these twenty amino acids in a laboratory, they failed every time. The proteins that make up living cells are composed of long, thin lines of amino acids only one-millionth the thickness of a human hair. The smallest living creature contains more than five hundred amino acids. All amino acids have side groups of atoms. Scientists found that 50 percent of the side groups of atoms that are attached to nonliving amino acids are on the left side and another 50 percent are on the right side.

When biologists examined proteins within living cells they discovered that all proteins are "left-handed." In other words, all living cells contain amino acids with their side groups of atoms on the left side only. Amino acids produced in a laboratory are exactly like those found in nonliving matter with 50 percent left-handed and 50 percent right-handed. Yet living cells can exist only when the atoms are solely left-handed. To determine the likelihood of life occurring by chance, scientists calculated the probability that amino acids would form chains of atoms solely on the left side. The odds against this happening are 1 chance in 10^{123}. In other words, it is absolutely impossible that *even a single protein* could have been formed by chance, let alone the staggering number of complex proteins that make up the multitude of living creatures. The only logical explanation is instantaneous creation by God.

The proteins in living creatures are composed of long chains of different amino acids that must be linked together in precise sequences to allow the protein to function. Evolutionary scientists believe these complex amino acids came together by chance in the exact sequences necessary to enable life. But mathematicians have calculated that the odds against these five hundred amino acids lining up in the correct order to produce one single living cell is equal to 1 chance in 10^{200}, which is 10 followed by 200 zeros. To put these numbers in perspective, remember that the number one trillion is 10^{12}, which is 1 followed by 12 zeros. Even if the amino acids and chemicals could combine together a trillion times faster than they do in the laboratory, and the experiment used every single atom on the planet, the odds against a single functioning protein forming by chance would be less than 1 chance in 10 followed by 166 zeros. This incredible number vastly exceeds the total number of atoms within the known universe.

The odds against a single correct protein being formed by chance alone is equal to the chance that a blindfolded man could locate a single grain of sand painted gold within a universe composed of fifty billion galaxies of two hundred million stars apiece composed of nothing but sand.

However, the formation of life requires far more complex structures than simple amino acids and proteins. Deoxyribonucleic acid (DNA) contains the genetic code that commands various structures in the cell to form the building blocks of life. Mathematicians have calculated that the odds against a single DNA gene forming by chance is equal to 1 chance in 10 followed by 155 zeros, a number that staggers the mind. Anyone who can believe that life on Earth evolved by random chance without the presence of a supernatural Intelligent Designer must do so on blind faith.

Fred Hoyle, one of the greatest biologists in the last century, wrote, "Precious little in the way of biochemical evolution could have happened on the earth. If one counts the number of trial assemblies of amino acids that are needed to give rise to the enzymes, the probability of their discovery by random shufflings turn out to be less than one in 10,400,000."[12] Hoyle eventually abandoned his agnosticism and became a believer in the special creation of life.

Several scientists have concluded that life must have been brought to Earth from outer space, based on the mathematical odds against the spontaneous development of life on Earth. Dr. Frances Crick theorized that life originated in some distant part of the universe and was imported to Earth by some extraterrestrial intelligence. However, this theory solves nothing. It only pushes the problem away from the Earth to some unknown place in space. How could life have been created by random chance in some far-off part of the universe? Obviously, only God could have created life with all of its incredible complexity and order.

The Population of the Earth

Those who reject the Bible's account of divine creation believe humanity has existed on Earth for more than one million years. In contradiction to this, the Bible declares that humanity was created approximately six thousand years ago—according to the chronological data presented in the Old Testament. While the Scriptures do not tell us when God created "the heaven and the earth" (Genesis 1:1), the Bible clearly declares, through a detailed list of the generations from Adam to Christ, that humanity was created approximately four thousand years before the birth of Christ. Obviously, a huge discrepancy exists between the evolutionists' suggestion of humanity's origin compared to the Bible's declaration of humanity's creation by God.

Which system of dating is consistent with the Earth's current human population? According to the Scriptures, eight people (four couples) survived the great Flood approximately forty-three hundred years ago (estimated date 2300 BC). To be conservative, we will make these calculations assuming that the human population got a new start forty-three hundred years ago with only one surviving couple and that all families produced only two and a half children on average. This rate of population growth is much slower than we are experiencing in this century.

Throughout history the average human life span has lasted approximately forty-three years per generation, so during forty-three hundred years there would have been one hundred generations. The calculations reveal that the human population should have grown from the time of the Flood until today to reach approximately six billion people. The Earth's population today (well over six billion) is almost identical with what we would expect if humanity began repopulating the Earth after the Flood. I am indebted to Professor Henry M. Morris for his brilliant study on this topic. I highly recommend his book *The Biblical Basis for Modern Science* for any reader who wishes to explore this topic in greater depth.[13]

Now let us consider what the Earth's population would be if the evolutionary theory were accurate. Using the same assumption of forty-three years for an average human generation, the population growth over one million years would produce 23,256 consecutive generations. We calculate the expected population by starting with one couple having children one million years ago and use the same assumptions of two and a half children per family. At this rate, the Earth would have a human population today of 10^{2700} people. The evolutionary theory of a million years of growth would produce trillions times trillions times trillions times trillions of people. To put this in perspective, this number is vastly greater than the total number of atoms in our universe. If humanity had lived on Earth for one million years, we would all be standing on very high mountains of bones from the trillions of skeletons of those who had died in past generations. However, despite the tremendous archaeological and scientific investigation in the last two centuries, scientists have not found a fraction of the trillions of skeletons predicted by the theory of evolution.

The only conclusion we can reasonably draw is this: the Bible's account of Noah's family repopulating the Earth following the Flood is consistent with the current population of the Earth.[14]

Our Universe and Our Bodies Are Composed of Almost Nothing

Two thousand years ago the writer of Hebrews revealed a remarkable truth that scientific research in astrophysics has only recently discovered. The book of Hebrews declares that all of the things that are visible were not made of things that are themselves visible. The inspired words of God declare, "Through faith we understand that the worlds were framed by the word of God, so that things which are seen were not made of things which do appear" (Hebrews 11:3). And indeed, scientific research has shown that everything we see in the universe is composed of things that we can't see: atoms.

Twenty-seven hundred years ago no philosophers even speculated that everything in our universe was composed of invisible bits of matter. Yet the prophet Isaiah wrote, "Behold, the nations are as a drop of a bucket, and are counted as the small dust of the balance: behold, he taketh up the isles as a very little thing" (Isaiah 40:15).

Everything in the universe is composed of atoms. Very few people, other than nuclear scientists, have a realistic grasp of just how small atoms are. The smallest unit of matter that can be seen by a human using a microscope contains more than ten billion atoms. "An atom is incredibly tiny—more than a million times smaller than the thickness of a human hair."[15] According to Bob Berman, who wrote about atoms for *Discover* magazine, "Each one of your fingertips contains a trillion atoms."

Another little-known fact is that most of what makes up the infinitely small mass of the atom is in the nucleus. At least

99.99 percent of the mass of each atom resides in a tiny nucleus composed of protons and neutrons (hydrogen being an exception). The rest of the atom is made up of a cloud of much smaller electrons circling the nucleus at an inconceivably fast speed. Electrons comprise only 1/200th of 1 percent of the atom's total weight. To place this in perspective, if we imagine the atom to be the size of an Olympic stadium, "the nucleus would be the size of a pea lying alone in the center of the track."[16] Everything else in the atom is empty space, a void. In other words, all that appears to be solid in the universe, including our bodies, is in fact virtually empty space.

In light of the fact that atoms, the building blocks of all matter, are themselves virtually empty space, we can see that Isaiah's statement is scientifically accurate: "Who hath measured...the dust of the earth in a measure, and weighed the mountains in scales, and the hills in a balance?" (Isaiah 40:12). But how could this ancient Hebrew prophet have known that the visible things of our universe are composed of that which is invisible to humans? Only God could have inspired Isaiah to reveal this astonishing but accurate truth.

The Dimensions of Noah's Ark

In Genesis 6, God gave Noah the dimensions of the one-and-a-half-million-cubic-foot ark he was commanded to build. The ark would save the animals and Noah's family from God's judgment of the people on Earth in the form of a worldwide flood. After the waters receded, Noah and his family would restore the human population on Earth. The pairs of animals aboard the ark would do the same for the Earth's animal population.

In 1609 at the port of Hoorn in Holland, biblically minded Christian shipbuilders created a ship after the same pattern Noah followed in constructing the ark. The inspired dimensions of Noah's ark more than forty-five hundred years ago are 300:50:30. "And this is the fashion which thou shalt make it of: The length of the ark shall be three hundred cubits, the breadth of it fifty cubits, and the height of it thirty cubits" (Genesis 6:15). The length of a perfectly stable oceangoing vessel should be six times the width.

The Lord specified to Noah, at a time when no one had ever

seen a ship, that the perfect proportions for a stable vessel were 30:5:3. Today's shipbuilders design ocean liners following similar proportions. These design specifications are recognized globally as the ideal dimensions to optimize a ship's stability in the ocean. This knowledge from the Bible revolutionized European shipbuilding in the last few centuries, saving countless cargoes and thousands of lives. By 1900 virtually every large oceangoing vessel was built according to these proportions.[17]

The Undeniable Wonders of Creation

The Bible claims that God created all living creatures on Earth. When we examine these creatures, we discover an awesome degree of complexity that defies the evolutionary theory.

The Particular Design of Birds

One of the most intriguing examples of God's design is found in the fact that birds have hollow bones. This makes them much lighter than they would be with solid bones and facilitates flight. As an example of God's providential design, consider the woodpecker.

As I write this, a beautiful woodpecker is perched on a branch of the tree only five feet beyond my library window, pecking away in diligent search for an insect beneath the bark. The woodpecker has two toes in front and two toes in the rear, allowing it to grip the trunk of a tree firmly while pecking for insects. While all other birds have a bill that is connected directly to their skull, only the woodpecker has between its bill and skull an unusual spongy tissue that acts as a shock absorber. Some woodpeckers have pecked through concrete in their quest for insects or to bury seeds for future food. The woodpecker's short tail feathers act as a support to brace its body against the trunk of a tree while it pecks. When it locates a tunnel bored through the tree by an insect, the woodpecker inserts its long tongue into the tunnel until it reaches its prey. Unlike other birds, the tongue of a woodpecker is not attached to the rear of its mouth. Remarkably, the woodpecker's tongue is five inches long and is coiled within its skull, allowing the bird to retrieve its insect prey from deep within a tree trunk.

Those who reject God's creation of the universe believe that the complexities of biological life occurred by simple chance. This argument appears ridiculous to people who examine the complexity of animal and human life. Those who carefully and objectively consider the evidence, without a predetermined bias, must conclude that God created this marvelous design.

Migratory Patterns in Birds

Another example of God's complex design is the migratory pattern of birds. The Manx shearwater birds that live in Wales migrate from South America every year, flying approximately 250 miles every day. In an experiment, a Manx shearwater captured in Wales was transferred by plane to North America. Scientists released the bird on the Atlantic coast in Boston, Massachusetts. Surprisingly, the bird flew back to Wales across the trackless expanse of the Atlantic Ocean. It made the 3,100-mile trip in only twelve days despite the fact that the bird had never flown that route before. How could this occur unless God planted within the bird the knowledge of where its home was located?

A Reptile's Hunting Method

Another example of God's creative design is found in the ability of a rattlesnake to detect its prey. This ability depends on a small sense organ found between the snake's nostril and eyes that is so sensitive it can detect a temperature difference of only one-thirty-third of a degree. (To put this in perspective, only a computerized thermometer device can detect such a small variance in temperature.) This ability to detect the precise temperature of an object in front of the snake enables it to measure the exact distance and direction of its prey. How could such a sensitive awareness of temperatures have evolved in the rattlesnake by chance?

Complex Sensory Processes in Humans

King David declared, "Thou [God] hast possessed my reins: thou hast covered me in my mother's womb. I will praise thee; for *I am fearfully and wonderfully made*" (Psalm 139:13–14). Consider the case of the human eye and ask yourself whether such an astonishingly intricate system could have occurred by chance alone.

When a baby is conceived in the womb, the genetic code governing the eye programs the baby's body to begin growing optic nerves from the brain as well as the eye. Each eye has one million nerve endings that begin growing through the flesh toward the baby's brain. Simultaneously, a million optic nerves in the brain begin growing through the flesh toward the baby's eye. Each of the million optic nerves must find and match up to its exact mate to enable the baby to see. We are impressed when highway engineers correctly align two thirty-foot-wide tunnels dug from opposite sides of a mountain. However, every day hundreds of thousands of children are born with the ability to see. Their bodies have aligned a million optic nerves from each eye, with each nerve meeting its matching nerve ending, which is growing from the baby's brain.

The human eye has the ability to transmit to the brain more than 1.5 million messages simultaneously. The retina at the back of the eye contains a dense area of rods and cones that gather and interpret information presented to the eye. The retina contains more than 137 million nerve connections, which the brain uses to evaluate data in its attempt to interpret the scene that appears in front of the eyes. One hundred thirty million of these cells are rods that enable us to have black and white vision. However, about 7 million cells are cone-shaped. They allow us to see color. Each of these 137 million cells communicates directly with the brain, allowing us to interpret the image in front of us. Amazingly, scientists have discovered that while the image we receive is upside-down, the cellular structure in our eye reverses the image within the eye. The eye then transmits the corrected image at three hundred miles per hour to the brain, where we "see" the image that is before us.

The Complexity of Your Brain

The human brain is the most complex organ in the universe. While it weighs less than three pounds, it contains an amazingly intricate network of nerves with *more than 30 billion* special cells known as neurons. In addition, there are another 250 billion glial cells that facilitate communication between neurons. Incredibly, every one of the 30 billion neurons is connected to other neurons in a staggeringly complex pattern. Every neuron is connected directly to more than 50,000 other neurons, which allows instantaneous transfers of messages across your brain.

In less than one second your brain can calculate the trajectory of a football that is suddenly thrown toward you at thirty miles per hour without warning. In a moment your brain calculates your position and the ball's ultimate trajectory and sends detailed messages to the muscles in your arms and legs at more than three hundred miles per second. The brain's split-second directions move you into a position to catch the ball. Despite hundreds of billions of dollars and fifty years of advanced research by computer scientists, there are no computers that can equal this instantaneous computing system!

Any unbiased person who examines the evidence must consider the possibility that only a supernatural Designer could account for the marvelously designed universe we live in. The accurate scientific statements found throughout the Bible—which was written in ancient times long before science had discovered these truths—provide some of the most convincing evidences of God's inspiration of Scripture. There are no scientific errors found in the Bible's thousands of passages. The remarkable scientific insights and revelations found throughout the Bible are God's genuine signature on the pages of the Scriptures.

Notes

1. "How Life on Earth Began," *Reader's Digest,* November 1982, 116.
2. Alexander Vilenkin, "Creation of the Universe from Nothing," *Physics Letters,* 1982, quoted in S. W. Hawking and G. F. R. Ellis, *The Large Scale Structure of Space-Time* (Cambridge: Cambridge University Press, 1973), 364.
3. Herman Bondi, letters section, in reference to a quote by Karl Popperp, published in *New Scientist,* November 21, 1980, 611.
4. Harold Jeffreys, *The Earth: Its Origin, History, and Physical Constitution* (Cambridge: Cambridge University Press, 1970), 359.
5. NASA made this announcement March 5, 1998, http://nssdc.gsfc.nasa.gov/planetary/ice/inc_moon.html.
6. Jean Audouze and Guy Israel, *The Cambridge Atlas of Astronomy* (Cambridge: Cambridge University Press, 1985), 219.
7. Mitchell Waldrop, "Delving the Hole in Space," *Science,* November 27, 1981.
8. Robert Jastrow, *The Intellectuals Speak Out About God* (Chicago: Regnery Gateway, 1984), 21.
9. For more on this phenomenon, see Sarah Simpson, "Big U.S. Population Uses Less Water," *Science News,* October 24, 1998, 260.
10. "Sea Floor Hot Springs as Teeming with Valuable Minerals and Microbes," SpaceDaily, www.spacedaily.com/news/life-03h.html (accessed November 23, 2009).
11. Quoted in Gershon Robinson and Mordechai Steinman, *The Obvious Proof: A Presentation of the Classic Proof of Universal Design* (New York: CIS, 1993), 87.
12. Fred Hoyle, "Where Microbes Boldly Went," *New Scientist,* August 13, 1991, 412–15.
13. See Henry M. Morris, *The Biblical Basis for Modern Science* (Grand Rapids: Baker, 1984), 414–26.
14. In this chapter I am greatly simplifying the calculations, but the results are consistent with the biblical account of

the Flood as well as with the assumptions inherent in the theory of evolution.

15. *World Book Encyclopedia,* 2004 ed., s.v. "Atoms."
16. For more on this comparison, see Lyall Watson, *Supernature: A Natural History of the Supernatural* (New York: Bantam Books, 1974).
17. This information is verified by *Lloyd's Register of Shipping,* as referenced in the *World Almanac.*

5

Advanced Medical Knowledge in the Bible

The level of medical knowledge and sanitation practices in the Western world prior to 1880 was surprisingly backward. Medicine and sanitation through most of the nineteenth century were nearly as primitive as the situation found in the Middle Ages and in the third world before Western medicine arrived in the twentieth century. Even the existence of germs was unknown until around 1890.

Yet the first five books of the Bible, recorded by Moses approximately 1491–1451 BC, reveal highly advanced knowledge about medicine, hygiene, and sanitation. The Scriptures contain God's medical instructions for Israel that go far beyond the level of knowledge possessed by the Egyptians and other ancient societies of that day. These records of advanced scientific and precise medical knowledge, written more than three and a half millenniums ago, provide strong evidence that God inspired the words of Scripture. It is impossible that Moses could have gained this advanced knowledge in Egypt. He could not have included it as he wrote the Torah unless God had inspired the words. As Moses recorded the first five books of the Old Testament, God made sure that Moses included the medical commandments to protect the health of God's chosen people.

A prime example of this is seen in the Bible's health recommendation against consuming excessive amounts of fat (see Leviticus 7:23). Only in recent decades has the medical community determined that fat clogs our arteries as well as contributes to heart disease. Also worthy of note is the Bible's declaration that life begins at conception (see Jeremiah 1:5). In addition, God tells us that He knew each one of us before we were born (see Psalm 139:13–15). So God's medical commands not only protected the health of His people, they also clarified crucial issues such as the beginning of human life, a person's worth in God's eyes, and the need to protect human life.

God's commitment to defending unborn human life is demonstrated in Exodus 21:22–23, where we read that the biblical penalty for causing the death of an unborn child was death. We know today that a woman's fertilized egg is truly the beginning of an entire human being. Growth is by cellular division. Nothing will be added to the first cell except nutrition and oxygen.

Healing in the Bible

In the Bible, it is God alone who heals. The only thing that humans can do is to serve as a helper who treats patients by following biblical rules that allow God to facilitate the actual healing. The Bible suggests numerous medical procedures that are remarkably advanced, given the era in which they were recorded. The medical knowledge contained in the Old Testament was so advanced, in fact, that even today modern medicine recommends many of these ancient biblical remedies in the treatment of disease. These procedures include:

- anointing a wound with oil
- washing with clean water
- applying the following to a wound or sore: balm, wine, compresses, baths
- the squeezing of an abscess to remove pus

- using soothing music to calm a patient (such as King Saul)
- using bandages with a roller to treat bone fractures (see Ezekiel 30:21)
- beneficial exposure to sunlight (see Malachi 4:2)

The various medicines mentioned in the Hebrew Scriptures include olibanum, mandrake, laudanum (pain medication), soda, borax, gall, wormwood, sweet cinnamon, and cassia.[1]

A great deal of the Old Testament laws, especially the books of Exodus, Numbers, and Leviticus, are comprised of health-related restrictions involving diet, cleansing, sanitation regulations, and quarantine. The fascinating books *None of These Diseases* and *Medicine in the Bible and the Talmud* demonstrate the wisdom of following this biblical advice. Human medicine did not discover this knowledge until thousands of years after it was originally written by Moses.

Biblical References to Physicians and Pharmacists
The prophet Jeremiah refers to physicians: "Is there no balm in Gilead; is there no physician there? why then is not the health of the daughter of my people recovered?" (Jeremiah 8:22). Moses wrote about pharmacists during the Exodus: "And the LORD said unto Moses, Take unto thee sweet spices, stacte, and onycha, and galbanum; these sweet spices with pure frankincense: of each shall there be a like weight: and thou shalt make it a perfume, a confection after the art of the apothecary, tempered together, pure and holy: and thou shalt beat some of it very small, and put of it before the testimony in the tabernacle of the congregation, where I will meet with thee: it shall be unto you most holy" (Exodus 30:34–36).

God's Promise: "The Lord Will Take Away from Thee All Sickness"

God promised that, if the ancient Hebrews obeyed all of His commandments and statutes, the Lord would protect them from plagues and sicknesses: "If thou wilt diligently hearken to the voice of the LORD thy God, and wilt do that which is right in his sight, and wilt give ear to his commandments, and keep all his statutes, I will put none of the diseases upon thee, which I have brought upon the Egyptians: for I am the LORD that healeth thee" (Exodus 15:26). Even today, following the Bible's medical laws and principles can protect us from devastating diseases.

For centuries the Jews lived as slaves among the pagan Egyptians. Obviously they learned and adopted the traditional folk medicine and remedies of their Egyptian masters. As a result, the Israelites would have been afflicted during their long captivity by the same diseases that repeatedly devastated the people of Egypt. Deuteronomy 28:27–28 records a number of the terrible diseases: "The LORD will smite thee with the botch of Egypt, and with the emerods, and with the scab, and with the itch, whereof thou canst not be healed. The LORD shall smite thee with madness, and blindness, and astonishment of heart."

However, if the Israelites would turn from their sins and follow the commandments of God, the Lord promised that "none of the evil diseases of Egypt, which thou knowest" would afflict the Jews from that moment on: "And the LORD will take away from thee all sickness, and will put none of the evil diseases of Egypt, which thou knowest, upon thee; but will lay them upon all them that hate thee" (Deuteronomy 7:15).

When the children of Israel left Egypt through the miraculous intervention of God, the Lord demanded that they obey His commandments. God's specific medical laws and sanitation commandments would protect the Jews from the most terrible diseases of the Egyptians and the attendant high mortality rates. An examination of the medical remedies of the ancient Egyptians and other pagan cultures of the Middle East reveals an appalling ignorance of even the most rudimentary medical knowledge. (We will look more closely at the medical practices of the Gentile nations later in this chapter.) However, the laws of Moses contained specific laws and sanitation procedures that, if faithfully followed, would eliminate these dreadful diseases.

God's Dietary Laws Protected the Israelites' Health

In addition to the Old Testament laws regarding medicine, sanitation, and personal hygiene, the Bible's dietary laws served to protect the Jews from a large number of diseases.

Avoid Eating Bottom Feeders
In Leviticus 11:9–12, the Jews were commanded to avoid eating sea creatures that have no fins or scales. We now know these creatures are bottom feeders, tending to get their food from among the accumulated centuries of waste in the Nile River and Delta (in Egypt), as well as along the Mediterranean coast. Sea creatures that nourish themselves on such food are likely to carry disease.

Avoid Consuming Predatory Birds
The Bible warns against eating birds of prey (see Leviticus 11:13–20). Scientists now recognize that predatory birds, because they eat carrion (putrefying flesh), often spread disease.

Avoid Eating Swine
The Bible prohibited the Israelites from eating swine (see Deuteronomy 14:8). We know today that eating undercooked pork can lead to an infection of parasites called trichinosis. How could Moses have known of this danger unless he was inspired by God to include these commands in the book of Deuteronomy?

Israel Was Given Highly Advanced Knowledge
The greatest medical treatise of ancient Egypt, known as the Ebers papyrus, is preserved in the library of the University of Leipzig, Germany. It is one of the two oldest surviving medical documents from the ancient Middle East. The 110-page Ebers papyrus is in remarkably good condition. Its text contains some seven hundred magical incantations as well as numerous so-called medical remedies. It was created by Egyptian royal scholars during the days of Moses (prior to the Exodus, approximately 1550 BC).

Egypt at that time was considered the most sophisticated and advanced scientific culture in the world. Phenomenal building projects, including the more ancient pyramids and the later temples built in Moses' generation, stand as powerful evidence of Egypt's advanced knowledge and engineering abilities. Their science, mathematics, and engineering expertise were far in advance of other ancient cultures. Their medical knowledge and health practices were remarkably backward compared to what we know today, and they certainly contributed to the spread of disease rather than helping to contain it. However, these "remedies" were taught to Egyptian scholars, including Moses, who was a prince of the royal house of the pharaoh (see Acts 7:22).

As an example of medical ignorance and primitive knowledge regarding infections, consider an Egyptian doctor's suggestion for healing an infected splinter wound, as documented in the Ebers papyrus. The prescription involves the application of an ointment mixture composed of the blood of worms mixed with the dung of a donkey. Various germs, including tetanus, contained in donkey dung must have assured that the patient would rapidly forget the pain of his splinter as he died from other diseases produced by his doctor's contaminated "medicine."

The cure for hair loss involved the application to the patient's scalp of a solution composed of various fats from a horse, a crocodile, a cat, and a snake, along with a donkey's tooth crushed in honey. Egyptian doctors had an equally wondrous cure for a poisonous snakebite. They poured "magical water" over a pagan idol and then gave the water to the poisoned victim for what probably turned out to be his last drink on earth.[2]

The pharmacies of ancient Egypt provided popular prescriptions including "lizards' blood, swines' teeth, putrid meat, stinking fat, moisture from pigs' ears, milk, goose grease, asses' hoofs, animal fats from various sources, excreta from animals, including human beings, donkeys, antelopes, dogs, [and] cats."[3] This list is quoted from the Ebers papyrus, as translated in S. E. Massengill's fascinating book *A Sketch of Medicine and Pharmacy.*

Another book, *An Ancient Egyptian Herbal*, describes a number of Egyptian cures that used ingredients such as hippopotamus dung, donkey's hoof, gazelle dung, snakeskins, and the ever-popular fly dung.[4]

The Egyptian doctor's remedy for constipation included zizyphus bread, gurma, cat's dung, sweet beer, and wine. In another passage, we find that "a painful tumour was treated with fly dung mixed with sycamore juice applied to the tumour so that it goes down by itself." Among these dangerous medicines we find an appalling suggestion for curing a baby of excessive crying: "A remedy for too much crying in a child: spn-seeds; fly dung from the wall; is made to a paste, strained and drunk for four days. The crying will cease instantly." No doubt the crying would cease permanently with the tragic and unnecessary death of the child.

Due to the lack of knowledge of germs and infection, almost any serious illness or injury treated by Egypt's medical system would result in a painful and virtually certain death. In light of this, we realize the tremendous, life-saving importance of the Hebrews having full access to God's true medical knowledge.

God's Truth Versus Ancient Egyptian "Wisdom"

The Ebers papyrus was discovered in 1862 during the investigation of an Egyptian tomb in the ancient capital of Upper Egypt, Luxor (Thebes). The manuscript was purchased a dozen years later by a German scholar, Georg Ebers, who taught Egyptology at the University of Leipzig. Despite the brilliant civilization of the ancient Egyptians, their understanding of medicine was abysmal.

However, when we examine the pages of the Bible, we find no instances of ignorant or harmful medical advice. Instead, the passages recorded by Moses display remarkably advanced medical knowledge regarding germs, plagues, the need for sanitation and personal hygiene, and quarantine regulations. Not only did the Torah's health and nutrition requirements go far beyond the medical advice contained in the Ebers papyrus, it was far in advance of the medical discoveries of humanity in general. The scientific world would not discover these truths until approximately AD 1890.

How is it possible that the pages of the Bible written more than thirty-five hundred years ago could contain the most advanced medical advice? Moses resisted any temptation he might have had to include any medical knowledge he had been taught in Egypt. There are no references to the dangerous Egyptian medical practices in the five books of Moses. In contrast, the Bible contains hundreds of accurate scientific and medical statements, including detailed laws regarding the careful inspection of meat and exacting sanitation regulations regarding the burial of bodies. In fact, 213 out of the 613 commandments found in the Torah are detailed medical regulations that ensured the good health of the children of Israel. This advanced, detailed knowledge proves that God inspired Moses to record these words. God was protecting His people from the dangerous health practices they had learned in Egypt.

The Bible's Laws on Sanitation

Since the beginning of civilization numerous diseases have spread through making contact with human waste. In the ages when most people lived in sparsely populated rural areas, there was little danger of infection. However, as people migrated to villages, towns, and cities, the danger of contamination increased geometrically. Throughout the medieval and Renaissance periods, and in many societies of the third world today, human waste is thrown into open gutters in the streets. Raw waste is then flushed through drains by occasional rains or floods. The presence of waste in the midst of densely populated areas, and the inevitable contamination of water supplies, guarantees the spread of infection and disease. The stench from such a primitive system is beyond imagination.

During the days of William Shakespeare, the river Thames in London was an open sewer. Even then, four hundred years ago, salmon could not survive in England's most famous river. People could not bear to walk near the Thames because of the overpowering smell. The stench was so terrible that burlap sacks saturated in chloride of lime were hung in the windows of Parliament in an ineffective attempt to minimize the odor.[5] However, modern sewage-treatment methods have succeeded in reclaiming the Thames to the point where fishermen are catching edible salmon from the bridges of London.

The result of the unsanitary conditions of centuries past is that people died in large numbers every year as they succumbed to a variety of diseases, including typhoid, dysentery, and cholera. Even the educated people of those days ignored the appalling threat to their health. Hundreds of millions of people died throughout history due to infectious diseases produced by the absence of even the most elementary sanitation treatment of human waste. Yet obedience to God's law of sanitation, proclaimed thousands of years ago, would have saved countless millions of lives.

My reason for dwelling on this unpleasant subject is to emphasize the extraordinary nature and life-saving impact of the advanced sanitation commands issued by God. At a time when no human understood the deadly nature of germs and infection, God instructed Moses about how he could ensure adequate sanitation for the huge Jewish refugee population. The Israelites were homeless for forty years, crossing the wilderness en route to Canaan. Consider the circumstances of refugees, who are removed from where they have been living and are faced with arduous travel and temporary shelter. Given these conditions, it is difficult to maintain hygiene and sanitation practices. The germs from untreated human waste, a huge threat to a large refugee group, could easily contaminate the ground water and lead to horrendous and deadly epidemics. God, however, took the necessary steps to protect His people from such diseases.

> Thou shalt have a place also without the camp, whither thou shalt go forth abroad: and thou shalt have a paddle upon thy weapon; and it shall be, when thou wilt ease thyself abroad, thou shalt dig therewith, and shalt turn back and cover that which cometh from thee. (Deuteronomy 23:12–13)

While such a basic sanitation law concerning latrines may seem obvious to us today, it is an extraordinary instruction when you consider that it was made thirty-five centuries before germs were discovered.

Consider the logistical headache of trying to meet the human needs of hundreds of thousands of Jews during their forty years spent in the wilderness. Most Israelites would have died due to infectious diseases if God had not instructed Moses to teach His people the laws of sanitation. Medical historian Arturo Castiglioni declared that Moses' sanitation commands were "certainly a primitive measure, but an effective one, which indicates advanced ideas of sanitation."[6]

The vast majority of soldiers killed during the world's countless wars have succumbed to infectious diseases rather than bullets or other weaponry. The history of wars fought prior to AD

1900 reveals that, typically, five times as many soldiers died of disease than from wounds sustained on the battlefield. Often the army that suffered the greatest diseases lost the war.

As late as the Boer War in South Africa (1899–1902), five times as many soldiers died or were incapacitated due to infections caused by exposure to germs generated from human waste than those who were wounded or killed by weapons. When armies marched across a country and besieged a city, tens of thousands of soldiers were forced to camp for months in the open. Unburied waste inevitably ended up in the ground water. Hence, simply from drinking water and using water in cooking, the troops were infected with disabling and deadly diseases. It is certain that strict obedience to the Law of God by the soldiers of Israel allowed them to escape many of the diseases that afflicted their pagan enemies.

God's Protection Against Unknown Germs

Prior to the medical advances of the past 130 years, doctors did not know that germs from human and animal waste caused infections that number among the greatest dangers to humanity. Yet we find advanced sanitation and medical knowledge in the Bible written thousands of years ago.

Neither did people know that deadly germs could exist on eating and cooking utensils. However, Leviticus 6:28, written more than thirty-five hundred years ago, commands the Jews to discard broken pottery (the cracks could contain germs): "But the earthen vessel wherein it is sodden shall be broken: and if it be sodden in a brasen pot, it shall be both scoured, and rinsed in water." A cracked vessel should not be used for cooking or eating. The Bible tells us further that a metal pot should be disinfected by scouring and rinsing in water. These instructions saved hundreds of thousands of Jews from infections at a time when the rest of the world didn't know germs existed.

Moses' writing also reveals a remarkable knowledge of germs associated with animal carcasses and anything a carcass might come into contact with. Throughout history, people stored and cooked their meat with ample spices to delay the rotting and to disguise the smell of decay. Without refrigeration, the eating of meat was often hazardous because of the danger of infection. In Leviticus 11:35, Moses revealed the danger of germs from animal carcasses: "And every thing whereupon any part of their carcase falleth shall be unclean; whether it be oven, or ranges for pots, they shall be broken down: for they are unclean and shall be unclean unto you."

God expanded on these health measures by inspiring Moses to record medical and sanitation instructions to protect the Israelites even further from infectious germs found in carcasses. Leviticus 7:24 forbids the eating of the flesh of any animal that died of disease or after being attacked by wild animals: "And the fat of the beast that dieth of itself, and the fat of that which is torn with beasts, may be used in any other use: but ye shall in no wise eat of it." An animal carcass found after its natural death would likely contain the germs that caused its death. An animal that had been killed by a predator would quickly start to rot and produce infectious germs.

Moses could not have learned this knowledge from his schooling in Egypt. Remember that one of the favorite ingredients found in the medicines of ancient Egypt was manure. How could Moses have written these incredibly accurate medical instructions unless God inspired him to do so?

Additional Laws to Prevent Infectious Diseases

This is the law, when a man dieth in a tent: all that come into the tent, and all that is in the tent, shall be unclean seven days. And every open vessel, which hath no covering bound upon it, is unclean. And whosoever toucheth one that is slain with a sword in the open fields, or a dead body, or a bone of a man, or a grave, shall be unclean seven days. And for an unclean person they shall take of the ashes of the burnt heifer of purification for sin, and running water shall be put thereto in a vessel. (Numbers 19:14–17)

Germs from a corpse are more dangerous to another human than germs from an animal carcass because of the greater likelihood of the transmission of infection. Deadly germs are especially prevalent in the bodies of those who have died due to disease.

However, the Bible gives instructions to protect people from many of these diseases.

Ignaz Semmelweis, a brilliant Hungarian doctor in the mid-nineteenth century, created a tremendous improvement in practical medical treatment and the control of infectious diseases.[7] An article in the *Encyclopaedia Britannica* documents that, as a young doctor in Vienna in 1845, Semmelweis was appalled by the staggering rate of death by infection of women who gave birth in hospitals. While most children were born at home, a number of women, usually the homeless or sick, gave birth in a hospital. The level of infectious puerperal (child-bed) fever was horrendous, with between 15 and 30 percent of such mothers dying. This tragic situation was generally accepted and considered normal at that time.

But Semmelweis was convinced there must be a way to protect more of these women from puerperal fever. He began to study the conditions under which the women were giving birth. He noted that every morning, young interns examined the bodies of the mothers who had died and then, without washing their hands, went to the next ward where they would examine expectant mothers. This was considered a normal medical practice in the mid-nineteenth century because the existence of germs was not yet known.[8]

However, Semmelweis insisted that the doctors under his supervision follow his new orders to wash their hands in water with chlorinated lime prior to examining living patients. Immediately, the mortality rate from infection among the expectant mothers fell to less than 2 percent. Despite such dramatic improvement, the senior hospital staff despised Semmelweis's medical innovations and eventually fired him. Most of his medical colleagues rejected his new techniques and ridiculed his demands that they wash their hands. They could not believe infections could be caused by something that was invisible to the naked eye.

Later Semmelweis took a position with a hospital in Pest (Budapest), Hungary, the St. Rochus Hospital, which was experiencing an epidemic of puerperal fever among pregnant women. Immediately, Semmelweis's new sanitary procedures again had a positive effect, with the mortality rate dropping to less than 1 percent.

During the next six years, the Hungarian government sent advisory letters to all district authorities demanding that all medical staff follow Semmelweis's instructions for hand washing and general hospital sanitation. Still, the medical establishments of Europe and North America continued to ignore his techniques. Decades of rejection by his colleagues drove Semmelweis to a nervous breakdown. Tragically, due to an infection he received through a cut on his hand while performing an operation in 1865, he succumbed to the infectious disease he spent his life trying to alleviate.

God, of course, was well aware of the threat posed to human health by germs and infection. Thousands of years ago He commanded the Israelites to wash their hands in "running water" when dealing with anyone who was afflicted with infectious disease: "And when he that hath an issue is cleansed of his issue; then he shall number to himself seven days for his cleansing, and wash his clothes, and bathe his flesh in running water, and shall be clean" (Leviticus 15:13). Until this last century most doctors who chose to wash their hands did so in a bowl of standing water, which allowed germs to remain on their hands. But God's Law specifies that when people are assisting those who are sick or in quarantine, their clothes and their bodies should be washed under running water. For centuries people naively washed in standing water. Today we recognize the need to wash away germs and remove them with fresh, running water, as the Bible advises—the only way to effectively protect against germs.

Quarantine Laws to Prevent Plague and Leprosy

There is some debate among medical scholars over whether the Hebrew word translated as *leprosy* in the Bible is the same disease as the modern variant more properly known as Hansen's disease. In biblical times it may have been a deadly disease that was different from modern forms of leprosy. But whether it was the same or a different affliction, it is amazing that the detailed laws contained in the books of Leviticus and Numbers established an advanced quarantine system for the control of infectious diseases. And these were instituted at a time when ancient pagan nations did not understand the dangers of infections.

The Bible commands that the priests act as medical control officers, examining all sick individuals and taking action to protect them and the community from the spread of disease: "Then the priest shall look upon it: and, behold, if the rising of the sore be white reddish in his bald head, or in his bald forehead, as the leprosy appeareth in the skin of the flesh; he is a leprous man, he is unclean: the priest shall pronounce him utterly unclean; his plague is in his head" (Leviticus 13:43–44). In addition to identifying the diseased individual, the priest was responsible for quarantining those afflicted with leprosy: "All the days wherein the plague shall be in him he shall be defiled; he is unclean: he shall dwell alone; without the camp shall his habitation be" (Leviticus 13:46).

The Lord's concern to protect His people was manifested in His command to forbid those who were infected with disease from participating in the three great annual festivals of the Jews, lest they infect others: "But the man that shall be unclean, and shall not purify himself, that soul shall be cut off from among the congregation, because he hath defiled the sanctuary of the LORD: the water of separation hath not been sprinkled on him; he is unclean" (Numbers 19:20). Even after a person recovered from a disease and returned from medical isolation, the individual was subject to strict medical supervision for seven days to ascertain that he or she was truly healed.

> He that is to be cleansed shall wash his clothes, and shave off all his hair, and wash himself in water, that he may be clean: and after that he shall come into the camp, and shall tarry abroad out of his tent seven days. But it shall be on the seventh day, that he shall shave all his hair off his head and his beard and his eyebrows, even all his hair he shall shave off: and he shall wash his clothes, also he shall wash his flesh in water, and he shall be clean. (Leviticus 14:8–9)

These ancient instructions are remarkably similar to medical quarantine orders that would be issued and enforced today by a modern public health official.

The Scourge of the Black Death

The continents of Europe and Asia have periodically been engulfed by epidemics of leprosy and plague, especially from 1200 to 1400. More than sixty million people, almost one-third of the population of Europe in the fourteenth century, are estimated to have died by the Black Death (bubonic plague). Those who survived described scenes that sounded like the haunting visions of Dante's descriptions of hell. Renowned doctors of the time were unable to respond effectively to the rapid spread of this disease due to their lack of knowledge. They were reduced to offering medical advice to prevent the plague such as, "Stop eating pepper or garlic." Some suggested the plague was caused by the position of the planets and stars. Mostly, doctors helplessly comforted their dying patients and finally succumbed to the disease themselves.

How was this dreaded plague finally stopped? During a trip to Vienna, in the center of the city I examined a strange-looking plague statue dedicated to the Black Death's countless victims and the actions of the church fathers to abolish the curse of that plague. In light of God's advanced health laws, one might expect to learn that it was only after the people began to follow the biblical laws of sanitation and disease control that the epidemic was broken.

Several church leaders began to search the Bible to discover whether there was a practical solution. They saw that in Leviticus 13:46 Moses laid down strict regulations regarding the treatment of those afflicted with leprosy or plague: "All the days wherein the plague shall be in him he shall be defiled; he is unclean: he shall dwell alone; without the camp shall his habitation be." God answered their prayers for deliverance when they finally began to obey His scriptural commands. This divine medical rule demanded that a person who contracted the plague must be isolated from the general population during his infectious period.

Fortunately, the church fathers of Vienna finally took the biblical injunctions to heart and commanded that those infected with the plague must be placed outside the city in special medical quarantine compounds. Caregivers fed them until they either died or survived the disease. Those who died in homes or streets were quickly removed and buried outside the city. These biblical sanitation measures quickly brought the dreaded epidemic under control. Other cities and countries rapidly followed the medical practices of Vienna until the deadly spread of the Black Death was halted.

Until the twentieth century, nearly every society other than the Israelites kept infected patients in their homes—even after death—unknowingly exposing other people to deadly disease. Even during the Black Death epidemic, patients who were sick or had died were kept in the same rooms as the rest of the family. People often wondered why the disease affected so many people at one time. They attributed the epidemic to "bad air" or evil spirits. However, careful attention to the medical commands of God as revealed in Leviticus would have saved untold millions of lives. Arturo Castiglioni characterized this biblical law with these words: "The laws against leprosy in Leviticus 13 may be regarded as the first model of a sanitary legislation."[9]

Moses' instruction to segregate infected patients from their families and other people was one of the most important medical advances in human history. Yet no other ancient nation followed this effective medical regulation. The only reasonable explanation is that Moses received this advanced medical knowledge from God's inspiration.

Laws of Cleanliness

While people repeat the phrase "Cleanliness is next to godliness," they often forget that God has provided stringent laws of cleanliness that, if followed, would prevent the spread of disease. Throughout the Scriptures we find God commanding His people to follow laws of hygiene and cleanliness. To put these laws and instructions in perspective, we need to understand that cleanliness and bathing were almost unknown through much of human history. Most people lived from the cradle to the grave without ever having a bath. In fact, most Europeans until the 1840s believed that taking a bath was the most dangerous thing you could do to your health.

Until the end of the nineteenth century, most Europeans took a bath less than once a year. James I of England, who ordered the translation of the Scriptures into English in 1611, never bathed once. He kept a bowl of talc beside him that he applied to his fingers and hands to keep them soft. When my wife, Kaye, and I visited the thousand-room Hampton Palace, the guide pointed out that King James's numerous guests did not have access to a single bathtub in the massive castle. One of the reasons they loved snuff and perfume so much was to mask dreadful body odors.

Even before God gave Moses the Ten Commandments, He told the Israelites to sanctify themselves by washing their clothes: "And the LORD said unto Moses, Go unto the people, and sanctify them to day and to morrow, and let them wash their clothes" (Exodus 19:10). Preparations for ministering in the Tabernacle required that Aaron and his sons wash their bodies before putting on their priestly garments: "And Aaron and his sons thou shalt bring unto the door of the tabernacle of the congregation, and shalt wash them with water" (Exodus 29:4). Likewise, "Moses and Aaron and his sons washed their hands and their feet thereat: when they went into the tent of the congregation, and when they came near unto the altar, they washed; as the LORD commanded Moses" (Exodus 40:31–32). This rule still applied centuries later when the priests ministered in the Temple.

When you consider that the priests were responsible for preparing and sacrificing animals—portions of which were later eaten—the need for strict rules of washing are obvious in light of the dangers from infectious germs. The Bible also contains detailed sanitation instructions concerning the purification following the birth of a child, and detailed instructions were laid out regarding hygiene for women.

Another of the medical commands that is unprecedented in its understanding of the need for disinfecting items is found in God's command regarding material captured from an enemy's camp. This command stated that "whosoever hath killed any person, and whosoever hath touched any slain, purify both yourselves and your captives on the third day, and on the seventh day. And purify all your raiment, and all that is made of skins, and all work of goats' hair, and all things made of wood" (Numbers 31:19–20). The instructions for disinfecting these items were as follows: "Every thing that may abide the fire, ye shall make it go through the fire, and it shall be clean: nevertheless it shall be purified with the water of separation: and all that abideth not the fire ye shall make go through the water. And ye shall wash your clothes on the seventh day, and ye shall be clean, and afterward ye shall come into the camp" (Numbers 31:23–24). These instructions would purify any contaminated materials captured in battle.

The Incineration of Animal Waste

One of the most intriguing of the Bible's sanitation commandments is the demand that the internal organs and waste of animals to be sacrificed were to be burned "without the camp" to prevent the possibility of transmitting infection. The Israelites were commanded to create, in effect, an incinerator outside the city of Jerusalem to safely dispose of dangerous materials produced by the Temple sacrifices.

> And the skin of the bullock, and all his flesh, with his head, and with his legs, and his inwards, and his dung, even the whole bullock shall he carry forth without the camp unto a clean place, where the ashes are poured out, and burn him on the wood with fire: where the ashes are poured out shall he be burnt. (Leviticus 4:11–12)

At a time when no one knew that animal waste and decaying organs would be dangerous, God commanded the Israelites to destroy these infectious agents in the most sanitary method available.

Laws Regarding Pest Control

Likewise, God commanded His people to rid the land of pests, an important measure that also helped control the spread of disease. Advanced pest-control procedures are revealed in Leviticus 25:1–24. The law of the Sabbath of the land demanded that every seventh year the land should be allowed to rest. God promised He would provide a much greater crop harvest in the sixth year to carry farmers through the year when the land was rested.

Throughout the third world today, multitudes of farmers are

plagued by multiplying insects that destroy up to one-third of their crops every year. Yet thirty-five hundred years ago, Moses commanded Israel to follow a plan of Sabbath years, a cycle of years that set aside one year in every seven when no crops were to be raised. Not only did this allow the land to lie fallow for twelve months, but it also mitigated the problem of destructive pests. Insects winter in the stalks of the previous year's crops, the eggs hatch the following spring, and the insect population is perpetuated by laying eggs in that year's new crop. If the crop is not grown one year in every seven, this disruption of the insect-producing environment and life cycle allows the pest population to be controlled. The law of the Sabbath of the land, a useful agricultural practice, is still observed today by some Orthodox Jewish farmers in Israel to promote soil conservation.

The Medical Importance of the Red Heifer Sacrifice

In the book of Numbers, Moses wrote these inspired instructions regarding the mysterious sacrifice of the Red Heifer:

> And one shall burn the heifer in his sight; her skin, and her flesh, and her blood, with her dung, shall he burn: and the priest shall take cedar wood, and hyssop, and scarlet, and cast it into the midst of the burning of the heifer. Then the priest shall wash his clothes, and he shall bathe his flesh in water, and afterward he shall come into the camp, and the priest shall be unclean until the even. And he that burneth her shall wash his clothes in water, and bathe his flesh in water, and shall be unclean until the even. And a man that is clean shall gather up the ashes of the heifer, and lay them up without the camp in a clean place, and it shall be kept for the congregation of the children of Israel for a water of separation: it is a purification for sin. And he that gathereth the ashes of the heifer shall wash his clothes, and be unclean until the even: and it shall be unto the children of Israel, and unto the stranger that sojourneth among them, for a statute for ever.

He that toucheth the dead body of any man shall be unclean seven days. He shall purify himself with it on the third day, and on the seventh day he shall be clean: but if he purify not himself the third day, then the seventh day he shall not be clean. Whosoever toucheth the dead body of any man that is dead, and purifieth not himself, defileth the tabernacle of the LORD; and that soul shall be cut off from Israel: because the water of separation was not sprinkled upon him, he shall be unclean; his uncleanness is yet upon him. (Numbers 19:5–13)

The primary spiritual significance of the sacrifice of the Red Heifer is the fact that it symbolically points to the ultimate sacrifice of Jesus Christ as our only hope of being cleansed from the uncleanness of our sins. The Talmud claims that the Red Heifer sacrifice was the only one of God's commands that King Solomon, the wisest man who ever lived, claimed he did not understand. Solomon apparently could not understand why the priest would be "unclean until the even." This unusual sacrifice symbolically pointed to Jesus Christ and His sacrifice because our Lord, who was perfectly sinless, judicially took upon Himself the sins of humans so that we who are sinful could become righteous before God.

Christ paid the spiritual and physical price for our sins. And just as the Red Heifer was sacrificed "without the camp"—in contrast to all other sacrifices that took place on the altar in front of the Tabernacle or Temple—Jesus also was sacrificed outside the city walls of Jerusalem. In contrast to the male animals typically used as a sacrifice, the Red Heifer was one of the few female animals the Law commanded to be sacrificed. Significantly, our Lord was betrayed for thirty pieces of silver, the price of a female slave.

In addition to the obvious spiritual significance of the law of the sacrifice of the Red Heifer, we now understand that the water of purification described in Numbers 19 actually had the ability to destroy germs and infection. The resulting water-of-purification solution contained ashes from the Red Heifer sacrifice combined with cedar, hyssop, and scarlet thread. The "cedar" oil in this water of purification came from a species of juniper tree that grew in Israel and the Sinai. The oil would irritate the skin, encouraging people to vigorously rub the solution into their hands. Most important, the hyssop tree—associated with mint and possibly marjoram—would produce hyssop oil. Hyssop oil is an effective antiseptic and antibacterial agent. It contains 50 percent carvacrol, which is an antifungal and antibacterial agent still used in medicine.[10] A new skin cleanser, Hyssop Health, kills most germs.

The waters of purification from the Red Heifer sacrifice were to be used to cleanse someone who had become defiled due to touching a dead body, which shows that this was an incredibly effective medical law as well as a spiritual law. The book of Hebrews reveals that Paul, an educated rabbi, understood that the Red Heifer sacrifice had a practical medical effect as well as its more obvious spiritual element. Paul declared that "the blood of bulls and of goats, and the ashes of an heifer sprinkling the unclean, sanctifieth to the purifying of the flesh" (Hebrews 9:13).

Life Is in the Blood

In ancient times, Moses declared, "For the life of the flesh is in the blood" (Leviticus 17:11). This statement revealed advanced scientific knowledge at a time when the level of pagan medical knowledge was abysmal. We know today that blood is essential to all of our body's life processes. Blood carries nutrients and material that produce growth and healing, store fat as energy, and support every organ in the body. When the blood supply is restricted to any part of the body, that part begins immediately to decline and die. Blood is essential to fighting disease, clotting open wounds, and growing new skin and cells. For centuries, doctors did the exact opposite of what they should have been doing to treat disease. Physicians used to bleed their patients by draining large amounts of blood from their bodies in a vain attempt to defeat disease. They did not realize that our blood is the key to our life. Truly, as the Bible declares, "The life of the flesh is in the blood."

We have more than seventy-five thousand miles of blood vessels in our bodies, enough to circle the world three times! Veins, arteries, and capillary vessels carry blood cells with nutrients to feed every one of the sixty trillion cells in our bodies. The sixty trillion amazingly complex cells that make up a human body are produced from a single microscopic cell formed when a father's sperm is joined to a mother's egg. This complex system of inter-connected blood vessels must bring the needed nutrients to the particular cells that require these chemicals.

This is the equivalent of a courier company delivering tril-lions of packages daily to sixty trillion business customers over a route covering seventy-five thousand miles. Each of our cells requires a number of different nutrients and chemicals. Special chemical sensors detect the nutrient needed as the blood passes through the bloodstream. The sensors allow that cell to connect with the necessary substance. In addition, we have more than one million special types of white blood cells, antibodies designed to fight a particular disease. As soon as the body detects that it has been invaded by a particular germ or virus, the blood system goes on special alert to produce an explosive increase in what-ever antibody is required to fight the disease.

The Hebrew word for the heart is *lev*. This word *lev* and variations of it appear at least 825 times in the Old Testament and another 160 times in Greek in the New Testament. The enor-mously complex blood system that allows human life to exist is pumped by the heart, the most powerful muscle in the body. Though it is only the size of a clenched fist, it is far stronger than one's legs or arms. However, while the heart works non-stop for eighty years or more, the muscles of our legs or arms are exhausted after only a short time of exertion. This fantastically reliable organ pumps more than one and a half million gallons of blood every year. In the course of a normal life span, the average human heart will pump forty million times, pushing almost one million pounds of blood.

The Circumcision Commandment

Following the instruction of God, Moses commanded the cir-cumcision of all Jewish boys on the eighth day following their birth (see Genesis 17:12; Leviticus 12:3). For thousands of years righteous Jews have obeyed the circumcision commandment as a sign that they accept the covenant with God. It is interesting that Muslims may choose to circumcise their male children at any point from age three until their thirteenth birthday.[11] Scientists have been examining the biological processes that lead to blood clotting. The rapid healing of a wound begins with clotting of the blood. Any wound that fails to clot and that continues to bleed, especially in a primitive environment, will provide a tremendous likelihood of infection and death.

Modern medical science has discovered that the blood-clotting chemical prothrombin peaks to its highest level when a newborn reaches the eighth day after birth. On this day as well, the liver is developing vitamin K, which assists in blood clotting. These two clotting agents, vitamin K and prothrombin, rise to the highest level (110 percent of normal) on the eighth day following birth. Without vitamin K and prothrombin, blood will not clot properly, and the possibility of severe bleeding as well as infection would make circumcision dangerous in a primitive medical situation.

It is remarkable that even a biblical command such as the circumcision of newborn males provides evidence of God's direct inspiration of the writing of the Scriptures. How would Moses have known that the eighth day of life was the ideal time to circumcise the male children of the Israelites unless God inspired him to write this command?

Notes

1. For more on the advanced medical advice that is provided in the Bible, see Fred Rosner, *Medicine in the Bible and the Talmud: Selections from Classical Jewish Sources* (Jersey City, NJ: Ktav Publishing, 1977).

2. For more on this, see S. E. Massengill, *A Sketch of Medicine and Pharmacy and a View of Its Progress by the Massengill Family from the Fifteenth to the Twentieth Century* (Bristol, TN: S. E. Massengill, 1943).

3. Massengill, *A Sketch of Medicine and Pharmacy.*

4. Lise Manniche, *An Ancient Egyptian Herbal* (London: British Museum Press, 1989).

5. This description comes from an article in the *Encyclopaedia Britannica.*

6. Arturo Castiglioni, *A History of Medicine,* trans. E. B. Krumbhaar (New York: Knopf, 1941), 71.

7. The story of Dr. Ignaz Semmelweis and his pioneering work is a fascinating one. I am indebted to S. I. McMillen, MD, and his thought-provoking book, *None of These Diseases* (Minneapolis, MN: Successful Living, 1972), for making me aware of the importance of Semmelweis's medical contributions.

8. See McMillen, *None of These Diseases.*

9. Castiglioni, *A History of Medicine,* 71.

10. McMillen, *None of These Diseases.*

11. See McMillen, *None of These Diseases.*

6

Precise Fulfillment of Bible Prophecy—the Signature of God

The study of the fulfillment of biblical prophecy provides overwhelming proof that God is controlling human history. The hand of God is moving behind the scenes to bring about His will on Earth (see Isaiah 42:9).

The history of God's chosen people was precisely prophesied throughout the Bible—down to the most detailed developments. Each of the three long captivities of Israel was foretold: the first exile in Egypt, which lasted 430 years; the 70 years of captivity in Babylon; and the final worldwide dispersion of the Jews that lasted for 2,000 years. Every time Israel was outside the Promised Land, the duration of the captivity was foretold. The date of the miraculous rebirth of Israel on May 15, 1948, was foretold by the prophet Ezekiel more than twenty-five centuries before it occurred.

If you have studied biblical prophecy and the fulfillment of those prophecies, you know already that history is following a purposeful pattern, a detailed design laid down in the Word of God. The two questions we must ask as we examine prophecy—both fulfilled and not yet fulfilled—are these:

1. Who is the Designer?
2. What is His purpose in history and in our own lives?

No one except God can accurately predict future events and in such great detail. Neither Satan nor his demons can predict the future. God Almighty told His people:

> Remember the former things of old: for I am God, and there is none else; I am God, and there is none like me, declaring the end from the beginning, and from ancient times the things that are not yet done, saying, My counsel shall stand, and I will do all my pleasure. (Isaiah 46:9–10)

The Bible contains 1,817 individual predictions concerning 737 separate subjects found in 8,352 verses. These predictions comprise 27 percent of the 31,124 verses in the whole of the Scriptures. The precise fulfillment of most of these prophecies are proven by ample historical evidence. Some of the biblical prophecies are yet to be fulfilled, but we can expect them to come to pass in our lifetime.

False Prophets

Despite the fact that the world is full of spiritual texts written by multitudes of religious writers, a close examination of this literature reveals that not one of these texts contains detailed prophecies that have been fulfilled. The reason is quite simple: since no one but God can accurately know the future, religious philosophers who wrote other texts were wise enough to avoid issuing detailed prophecies. God, however, knows the end from the beginning.

> Thus saith the LORD the King of Israel, and his redeemer the LORD of hosts; I am the first, and I am the last; and beside me there is no God. And who, as I, shall call, and shall declare it, and set it in order for me, since I appointed the ancient people? and the things that are coming, and shall come, let them shew unto them. (Isaiah 44:6–7)

The classical and religious literature of the Greeks, Romans, and Middle Eastern cultures contains no specific, detailed prophecies regarding future events, people, or trends. There were no prophecies concerning the coming of Buddha, Muhammad, or any other religious leader. However, the Old Testament prophecies predicted numerous precise details about the life, death, and resurrection of Jesus.

Despite the impossible odds against correctly *guessing* future events, multitudes of false prophets have attempted to make accurate predictions. However, human predictions are almost always wrong—with the exception of a very few lucky guesses. A study of the predictive claims of New Age psychics was published in *Reader's Digest* magazine. The study proved that psychics are hopelessly wrong in their predictions. "The study analyzed the accuracy of the ten top psychics whose prophecies were published over a three-year period, 1976 to 1979. The study compared all of the published predictions with their subsequent success or failure rate. The results are certainly intriguing: 98 percent of their predictions were totally incorrect! Only 2 percent of their predictions were fulfilled…six out of the ten psychics were wrong 100 percent of the time."[1]

Some New Age writers have claimed that several nonbiblical prophets such as Nostradamus (AD 1555) were able to correctly predict the future. Many New Age writers have claimed that Nostradamus predicted that Adolf Hitler would be the future leader of Germany. In fact, Nostradamus never mentioned Adolf Hitler by name in any of his predictions. The closest he came to the surname Hitler was his mention of the word *Ister* in several predictions. The majority of interpreters admit that *Ister* refers to a European river, a tributary of the river Danube. However, some writers who wrote their analyses after World War II falsely claimed that Nostradamus predicted the history of Hitler.

New Age writer Erika Cheetham, who authored *The Final Prophecies of Nostradamus*, admitted that "until 1936, approximately, all commentators on the *Centuries* [of Nostradamus] thought that the word referred to the River Danube, the Ister."[2] Even strong supporters of Nostradamus, such as Henry C. Roberts, editor of *The Complete Prophecies of Nostradamus*, admitted that the "Ister" writings of Nostradamus are "unintelligible." He further described the writings as "garbled to the uninitiate. The strange, broken, and often incoherent nature of the quatrains, both in French and English, is the hallmark of prophetic media."[3]

Other New Age writers have made great claims for the accuracy of the predictions of Edgar Cayce, the so-called American sleeping prophet. I had the opportunity to interview Hugh Lynn Cayce, the son of Edgar Cayce, and his grandson in the early 1970s at their research center in Virginia Beach, Virginia. It was fascinating to listen to them describe the research they had completed for a manuscript that would reveal numerous mistaken predictions that the famed Edgar Cayce had made. Some of these false predictions were prophecies Cayce made about where oil wells or mineral deposits could be located. Not surprisingly, Hugh Lynn Cayce indicated he did not intend to publish the manuscript.

No One but God Knows the Future

Despite the genius of humanity, we are unable to correctly predict future events and trends. For instance, the director of the U.S. Patent Office resigned in 1875. He complained in his resignation letter that there was no point in continuing the Patent Office because "there's nothing left to invent." Only a few years later, in 1887, the brilliant French chemist Marcellin Berthelot wrote, "From now on there is no mystery about the universe."

During the 120 years that followed we have seen the mysteries of the atomic structure of matter unfold, and the creation of new sciences including biophysics, astrophysics, and molecular biology. We have seen the development of commercial air travel, mass communications, supercomputers, and cellular technology. We have landed men on the moon, sent spacecraft to Mars, and probed deep space. New diseases have been identified and cures found. The human genome has been mapped and sequenced. And this short list doesn't even begin to address all the major advances in science, medicine, and technology in the twentieth and twenty-first centuries.

Another great scientist of the nineteenth century, Simon Newcomb, wrote that it was mathematically impossible for any machine that was heavier than a balloon to fly. An equally brilliant French mathematician by the name of Henri Poincaré ridiculed a scientist's speculations about unleashing the power of the atom through chain reactions in uranium: "Common sense alone is enough to tell us that the destruction of a town by a pound of metal is an evident impossibility." Tragically, the discoveries of awesome nuclear energies allowed scientists to create atomic weapons that annihilated two Japanese cities in World War II with only a few pounds of metal.[4]

Inaccurate predictions by noted experts reveal the profound limitations of human intelligence and our inability to correctly predict future developments, trends, personalities, and events. However, when we turn to the pages of the Scriptures we discover a staggering number of precise predictions that were made thousands of years ago. A careful analysis reveals that every biblical prophecy that has been fulfilled to date came to pass with an awesome precision that can only be explained by divine foreknowledge. God knows exactly what the future holds, and He inspired His prophets to proclaim and write exactly what is to come in the world. God predicted future events and made those events known through His messengers. And God is the One who is bringing the events to pass.

Detailed Predictions of the Future of Israel

One of the most incredible biblical prophecies is the prediction of the rebirth of the nation of Israel. Overall, the relationship of the nation of Israel to the geography of the Holy Land is a major focus of biblical prophecy, both fulfilled and unfulfilled. God prophesied precisely when Israel would return to the Promised Land after her citizens went into exile in the first two captivities, the Egyptian bondage and the Babylonian captivity.

While students of prophecy know that the Scriptures contain numerous prophecies that the Jews would return to Israel in the last days, God's prediction about the exact time of Israel's return was not revealed until *after* the fulfillment of the prophecy. Many details about the prophecies concerning the last days were sealed in biblical visions in such a way that they could not be clearly discerned prior to their accomplishment. But in hindsight, it is possible to read the prophecies and see that they already had revealed the timing of many of the major events that the prophets foretold.

A careful examination of the prophecies reveals that God often specified in great detail the exact duration of time involved in various predictions concerning Israel. However, there are no prophecies that reveal the date of the Rapture or other last-days events related to the Church. The Lord has specifically hidden the time of the future resurrection of the saints. The Lord Himself told us, "But of that day and hour knoweth no man, no, not the angels of heaven, but my Father only" (Matthew 24:36).

Israel's First Captivity and Return from Egypt

On the fourteenth day of Nisan, the exact day that would later become the date of Passover, the Lord appeared to Abraham to proclaim the covenant for the Promised Land. God also prophesied that Abraham's descendants would be in affliction and bondage for a period of four hundred years: "And he [God] said unto Abram, Know of a surety that thy seed shall be a stranger in a land that is not theirs, and shall serve them; and they shall afflict them four hundred years" (Genesis 15:13). The affliction of the seed of Abraham (meaning Abraham's descendants) had its beginnings just thirty years after God gave Abraham the promise of the land. The enmity grew from an incident within Abraham's family:

> And the child [Isaac] grew, and was weaned: and Abraham made a great feast the same day that Isaac was weaned. *And Sarah saw the son of Hagar the Egyptian, which she had born unto Abraham, mocking.* Wherefore she said unto Abraham, Cast out this bondwoman and her son: for the son of this bondwoman shall not be heir with my son, even with Isaac. (Genesis 21:8–10)

This jealous mocking of Isaac by his older half brother, Ishmael, began the affliction of Abraham's seed in Canaan. It ended four centuries later, with the exodus of the Hebrew slaves from Egypt. Significantly, the four-hundred-year period prophesied in Genesis 15:13 ended precisely to the day when the Jewish captivity ended: "And it came to pass at the end of the four hundred and thirty years, even the selfsame day it came to pass, that all the hosts of the LORD went out from the land of Egypt" (Exodus 12:41). On that day, God fulfilled His promise and brought Israel out of bondage. The apostle Paul confirmed that God fulfilled His promise to end the captivity precisely 430 years after the promise was given to Abraham (see Galatians 3:17).

Israel's Second Captivity and Return from Babylon

Jeremiah predicted that the duration of the captivity of the Jewish exiles in Babylon would be exactly seventy years (see Jeremiah 25:11). The Babylonian army conquered Israel in the spring of 606 BC. The captivity ended seventy years later in the spring of 536 BC, in the Jewish month Nisan (see Ezra 1:1–3). This is yet another example of the precision of God's prophecies.

Israel's Third Captivity and Return in 1948

The prophet Ezekiel (590 BC) was aware of Jeremiah's prophecy that the Jews would be able to return to their land from Babylon after seventy years (in 536 BC). However, God gave Ezekiel a new revelation that looked much further into the future, revealing how long it would be until the Jews would finally reestablish their nation in the last days. The prediction is found in Ezekiel 4:3–6:

> This shall be a sign to the house of Israel. Lie thou also upon thy left side, and lay the iniquity of the house of Israel upon it: according to the number of the days that thou shalt lie upon it thou shalt bear their iniquity. For I have laid upon thee the years of their iniquity, according to the number of the days, three hundred and ninety days: so shalt thou bear the iniquity of the house of Israel. And when thou hast accomplished them, lie again on thy right side, and thou shalt bear the iniquity of the house of Judah forty days: I have appointed thee each day for a year.

In this passage, Ezekiel declares that each day represents one biblical year. This means Israel would be punished for a combined period of 430 years (arrived at by adding 390 years plus another 40 years). The beginning point occurred in the spring of 536 BC, at the end of the first 70 years of predicted captivity in Babylon (see Jeremiah 25:11). However, in the month of Nisan in 536 BC, only a small remnant of the Jews from the southern kingdom (Judah) chose to leave Babylon and return to Jerusalem. The Jewish exiles who remembered their former homes in Israel were now more than 70 years old. Their children who had been born in Babylon had little attachment to the former home of their parents. The vast majority were happy to remain in the Persian Empire as colonists rather than travel six hundred miles to rebuild the devastated colony of Israel.

God decreed to Ezekiel a period of punishment of 430 years for Israel's and Judah's sin (390 years + 40 years = 430 years). However, when we deduct the 70 years of punishment that the Jews already had endured during the 70-year Babylonian captivity, there still remained 360 years of further punishment beyond the year 536 BC. When we examine the history of that period we see that the Jews did not return to establish an independent country at the end of either 360 or 430 years of additional punishment. In light of the precision of Ezekiel's prophecy, this raises a question. It is difficult to understand why nothing occurred at that time.

Both the Bible and history reveal that Israel did not repent of its sins at the end of the 70-year captivity in Babylon. In fact, the Scriptures record in the books of Ezra and Nehemiah that the minority of fifty thousand Jews who chose to return with Ezra to the Promised Land did so with little faith. The vast majority of the Jews willingly remained in pagan Babylon. They failed to repent of their disobedience, which was the reason God sent them into captivity in the first place. This majority who refused to immigrate home to Israel, comprising more than 95 percent of the Jewish captives, settled as colonists in what is now Iraq and Iran. Over the centuries that followed, travelers such as Benjamin of Tudela, in the twelfth century, reported that thousands of Jews still lived in several of the cities of what are present-day Iraq, Iran, and Afghanistan.

I have discovered the solution to the mystery of the duration of Israel's worldwide dispersion and subsequent return to the

Holy Land. The answer is found in a divine principle that God revealed to Moses in Leviticus 26. In this chapter the Lord established promises and punishments for Israel based on her obedience (the promises) and her disobedience (the punishments). God declared to Israel four times in this passage that if, after being punished for her sins, Israel still did not repent, the punishments previously specified would be multiplied by seven (the number of completion). "And if ye will not yet for all this hearken unto me, then I will punish you seven times more for your sins" (Leviticus 26:18; see also verses 21, 23–24, 27–28). Since the majority of the Jews refused to repent after the Babylonian captivity ended, the period of 360 years of further punishment declared by Ezekiel 4:3–6 was to be multiplied by seven. This meant that the Jews would remain without an independent nation for another 2,520 biblical years, starting from 536 BC. The period of punishment was to last 2,520 *biblical* years (of 360 days each), rather than 2,520 calendar years (of 365.25 days).

The Biblical Year of 360 Days

The Bible always follows the ancient Jewish calendar, in which 360 days make up a biblical year. It is a lunar-solar year composed of twelve months of 30 days each. According to articles in the *Encyclopaedia Britannica* (6th ed.) and *Smith's Bible Dictionary*, Abraham used a 360-day year. The Genesis record of the Great Flood (see 7:11–8:4) confirms that the ancient year consisted of twelve months of 30 days each. (Moses declared that the period of 150 days when the floodwaters were at their height lasted five months, from the seventeenth day of the second month to the seventeenth day of the seventh month.)

If we wish to understand the precise times involved in the fulfillment of biblical prophecy, we need to calculate using the 360-day year. The failure to understand this has prevented some prophecy students from clearly understanding many prophecies that contain a precise time element. The 360-day prophetic year is also borne out in the book of Revelation, where John describes the Great Tribulation of three and a half years as lasting precisely 1,260 days (see Revelation 12:6).

Ezekiel's prophecy declared that the end of Israel's punishment and her final restoration to the Promised Land would be accomplished in 2,520 biblical years of 360 days each, or 907,200 days. To convert this into our calendar year of 365.25 days we simply divide 907,200 days by 365.25 days, or 2,483.8 of our modern calendar years. So Israel's worldwide captivity would end precisely 2,483.8 calendar years after the end of the Babylonian captivity (the spring of 536 BC). In these calculations we must keep in mind that the year 1 BC was immediately followed by the year AD 1. There was no year zero.

The Date of Israel's Rebirth as a Nation

The Babylonian captivity ended in the spring of 536 BC, or 536.4 BC. Subtract 536.4 from the duration of Israel's captivity (see Ezekiel 4:3–6, as discussed above), which is 2,483.8 calendar years. The result is AD 1947.4. Now adjust for the fact there was no year zero between 1 BC and AD 1, so the end of Israel's captivity would occur, on our modern calendar, in the year 1948.4.

On the afternoon of May 14, 1948, the Jews proclaimed the independence of the reborn State of Israel. As an old rabbi blew on the *shofar*, a ram's horn, the Jewish people celebrated the end of their worldwide dispersion and captivity. At midnight, as May 15, 1948, began, Israel officially became an independent nation. This great day marked the first time since the days of Solomon that a united Israel took its place as a sovereign, independent state among the nations of the world.

This was the fulfillment of prophecy of such remarkable precision that one is forced to marvel at the power of God to control all of humanity's plans and their outcomes. God remains in full control of the events of humanity and the world. The universe is unfolding precisely as our Lord ordained millenniums ago. In addition, this amazingly accurate fulfillment of prophecy should focus our attention on the prophecy of Jesus Christ about the budding of the fig tree.

The Bible used the symbol of the fig tree or figs in five different passages as an exclusive symbol of the nation Israel (see Judges 9:8–15; Jeremiah 24:1–10; Hosea 9:10; Matthew 21:18–20; 24:32–34).

Now learn a parable of the fig tree; When his branch is yet tender, and putteth forth leaves, ye know that summer is nigh: so likewise ye, when ye shall see all these things, know that it is near, even at the doors. Verily I say unto you, This generation shall not pass, till all these things be fulfilled. (Matthew 24:32–34)

Consider two things. First, keep in mind the startling precision of the fulfillment of Ezekiel's prophecy about Israel's rebirth, which calculates out to the year AD 1948.4, or May 1948. Second, recall the prophecy of Jesus that the generation that would witness this rebirth of a nation "shall not pass [away], till all these things be fulfilled" (Matthew 24:34). You and I are now living in the generation when Christ indicated He will return to judge humanity.

Prophecy of the Destruction of Tyre

One of the most unusual of all the biblical prophecies is the prediction and history of the destruction of the ancient city of Tyre. The famous Phoenician trading city, known as the "Queen of the Sea," was located twenty miles south of the present-day city of Sidon on the Lebanese coast of the Mediterranean Sea. Tyre was enormously powerful, proud, and rich, receiving the trade and tribute of many lesser cities. In its day, it was the equivalent of present-day New York City. Despite the city's overwhelming naval military power and dominant defensive position, the prophet Ezekiel (592–570 BC) described a vision that outlined an unprecedented series of military invasions that would ultimately bring about the destruction of the famous city of Tyre.

The Vision of Tyre's Destruction

Therefore thus saith the Lord GOD; Behold, I am against thee, O Tyrus, and will cause many nations to come up against thee, as the sea causeth his waves to come up. And they shall destroy the walls of Tyrus, and break down her towers: I will also scrape her dust from her, and make her like the top of a rock. It shall be a place for the spreading of nets in the midst of the sea: for I have spoken it, saith the Lord GOD: and it shall become a spoil to the nations....

For thus saith the Lord GOD; Behold, I will bring upon Tyrus Nebuchadrezzar king of Babylon, a king of kings, from the north, with horses, and with chariots, and with horsemen, and companies, and much people. He shall slay with the sword thy daughters in the field: and he shall make a fort against thee, and cast a mount against thee, and lift up the buckler against thee.... And they shall make a spoil of thy riches, and make a prey of thy merchandise: and they shall break down thy walls, and destroy thy pleasant houses: and they shall lay thy stones and thy timber and thy dust in the midst of the water.... And I will make thee like the top of a rock: thou shalt be a place to spread nets upon; thou shalt be built no more: for I the LORD have spoken it, saith the Lord GOD....

I will make thee a terror, and thou shalt be no more: though thou be sought for, yet shalt thou never be found again, saith the Lord GOD. (Ezekiel 26:3–5, 7–8, 12, 14, 21)

To better understand these predictions, it may help to list them:
1. God will "bring upon [Tyre] Nebuchadnezzar," the king of Babylon (verse 7).
2. God will "cause many nations to come up against thee, as...waves...come up" (verse 3).
3. Enemies will destroy the walls of Tyre and "make her like the top of a rock" (verse 4).
4. The destroyed city will be "a place for the spreading of nets" (verse 5).
5. Tyre's enemies will lay the destroyed city's debris "in the midst of the water" (verse 12).
6. The original city of Tyre will be "built no more" (verse 14).
7. The ancient city will "never be found again" (verse 21).

The subsequent history of this area, borne out in secular histories and records, reveals the unprecedented way in which these predictions were fulfilled. When one compares Ezekiel's prophecies with the history of the city, one can't help but be amazed by the remarkable fulfillment of the prophecies in the Word of God.

First Prophecy: King Nebuchadnezzar's Defeat of Mainland Tyre

Only three years after Ezekiel received and published his prophecy, the king of Babylon, Nebuchadnezzar, launched a prolonged siege against the powerful city of Tyre. The *Encyclopaedia Britannica* reports, "After a 13-year siege (585–573 BC) by Nebuchadnezzar II, Tyre made terms and acknowledged Babylonian sovereignty."[5] However, when King Nebuchadnezzar's army broke through the gates of Tyre, he was disappointed to discover that the city was virtually deserted.

Most of the population had evacuated the mainland city by ship and relocated to a small island a half mile off the coast. The resourceful citizens of Tyre used their incredible wealth and the help of strong allies to fortify the city walls that they rapidly erected on the island. The mainland city was destroyed in 573 BC by the armies of Babylon. However, the newly built island city of Tyre remained a powerful and well-defended city for several centuries, protected by its strong naval fleet, its allies, and its unique defensive position as an island fortress.

Second Prophecy: A Series of Attacks like Waves of the Sea

The next prophecy was fulfilled during the Greek invasion of the Middle East by the victorious armies of Alexander the Great (333 BC). According to the *Encyclopaedia Britannica,*

> In his war on the Persians Alexander III [the Great], after defeating Darius III at the Battle of Issus, marched southward toward Egypt, calling upon the Phoenician cities to open their gates to him, as it was part of Alexander's general plan to deny their use to the Persian fleet.
>
> The citizens of Tyre refused to do so, and Alexander laid siege to the city. Possessing no fleet, he demolished the old city of Tyre, on the mainland, and with the debris of the city

he built a causeway some 200 feet wide across the half-mile wide straits separating the old and new towns, erecting towers and war engines at the farther end.[6]

Alexander built up his fleet of ships from the contributions of his allies and eventually completed a causeway that made possible the destruction of the island city of Tyre. He captured the city and then sold thirty thousand citizens into slavery and killed more than eight thousand of its defenders.

The ancient Roman historian Quintus Curtius wrote about the construction of Alexander's causeway. He recorded that Alexander the Great used material that was available from both Mount Libanus and the old city of Tyre to supply stones and dirt for the causeway.[7]

Just as ocean waves come in a series or succession, the armies of Tyre's enemies came one after another over the centuries to destroy the greatest and richest city on the ancient Mediterranean coast.

Third Prophecy: Tyre's Walls Would Be Destroyed

Historian Philip Myers wrote about the Greek army's total destruction of the island city of Tyre. "Alexander the Great... reduced it to ruins (332 BC). She recovered in a measure from this blow, but never regained the place she had previously held in the world."[8]

Fourth Prophecy: Tyre Would Be "a Place for the Spreading of Nets"

Despite the city's ideal location based on its excellent harbor, its location on a major trading route, and its tremendous fresh water supply, the mainland city was left bare as a rock. This is an exact fulfillment of Ezekiel's prophecy. Philip Myers wrote, "The larger part of the site of the once great city is now bare as the top of a rock, where the fishermen that still frequent the spot spread their nets to dry."[9]

Archaeologist Hanns-Wolf Rackl described the present situation of the site of ancient Tyre: "Today hardly a single stone of the old Tyre remains intact.... Tyre has become a place to dry fish nets, as the prophet predicted."[10]

Fifth Prophecy: Tyre's Debris "in the Midst of the Water"

As was mentioned earlier, Alexander the Great's army took the debris of stone and timber from the destroyed mainland city of Tyre and cast it into the sea to create a causeway to enable his army to approach the satellite island city. The causeway, measuring two hundred feet in width, stretched across a half mile of sea so Alexander's army could invade the island city.

Sixth Prophecy: Ancient Tyre Was to Be "Built No More"

Many people have assumed that this prophecy was incorrect, in that any current map of the Middle East reveals a city named Tyre on the Mediterranean coast of Lebanon. However, the modern city of Tyre is not the rebuilt city of ancient Tyre. The ancient ruins remain as they were in biblical times, still abandoned. It would be the equivalent of the destruction of New York City and, centuries later, the building of a new city many miles to the north, albeit a city that took the ancient name to honor the historical memory.

Others have complained that there is a small fishing village built near the ancient ruins. However, this is not a development that contradicts Ezekiel's detailed prophecy. The prophecy that fishermen would dry their nets on the bare rocks of the ruined city of Tyre necessarily implies that fishermen would live nearby. One writer described it in these words: "The 'Sidonian' port of Tyre is still in use today. Small fishing vessels lay at anchor there. An examination of the foundations reveals granite columns of the Roman period which were incorporated as binders in the walls by the Crusaders. The port has become a haven today for fishing boats and a place for spreading nets."[11]

Although almost all destroyed ancient cities were rebuilt because of the obvious advantages of their geographical location, trade routes, water sources, roads, and so forth, the ancient ruins of Tyre remain today as silent testimony to the accuracy of the Bible's prophecies. Scientist Peter Stoner wrote of the incredible odds against Tyre ever being rebuilt: "The great freshwater springs of Reselain are at the site of the mainland city of Tyre, and no doubt supplied the city with an abundance of fresh water. These springs are still there and still flow, but their water runs into the sea. The flow of these springs was measured by an engineer, and found to be about 10,000,000 gallons daily. It is still an excellent site for a city and would have free water enough for a large modern city, yet it has never been rebuilt."[12]

Seventh Prophecy: The Ancient City Will "Never Be Found Again"

The prophet Ezekiel's expression that the destroyed city of Tyre will "never be found again" obviously does not mean that the physical site could never be located. Ezekiel's expression logically refers to the fact that, although people would desire to see the magnificent city rebuilt, Tyre would never be found as a rebuilt city.

Floyd E. Hamilton wrote in his book *The Basis of the Christian Faith*:

> Other cities destroyed by enemies had been rebuilt; Jerusalem was destroyed many times, but always has risen again from the ruins.... The voice of God has spoken and Old Tyre today stands as it has for twenty-five centuries, a bare rock, uninhabited by man! Today anyone who wants to see the site of the old city can have it pointed out to him along the shore, but there is not a ruin to mark the spot. It has been scraped clean and has never been rebuilt.[13]

Some critics have questioned an apparent contradiction in the book of Ezekiel. In chapter 26, the prophet predicts the imminent destruction of the city of Tyre by the armies of King Nebuchadnezzar. However, there is a statement just a few chapters later (Ezekiel 29:18) that describes the failure of King Nebuchadnezzar to capture the riches of the city. The king had intended to use the spoils of war to pay his army: "Son of man, Nebuchadrezzar king of Babylon caused his army to serve a great service against Tyrus: every head was made bald, and every shoulder was peeled: yet had he no wages, nor his army, for Tyrus, for the service that he had served against it" (29:18).

On the surface, there appears to be a contradiction. However, there was no contradiction in the mind of Ezekiel nor in the actual historical statement. Although the Babylonian army destroyed the mainland city of Tyre, they obviously failed to profit from the spoils, possibly because the total burning of Tyre at the end of the thirteen-year siege prevented the successful looting of the city.

The Site of the City of Tyre Today

Nina Jidejian concludes in her excellent book *Tyre Through the Ages* that the city of Tyre's

> stones may be found as far away as Acre and Beirut. Yet evidences of a great past are abundant and recent excavations have revealed successive levels of this proud Phoenician seaport.... The great ancient city of Tyre lay buried under accumulated debris. The ruins of an aqueduct and a few scattered columns and the ruins of a Christian basilica were the only remains found above ground.... Looking down into the water one can see a mass of granite columns and stone blocks strewn over the sea bottom. Until recently the ruins of Tyre above water were few.[14]

The detailed prophecy about the repeated invasions and final defeat of the rich and powerful city of Tyre is clearly one of the most fascinating and improbable predictions made in the Word of God. Yet every detail of this complicated prophecy, which was made twenty-six centuries ago, ultimately came true exactly as Ezekiel described it. The history of Tyre, once the greatest city of the ancient world, stands as a silent and profound witness to the prophetic authority and supernatural inspiration of the Word of God.

As we examine the various categories of evidence that support the reliability, accuracy, and authority of the Scriptures, there is no evidence that speaks more loudly or with more persuasiveness than the testimony of fulfilled prophecy. And there is no area of prophecy more important, nor more compelling, than the prophecies of Israel's Messiah, Jesus Christ.

We will now turn to those prophecies, where we will again see that God has a plan and a purpose for humanity. He has revealed His plan from the beginning, not wanting anyone to be unaware that He has provided for our salvation (see Genesis 3:15).

Notes

1. The study, titled "The Shattered Crystal Ball," appeared in *Reader's Digest* magazine. Cited in Grant R. Jeffrey, *Armageddon* (Colorado Springs: WaterBrook, 1997), 14–15.
2. Erika Cheetham, *The Final Prophecies of Nostradamus* (New York: Putnam, 1989).
3. Henry C. Roberts, ed., *The Complete Prophecies of Nostradamus* (Jericho, NY: Nostradamus, 1976).
4. This topic is worthy of additional reading. Louis Pauwels and Jacques Bergier, in their fascinating book *Morning of the Magicians*, explore the massive changes in technology that challenged the assumptions of modern civilization. See Pauwels and Bergier, *Morning of the Magicians*, trans. Rollo Myers (New York: Stein and Day, 1964), 9–10, 14.
5. *Encyclopaedia Britannica*, 1970 ed., s.v. "Tyre."
6. *Encyclopaedia Britannica*, 1970 ed., s.v. "Tyre."
7. Quintus Curtius, *History of Alexander*, trans. John C. Rolfe, Loeb Classical Library, 2 vols. (Cambridge, MA: Harvard University Press, 1946), 1:18–19.
8. Philip Myers, *A General History for Colleges and High Schools* (Boston: Ginn and Co., 1889).
9. Myers, *General History for Colleges and High Schools.*
10. Hanns-Wolf Rackl, *Diving into the Past: Archaeology Under Water*, trans. Ronald J. Floyd (New York: Scribner, 1968), 179.
11. Nina Jidejian, *Tyre Through the Ages* (Beirut: Dar el-Mashreq, 1969), 139.
12. Peter Stoner, *Science Speaks: An Evaluation of Certain Christian Evidences* (1953; repr., Chicago: Moody, 1963), 76–77.
13. Floyd E. Hamilton, *The Basis of the Christian Faith* (New York: George H. Doran, 1927), 299.
14. Jidejian, *Tyre Through the Ages*, 139.

7

The Promised Messiah— Proof That the Scriptures Are Inspired by God

The Old Testament contains more than three hundred passages that refer to the first coming of the promised Messiah. These references are remarkably detailed, and taken together they present a clear portrait of God's Anointed One. Within the prophecies, Bible scholars have found forty-eight specific details that match the life, death, and resurrection of Jesus. We will discuss only seventeen of these prophecies, which present undeniable evidence that only one person, Jesus of Nazareth, could be Israel's promised Messiah.

The Laws of Probability

The study of statistics includes the theory and laws of mathematical probability. The laws of probability are so reliable that life insurance companies write policies promising to pay staggering amounts of money to the beneficiary of a thirty-year-old male in return for only a small premium. How can an insurer take on such a huge risk in return for modest premiums? The answer is found in the laws of probability. After careful analysis of mortality tables, insurance companies know that only a tiny fraction of thirty-year-old clients will die within the next twelve months. Every day insurance companies risk billions of dollars based on their analysis of and reliance on mathematical probability.

When you calculate the likelihood of several events taking place at or near the same time, you have to multiply all the probabilities together. For instance, if the probability of a single event occurring randomly is 1 chance in 5 and the probability of a separate event occurring is 1 chance in 10, then the probability that *both* events will occur together or in sequence is 1 in 5 multiplied by 1 in 10, which yields 1 in 50. For example, if the New York Yankees have a 1-in-5 chance of making it to the World Series this year and the St. Louis Cardinals have a 1-in-10 chance, the odds against these two teams facing each other in October is 1 chance in 50.

Consider the odds when you toss a coin in the air. Since a coin has two sides, the odds are 50 percent, or 1 chance in 2, that you will get heads when you toss a quarter. However, suppose you toss the quarter two times. What are the odds against getting heads twice in a row? The answer is 1 in 4. The combined odds are $2 \times 2 = 4$. The odds of tossing ten coins in a row and getting ten heads are staggering at 1 chance in 1,024. Don't bet your salary that you can beat such odds.

However, when we look at biblical prophecy, we can trust fully that every event that was foretold will come to pass. The odds against the hundreds of Messianic prophecies coming true are beyond comprehension. And even when we narrow the discussion down to just seventeen of these prophecies coming true in the life of just one person, the odds are overwhelming. But no matter what the laws of probability might say about seventeen diverse predictions all being perfectly fulfilled in the life of the same person, the evidence is compelling that Jesus Christ was the promised Messiah.

In this chapter we will examine a series of very specific predictions that were made by different Jewish prophets who lived in widely separated communities over a period of a thousand years. These predictions were fulfilled more than five hundred years after they were recorded. We also will examine the argument that these individual predictions all could have come to pass by random chance alone. After considering the evidence presented in this chapter, you will understand that the fulfillment of all these predictions in the life of only one man was so improbable that any unbiased observer must accept that the Bible was inspired by God and that Jesus Christ is the promised Messiah.

Seventeen Incredible Prophecies of the Messiah

As you consider the likelihood that any one of these seventeen prophecies could have occurred by chance, ask yourself if it could have been possible that *all seventeen* could have been fulfilled by random chance in the life of Jesus Christ.

The First Prediction

The Messiah would be born in the town of Bethlehem, and his ancestry would be from the tribe of Judah.

Probability: 1 chance in 2,400

The Old Testament prediction

But thou, Bethlehem Ephratah, though thou be little among the thousands of Judah, yet out of thee shall he come forth unto me that is to be ruler in Israel; whose goings forth have been from of old, from everlasting. (Micah 5:2)

The sceptre shall not depart from Judah, nor a lawgiver from between his feet, until Shiloh come; and unto him shall the gathering of the people be. (Genesis 49:10)

The New Testament fulfillment

Now when Jesus was born in Bethlehem of Judaea in the days of Herod the king, behold, there came wise men from the east to Jerusalem. (Matthew 2:1)

There were twelve tribes in ancient Israel from which the Messiah could have been born. Yet He was born from the tribe of Judah, as Moses predicted fifteen hundred years earlier. Since there were twelve tribes, the odds of this happening were twelve to one against Moses' correctly guessing the tribe of Christ's birth. The odds of Jesus' place of birth matching prophecy by mere chance are based on the fact that there were more than two thousand villages and towns in the densely populated area allotted to the tribe of Judah during the first century of this era. However, to be conservative, I used the figure of 1 chance in 2,400 to estimate the odds against anyone guessing that the Messiah would be born in Bethlehem *and* that He would descend from the tribe Judah.

The Second Prediction
The Messiah would be preceded by a messenger.
>   Probability: 1 chance in 20
>   *The Old Testament prediction*

> The voice of him that crieth in the wilderness, Prepare ye the way of the LORD, make straight in the desert a highway for our God. (Isaiah 40:3)

> *The New Testament fulfillment*

> In those days came John the Baptist, preaching in the wilderness of Judaea, and saying, Repent ye: for the kingdom of heaven is at hand. (Matthew 3:1–2)

I estimated the odds as 1 in 20, but to my knowledge historical records do not reveal any other king—in ancient Palestine or any other part of the Middle East—who was preceded by a messenger such as John the Baptist. As we keep a running count, to calculate the combined probability of these first two predictions taking place, we must multiply 2,400 times 20, which equals 1 chance in 48,000 that Jesus would fulfill both prophecies simply by random chance.

The Third Prediction
The Messiah would enter Jerusalem on a colt.
>   Probability: 1 chance in 50
>   *The Old Testament prediction*

Rejoice greatly, O daughter of Zion; shout, O daughter of Jerusalem: behold, thy King cometh unto thee: he is just, and having salvation; lowly, and riding upon an ass, and upon a colt the foal of an ass. (Zechariah 9:9)

The New Testament fulfillment

And they brought him [the colt] to Jesus: and they cast their garments upon the colt, and they set Jesus thereon. And as he went, they spread their clothes in the way. And when he was come nigh, even now at the descent of the mount of Olives, the whole multitude of the disciples began to rejoice and praise God with a loud voice for all the mighty works that they had seen. (Luke 19:35–37)

Of all the kings in history, I do not know of a single one who entered his capital city riding on a colt, as Jesus did on Palm Sunday, AD 32, in fulfillment of this prophecy. The combined odds of the first three predictions occurring by chance are 50 × 48,000, which equals 1 chance in 2.4 million. With the addition of every subsequent prediction in this list of seventeen, the laws of probability reveal that the combined odds against anyone fulfilling these multiple prophecies are simply astronomical.

The Fourth Prediction
He would be betrayed by a friend.
  Probability: 1 chance in 10
  The Old Testament prediction

Yea, mine own familiar friend, in whom I trusted, which did eat of my bread, hath lifted up his heel against me. (Psalm 41:9)

The New Testament fulfillment

And while he [Jesus] yet spake, lo, Judas, one of the twelve, came, and with him a great multitude with swords and staves, from the chief priests and elders of the people. Now he that betrayed him gave them a sign, saying, Whomsoever I shall kiss, that same is he: hold him fast. (Matthew 26:47–48)

Although throughout history it was not at all unusual for a secular king to be betrayed by a close associate, the betrayal of a religious leader is quite unusual. However, to be conservative, I have assigned the odds of this occurring by chance as only 1 in 10. The combined probability for these four predictions (10 × 2,400,000) is now 1 chance in 24 million.

The Fifth Prediction
The Messiah's hands and feet would be pierced.
> Probability: 1 chance in 100
> *The Old Testament prediction*

> For dogs have compassed me: the assembly of the wicked have inclosed me: they pierced my hands and my feet. (Psalm 22:16)

> *The New Testament fulfillment*

> And when they were come to the place, which is called Calvary, there they crucified him, and the malefactors, one on the right hand, and the other on the left. (Luke 23:33)

Because first-century Judea was under Roman occupation and rule, and taking into account that the Roman form of capital punishment was crucifixion, the odds are low but not unheard of that a Jew in the first century might meet such an end. The combined probability of these first five predictions (100 × 24,000,000) has now reached an astonishing 1 chance in 2.4 billion. We are not yet one-third of the way through this abbreviated list of Messianic predictions, and already Jesus has fulfilled more prophecies than could ever occur by random chance.

The Sixth Prediction
The Messiah would be wounded by His enemies.
> Probability: 1 chance in 10
> *The Old Testament prediction*

> But he was wounded for our transgressions, he was bruised for our iniquities: the chastisement of our peace was upon him; and with his stripes we are healed. (Isaiah 53:5)

The New Testament fulfillment

> Then released he [Pilate] Barabbas unto them: and when he had scourged Jesus, he delivered him to be crucified. (Matthew 27:26)

Throughout history, most kings who were killed were murdered suddenly. Very few were subjected to torture, much less the excruciating punishment that was inflicted on our Lord Jesus Christ. The odds against this occurring by chance are less than 1 chance in 10. The combined odds for the six predictions (10 × 2,400,000,000) now rises to 1 chance in 24 billion.

The Seventh Prediction
He would be betrayed for thirty pieces of silver.
>> Probability: 1 chance in 50
>> *The Old Testament prediction*

> And I said unto them, If ye think good, give me my price; and if not, forebear. So they weighed for my price thirty pieces of silver. (Zechariah 11:12)

The New Testament fulfillment

> And [Judas Iscariot] said unto them, What will ye give me, and I will deliver him unto you? And they covenanted with him for thirty pieces of silver. (Matthew 26:15)

Consider how impossible it would be to correctly predict five hundred years in advance the exact amount of silver that a betrayer would be given in exchange for the betrayal of a trusted friend. Or how could anyone guess hundreds of years in advance the price that would be paid for the death of a king? The odds (50 × 24,000,000,000) now rise to 1 chance in 1.2 trillion.

The Eighth Prediction
The Messiah would be spit upon and beaten.
>> Probability: 1 chance in 10
>> *The Old Testament prediction*

I gave my back to the smiters, and my cheeks to them that plucked off the hair: I hid not my face from shame and spitting. (Isaiah 50:6)

The New Testament fulfillment

Then did they spit in his face, and buffeted him; and others smote him with the palms of their hands. (Matthew 26:67)

Although many kings throughout history were killed, very few were tormented, beaten, and ridiculed. However, Jesus Christ had to endure a remarkable amount of abuse, mocking, and physical punishment before He was nailed to the cross. He bore those stripes for our healing and salvation. The odds of these eight predictions (10 × 1,200,000,000,000) occurring by chance are now 1 chance in 12 trillion.

The Ninth Prediction
His betrayal money would be thrown in the Temple and then given to buy a potter's field.
Probability: 1 chance in 200
The Old Testament prediction

And the LORD said unto me, Cast it unto the potter: a goodly price that I was prised at of them. And I took the thirty pieces of silver, and cast them to the potter in the house of the LORD. (Zechariah 11:13)

The New Testament fulfillment

And he [Judas] cast down the pieces of silver in the temple, and departed, and went and hanged himself. And the chief priests took the silver pieces, and said, It is not lawful for to put them into the treasury, because it is the price of blood. And they took counsel, and bought with them the potter's field, to bury strangers in. (Matthew 27:5–7)

This is a complicated story. It involves multiple decisions and actions made by a number of people, primarily Judas Iscariot and the chief priests of Israel. In order for this prophecy to be fulfilled, each character in the story had to make the right choices and follow those choices with the appropriate actions, as predicted by

Zechariah. How could all these parties have followed the prophetic script by random chance?

And it doesn't end there. The prophecy itself seems contradictory, at least on its surface. However, in spite of its apparent impossibility, every detail of the prophecy was fulfilled. Judas threw the thirty pieces of betrayal money into the Temple. Later, the priests had a crisis of conscience over a relatively minor point, considering they had just conspired to assure the execution of an innocent man. At any rate, the priests used the betrayal money to purchase a potter's field, to be used for the burial of strangers. Ironically, Judas was buried in that field. Overcome with guilt, he went out and hanged himself. I calculated the odds extremely conservatively as 1 chance in 200. However, the combined odds (200 × 12,000,000,000,000) against these nine predictions occurring have risen to 1 chance in 2,400 trillion.

The Tenth Prediction
He would be silent before His accusers.
Probability: 1 chance in 100
The Old Testament prediction

He was oppressed, and he was afflicted, yet he opened not his mouth: he is brought as a lamb to the slaughter, and as a sheep before her shearers is dumb, so he openeth not his mouth. (Isaiah 53:7)

The New Testament fulfillment

And when he was accused of the chief priests and elders, he answered nothing. Then said Pilate unto him, Hearest thou not how many things they witness against thee? And he answered him to never a word; insomuch that the governor marvelled greatly. (Matthew 27:12–14)

When a person is accused of a crime, it is natural for him to defend himself—even if he is guilty. Consider how unlikely this prediction was that a totally innocent man would stand in front of his accusers and remain absolutely silent. Even when Jesus was invited to defend Himself, He chose not to speak up. While I assigned the odds as 1 chance in 100, the realistic chances against this event occurring are much higher. The odds against these ten predictions occurring (100 × 2,400,000,000,000,000) is now 1 chance in 240 quadrillion.

The Eleventh Prediction
He would be crucified with thieves.
> Probability: 1 chance in 100
> *The Old Testament prediction*

> Therefore will I divide him a portion with the great, and he shall divide the spoil with the strong; because he hath poured out his soul unto death: and he was numbered with the transgressors; and he bare the sin of many, and made intercession for the transgressors. (Isaiah 53:12)

> *The New Testament fulfillment*

> Then were there two thieves crucified with him, one on the right hand, and another on the left. (Matthew 27:38)

At the tenth prediction, the running count on the odds stood at 1 chance in 240 quadrillion. I will not continue to supply the multiplication of odds for each of the next six prophecies since we already have arrived at a staggering number. At the end of this analysis, however, I will give the final calculation to show the impossibility that all seventeen prophecies could have been fulfilled by random chance in the life of just one man.

The Twelfth Prediction
People would gamble for the Messiah's garments.
> Probability: 1 chance in 100
> *The Old Testament prediction*

> They part my garments among them, and cast lots upon my vesture. (Psalm 22:18)

> *The New Testament fulfillment*

> Then the soldiers, when they had crucified Jesus, took his garments, and made four parts, to every soldier a part; and also his coat: now the coat was without seam, woven from the top

throughout. They said therefore among themselves, Let us not rend it, but cast lots for it, whose it shall be: that the scripture might be fulfilled, which saith, They parted my raiment among them, and for my vesture they did cast lots. (John 19:23–24)

Think of how unlikely it was that Roman soldiers would bother to gamble to see who would win the right to claim the garments of a crucified prisoner. Yet the prophecy was fulfilled precisely.

The Thirteenth Prediction
His side would be pierced.
> Probability: 1 chance in 100
> *The Old Testament prediction*

> And I will pour upon the house of David, and on the inhabitants of Jerusalem, the spirit of grace and of supplications: and they shall look upon me whom they have pierced, and they shall mourn for him, as one mourneth for his only son, and shall be in bitterness for him, as one that is in bitterness for his firstborn. (Zechariah 12:10)

> *The New Testament fulfillment*

> But one of the soldiers with a spear pierced his side, and forthwith came there out blood and water. (John 19:34)

The cruelty of the Romans was expressed in the unspeakable pain inflicted on condemned prisoners during their lengthy death on a cross. However, despite receiving orders to assure a drawn-out death, the Roman centurion on duty at Jesus' crucifixion was motivated by God to use a spear to pierce Christ's side. The blood and water flowing out of Christ's side proved that He already had died before the spear entered His body. The odds against anyone plunging a spear into the side of a man being crucified is estimated conservatively as 1 chance in 100.

The Fourteenth Prediction
None of His bones would be broken.
> Probability: 1 chance in 20
> *The Old Testament prediction*

> He keepeth all his bones: not one of them is broken. (Psalm 34:20)

The New Testament fulfillment

> But when they came to Jesus, and saw that he was dead already, they brake not his legs. (John 19:33)

When a prisoner of Rome was crucified, his body was placed on a cross in such a manner that the only way he could breathe was by painfully lifting his upper body, using the strength of his legs, to expand his diaphragm. When Roman soldiers wished to speed up a prisoner's death, they would break his legs with a club and thus prevent him from lifting himself up to breathe. Within minutes the prisoner would die due to oxygen deprivation and fluid accumulation in his lungs. To avoid desecrating the Sabbath, which was about to begin, the soldiers broke the legs of the prisoners on either side of Jesus to assure their quick death. However, in fulfillment of the ancient prophecy, Jesus already had died. Therefore, they did not break Christ's legs, and thus the prophecy was fulfilled.

The Fifteenth Prediction
His body would not decay.
> Probability: 1 chance in 10,000
> *The Old Testament prediction*

> For thou wilt not leave my soul in hell; neither wilt thou suffer thine Holy One to see corruption. (Psalm 16:10)

The New Testament fulfillment

> He [King David] seeing this before spake of the resurrection of Christ, that his soul was not left in hell, neither his flesh did see corruption. (Acts 2:31)

Obviously, the odds against anyone dying and his body not decaying, but later rising from the dead, are astronomical. However, I have estimated the odds as 1 chance in 10,000 because several other individuals were resurrected in the Old Testament, such as the Shunammite widow's son who was raised from the dead by Elisha (see 2 Kings 4:28–37), and in the New Testament, Lazarus, who was resurrected by Jesus (see John 11:43–44).

The Sixteenth Prediction
He would be buried in a rich man's tomb.
> Probability: 1 chance in 100
> *The Old Testament prediction*

> And he made his grave with the wicked, and with the rich in his death; because he had done no violence, neither was any deceit in his mouth. (Isaiah 53:9)

> *The New Testament fulfillment*

> When the even was come, there came a rich man of Arimathaea, named Joseph, who also himself was Jesus' disciple: he went to Pilate, and begged the body of Jesus. Then Pilate commanded the body to be delivered. And when Joseph had taken the body, he wrapped it in a clean linen cloth, and laid it in his own new tomb, which he had hewn out in the rock: and he rolled a great stone to the door of the sepulchre, and departed. (Matthew 27:57–60)

The probable site of the tomb of Christ, the Garden Tomb, is located just north of the Damascus Gate of the old walled city of Jerusalem. The tomb is located only a few hundred yards from the probable site of Golgotha, or Calvary. When the tomb was discovered in the last century, archaeologists found that only one body depression was ever used. The owner did not complete the stone carving work to bury a second body in the same tomb. In addition, they found a huge cistern capable of holding two hundred thousand gallons of water beneath the garden, indicating that it was a rich man's garden tomb.

The Seventeenth Prediction
Darkness would cover the earth.
> Probability: 1 chance in 1,000
> *The Old Testament prediction*

> And it shall come to pass in that day, saith the Lord GOD, that
> I will cause the sun to go down at noon, and I will darken
> the earth in the clear day. (Amos 8:9)

The New Testament fulfillment

> Now from the sixth hour there was darkness over all the
> land unto the ninth hour. (Matthew 27:45)

Although this prophecy is one of the most incredible of the seventeen, the *Third History* of Thallus, a pagan Greek historian of the third century, reported that there was an unusual darkness that blotted out the sun for a number of hours at the time of Passover in the year AD 32, the year of Christ's crucifixion. Although Thallus speculated that this darkness was the result of an eclipse, it is impossible that an eclipse could have occurred at that time, because Passover was calculated to occur at the time of a full moon. The high priest of Israel would carefully calculate the timing of the full moon, because the Jewish liturgical calendar, especially the feast of Passover, depended on determining the precise lunar position. The position of the sun, moon, and Earth at the time of a full moon makes it impossible that the midday darkness could have been the result of a natural eclipse. (This detail in the Messianic prophecies is so crucial that we will devote a more in-depth discussion of it later in this chapter.)

Could Anyone Else Have Been the Messiah?

Our quick analysis of just seventeen of the hundreds of Messianic prophecies has shown a number of things to be true. First, it is obvious that the seventeen detailed prophecies, made five centuries before the birth of Jesus of Nazareth, were fulfilled with absolute precision in the life, death, and resurrection of Jesus Christ. The question to consider is this: what are the chances that all seventeen of these predictions occurred by chance rather than by the plan and will of God? The combined probability against these seventeen predictions occurring is equal to

1 chance in 4,800,000,000,000,000,000,000,000,000,000,000
or
1 chance in 4.8 trillion × 1 billion × 1 trillion.

There is only 1 chance in 4.8 trillion × 1 billion × 1 trillion that the Old Testament prophets could have accurately made these seventeen predictions about the life, death, and resurrection of Jesus Christ by chance alone. The odds are equally impossible that any man could have fulfilled these prophecies by chance alone.

You might take issue with the level of probability that I have assigned to each of these predictions being fulfilled. Feel free to do the calculation with your own estimates of probability. But regardless of the estimates that you might assign for each one of the seventeen prophecies, whether higher or lower than mine, you still will be confronted with a combined probability that exceeds comprehension. The odds are so staggering in their magnitude that it will be impossible to convince yourself that these events could have occurred by chance.

In the unlikely event that you still are not convinced, consider the fact that we examined only seventeen of the forty-eight major prophecies given in the Old Testament about the promised Messiah. If we were to calculate the odds against all forty-eight predictions occurring by chance in the life of the same person, we would arrive at a number so large it would dwarf even the astounding number we arrived at in this chapter: 1 chance in 4.8 trillion × 1 billion × 1 trillion.

Answering the Critics

Some Bible critics have suggested that Jesus of Nazareth, as a rabbi, knew about these predictions and simply arranged the events of His life to fulfill the predictions. However, consider the impossibility of such a thing. How could you arrange in advance to be born in Bethlehem? How could you manage to manipulate circumstances so that you would be descended from the tribe of Judah? How could you arrange with your enemies for the price of your betrayal to be precisely thirty pieces of silver? How could you set it up with the Roman authorities that you would be crucified with thieves? And how could you ensure that a rich man who is not related to you would take responsibility for your body and bury it in his tomb?

If you could arrange to have all of these remarkable events

happen, you are the Son of God. Obviously, only God could foresee these events and arrange in advance to fulfill the precise predictions in the life of Jesus Christ.

The Darkness at Noon
One of the most intriguing of the Messianic prophecies is the account of the supernatural darkness that covered the light from the sun for three hours during the afternoon of the Passover Feast, when Jesus Christ's body hung on the cross. In the gospel of Matthew, the disciple records, "Now from the sixth hour [12:00 noon] there was darkness over all the land unto the ninth hour [3:00 p.m.]" (Matthew 27:45). The three hours of darkness also were described in Mark 15:33: "And when the sixth hour was come, there was darkness over the whole land until the ninth hour." Finally, Luke 23:44–45 records, "And it was about the sixth hour, and there was a darkness over all the earth until the ninth hour. And the sun was darkened, and the veil of the temple was rent in the midst."

Although it would be impossible for a natural solar eclipse to occur at that phase of the moon, all three of the Synoptic Gospel writers independently recorded the miracle. In addition, two pagan Greek historians, Phlegon of Tralles and Thallus, independently recorded the supernatural event in their histories. If this miracle had not actually taken place, the entire Christian message would have been discredited. The thousands of people who witnessed Jesus' crucifixion would have easily repudiated the claims of the gospel writers.

In light of the ample historical evidence we have available, we know that not one of the early critics of Christianity ever claimed that accounts of the darkness at noon were false. On the contrary, independent sources confirmed the occurrence of one of the greatest miracles ever recorded. We will take a close look at the evidence from five of these witnesses.

Amos Prophesied a Special Darkness at Noon
Seven centuries before the event, the prophet Amos predicted that a day would come when the sun would appear to "go down at noon." Amos (750 BC) lived as a shepherd near Bethlehem.

The Lord gave him a prophecy to announce to the Jewish people that God would supernaturally cause the sky to darken in the middle of the day as a sign of the judgment that was coming because of their disobedience. Amos wrote:

> And it shall come to pass in that day, saith the Lord GOD, that I will cause the sun to go down at noon, and I will darken the earth in the clear day: and I will turn your feasts into mourning, and all your songs into lamentation; and I will bring up sackcloth upon all loins, and baldness upon every head; and I will make it as the mourning of an only son, and the end thereof as a bitter day (Amos 8:9–10)

Notice that this prophecy declares that the darkness will occur as "the sun [will] go down at noon." This identifies the precise hour when the miracle of supernatural darkness occurred. Amos also predicted that the miracle would occur during the time of a feast day (see verse 10). He even refers to it "as the mourning of an only son" (verse 10), reminding us of John's mention of God's "only begotten Son" (see John 3:16).

Confirmation of the Miracle by Secular Historians

A very early confirmation of the darkness at noon in connection with Jesus' crucifixion is found in the writings of the pagan historian Thallus in his *Third History*. This account from the middle of the first century AD is significant because it may have been written close to the time when the Synoptic Gospels were being composed by Matthew, Mark, and Luke. Further, it is one of the earliest historical records of an event connected with the Crucifixion and the miracle of the midday darkness.

Thallus wrote in Syria in AD 52, only twenty years after the death and resurrection of Christ. He wrote that darkness covered the land at the time of the Passover in the year we now call AD 32. Julius Africanus, a North African Christian leader writing in AD 215, mentions Thallus's account of the supernatural darkness:

> As to [Jesus'] works severally, and His cures effected upon body and soul, and the mysteries of His doctrine, and the resurrection from the dead, these have been most authoritatively

set forth by His disciples and apostles before us. On the whole world there pressed a most fearful darkness; and the rocks were rent by an earthquake, and many places in Judea and other districts were thrown down. This darkness, Thallus, in the third book of his History, calls as appears to me without reason, an eclipse of the sun. For the Hebrews celebrate the passover on the 14th day according to the moon, and the passion of our Saviour falls on the day before the passover; but an eclipse of the sun takes place only when the moon comes under the sun.[1]

Julius Africanus explained that Thallus's theory of a solar eclipse as the explanation for the three hours of darkness was without merit because an eclipse of the sun cannot occur at the same time there is a full moon. At the Feast of Passover, with a full moon in the sky, the moon's position is almost diametrically opposite to the sun's position, which would make a solar eclipse impossible. Though Thallus's explanation of a solar eclipse was wrong, his historical reference to the three hours of darkness at noon during the Feast of Passover confirms the gospel account.

Modern astronomers confirm that Julius Africanus was right in his conclusion that a solar eclipse could not occur at the time of a full moon, which was in the sky at the time of the Jewish Passover. There are two important points here. First, Thallus, who was alive at the time of Jesus' death, confirmed that darkness covered the earth at Passover at the same time recorded by the Synoptic Gospel writers. Second, the fact that there was a full moon makes it certain that this darkness was not a natural eclipse, but rather that it was a supernatural event.

The Greek Historian Phlegon

A second fascinating historical reference to the supernatural darkness is found in the manuscript of Phlegon of Tralles, a pagan writer originally from Lydia. Phlegon was a Greek who was granted freedom as a Roman citizen by Emperor Hadrian. Phlegon lived in Tralles, a town in Asia Minor near Ephesus. In approximately AD 138, Phlegon noted the astonishing fact that this "great and extraordinary eclipse of the sun distinguished among all that had happened [occurred] in the fourth year of the two hundred and second olympiad." This was the nineteenth year of the reign of Emperor Tiberius, which corresponds with the year AD 32 on our calendar. In his *Chronicle* (AD 300), the Christian historian Eusebius quoted from Phlegon's sixteen-volume *Collection of Olympiads and Chronicles* as follows:

> All which things agree with what happened at the time of our Saviour's passion. And so writes Phlegon, an excellent compiler of the Olympiads in his thirteenth book, saying: "In the fourth year of the two hundred and second olympiad there was a great and extraordinary eclipse of the sun, distinguished among all that had happened before. At the sixth hour the day was turned into dark night, so that the stars in the heavens were seen, and there was an earthquake in Bithynia which overthrew many houses in the city of Nice." So writes the above named author.[2]

Furthermore, Phlegon indicated that the darkness that covered the earth began at the sixth hour, which is equivalent to 12:00 p.m., or noon, precisely the hour recorded in Matthew 27:45.

Another source confirms that Phlegon wrote in his book *Olympiades* that an unprecedented darkness and a devastating earthquake occurred at noon, when Christ was dying on the cross:

> In the 4th year of the 202nd Olympiad, there was a great eclipse of the Sun, greater than had ever been known before, for at the 6th hour the day was changed into night and the stars were seen in the heavens. An earthquake occurred in Bythinia and overthrew a great part of the city of Nicea.[3]

The Roman Government Archives

The Christian writer Tertullian (AD 160–220) wrote that the event of supernatural darkness was recorded in the official Roman government archives and that the record could still be consulted in his day. Tertullian authored a book titled *Apology*, which defended the Christian faith and the gospel account of Christ's crucifixion:

> At the same time at noonday there was a great darkness.
> They thought it to be an eclipse, who did not know that this
> also was foretold concerning Christ. And some have denied
> it, not knowing the cause of such darkness. And yet you
> have that remarkable event recorded in your archives.[4]

Tertullian knew that the Roman government archives contained official records confirming these events.

In discussing the death of Jesus, Tertullian also wrote about the supernatural darkness:

> And yet, nailed upon the cross, He exhibited many notable
> signs, by which His death was distinguished from all oth-
> ers. At His own free-will, He with a word dismissed from
> Him His spirit, anticipating the executioner's work. In the
> same hour, too, the light of day was withdrawn, when the
> sun at the very time was in his meridian blaze. Those who
> were not aware that this had been predicted about Christ,
> no doubt thought it an eclipse.[5]

The Christian teacher Lucian of Antioch died as a martyr in Nicomedia during the reign of Emperor Maximinus II in AD 312. Lucian confirmed that the Roman Empire's public archives contained a record of this supernatural event that established the miraculous nature of Christ's death on the cross: "Look into your annals; there you will find that in the time of Pilate, when Christ suffered, the sun was obscured, and the light of the day was interrupted with darkness."

During the first few centuries of the Christian era, the government archives were available to be studied by scholars and government officials. Every year the governor of each Roman province had to submit an official report to the Roman Senate concerning wars, laws, taxes, trials, and unusual events that occurred during their watch. The fact that Christian teachers and writers appealed to their readers to check out the official government account of Jesus Christ's trial provides compelling evidence that official records confirming the darkness at noon must have existed in their day.

Detailed, Fulfilled Prophecy Proves the Inspiration of Scripture

I have studied biblical prophecy for decades, and I am convinced it is among the most important disciplines we can pursue. However, its highest value does not lie in the fascinating details or the intrigue and mystery that you encounter as you explore the predictions of God's prophets. Those aspects of the study hold your attention, to be sure. But the true value is found in what prophecy and its fulfillment tells us about God's trustworthiness and the pains He went to in order to make us aware of what is to come.

In this book we are looking at the best arguments for the reliability, truth, and divine inspiration of the Bible. Fulfilled prophecy stands among the most convincing of these proofs. As we studied seventeen of the Messianic prophecies, we have seen that it is impossible that the Old Testament prophets were just lucky in guessing what the future would hold. We also have seen that Jesus of Nazareth could not possibly have accidentally lived a life that conformed to the precise description we have of the Messiah from the predictions provided by the Jewish prophets.

The odds against such things happening by random chance are astronomical. To fully grasp the reality that these fulfilled prophecies prove that Jesus Christ is the promised Son of God, consider the following illustration.

First, as I've said, the odds against the prophets correctly guessing all seventeen prophecies are 1 chance in 4.8×10^{33} (4.8 trillion × 1 billion × 1 trillion)!

To understand these odds, imagine that every one of these chances is represented by a single grain of sand. Then imagine that one grain of sand is painted gold and represents the one chance out of this astronomical number that Christ fulfilled the predictions by chance. We will blindfold you and ask you to search for the single gold-painted grain of sand. Imagine that the entire Milky Way galaxy, encompassing billions of stars plus millions of planets, moons, and asteroids is composed only of these

4.8×10^{33} grains of sand. Out of the entire galaxy and all that it contains, your target is the one grain of sand that is painted gold.

Finding it will be a challenge, because even if you could travel in the starship *Enterprise* at the speed of light—187,000 miles per second—it would still take you a hundred thousand years to cross the Milky Way. If we were to blindfold you and send you out to search through the galaxy to find the one gold-painted grain of sand, with no direction whatsoever, you would face the same impossible odds as the probability against these seventeen prophecies occurring by chance.

With such odds against you, would you bet a thousand dollars that you would find the gold-painted grain of sand? I doubt it. Yet, tragically, every year millions of people will die who have bet their lives and their eternal souls on the chance that the prophecies about Jesus are not reliable. They believe they can safely ignore the claims that Christ has made about Himself, about salvation, and about heaven and hell. However, in light of the overwhelming evidence for the authority of the Bible and the reality of Jesus Christ as God's Messiah, each of us needs to consider the decision we must make about our response to Christ's life, death, and resurrection.

The Testimony of a New Believer

I found a Web site that deals with answering the questions of Muslims who are searching for information about Jesus Christ. This site contains a letter from a former Palestinian named Walid. He had chosen sides, living as a Muslim terrorist and filled with hatred for the Jews. However, one day he happened to find my book *Armageddon*, which included an analysis of several of the key prophecies about Jesus. To demonstrate the power of fulfilled prophecy to reach a person's mind and soul, I will share a portion of this man's story.

> Sometime in 1992, I was fascinated when I read a book titled *Armageddon: Appointment with Destiny,* by Grant Jeffrey. Some of the things explained in this book had many detailed prophecies about Jesus: his birth, life, death and resurrection; and the re-creation of the state of Israel. Many

of these prophecies came to pass just as God put them down in the Bible! What also amazed me was to find out that the chances for a man to predict hundreds of historic events written hundreds and thousands of years before their occurrences are one in zillions… What is more fascinating is that the margin of error had to be zero, especially when the fulfillment of many of these prophecies was happening in my generation. This kind of evidence had to come from a divine origin; that origin had to be God Almighty.[6]

Walid communicated with me later and confirmed that he had accepted Jesus Christ as his Savior. He had been motivated to read the Gospels after becoming convinced that fulfilled prophecies proved that Jesus was the promised Messiah and Son of God. He now loves the Jews as he loves his own Arab people and prays for their salvation.

The Bible declares that fulfilled prophecy is the absolute proof that the Scriptures were written under the direct inspiration of God. I am convinced that the material in this chapter provides compelling evidence of the authority and inspiration of the Scriptures.

Many people resist the idea of adopting a belief or following religious teachings based on the influence or traditions of people close to them. Many of us want to examine the evidence for ourselves, just as Walid did. We want to compare the arguments of the critics with the evidence that supports the truth of the biblical text. In this chapter we examined evidence that relies not on anyone's personal story or experience but on the facts as they are set down both in Scripture and in ancient history. These facts demonstrate that the Christian faith is not just an idea, a system of morality, a religion, or a personal preference. It is the one set of teachings and beliefs—and the only way of life—that aligns with God's truth, His revelation, and His work in the world.

In the next chapter we will see that prophecy is not limited to events that occurred in the distant past. Indeed, many of the most intriguing of God's prophecies have become reality in our lifetime. And much of God's prophesied activity is yet to come. We can expect to see the fulfillment of God's plan for the last days in our generation.

Notes

1. Julius Africanus, *Extant Writings 18*, Ante-Nicene Fathers, 10 vols. (Grand Rapids: Eerdmans, 1987), vol. 6.
2. Phlegon, *Collection of Olympiads and Chronicles*, quoted in Eusebius, *Church History*, Ante-Nicene Fathers, 3–4.
3. Karl Muller, *Fragmenta Historicum Graecorum*, 4 vols. (Paris: Didot, 1841–51), 3:607.
4. Tertullian, *Apology*, Ante-Nicene Fathers, 10 vols. (Grand Rapids: Eerdmans, 1987), 3:21.
5. Tertullian, *Apology*, 3:21.
6. Found at www.answering-islam.org/Testimonies/walid.html (accessed December 20, 2009).

8

Evidence from Prophecies Fulfilled in Our Generation

As we have noted earlier, one of the most convincing proofs that the Bible is inspired is the evidence of thousands of detailed prophecies that were fulfilled throughout history. Centuries before the events occurred, prophets foretold the rise and fall of empires and cities, including Babylon, Tyre, and Nineveh. However, several prophecies that have been fulfilled in our lifetime deserve a closer look. These prophecies prove not only that the Bible is inspired by God but also point to the nearness of Christ's return.

Many Christians today long for the return of Jesus Christ. Even Jesus' first disciples, the twelve who spent the greatest amount of time with Him during His three years of ministry on Earth, were curious about His return: "And as he sat upon the mount of Olives, the disciples came unto him privately, saying, Tell us, when shall these things be? and what shall be the sign of thy coming, and of the end of the world?" (Matthew 24:3). It is understandable that those who love and worship Christ also long for Him to come back to Earth, just as He said He would.

Naturally, skeptics remind us that the generations in the past looked for the Second Coming but never saw the promise fulfilled. So why should we believe our generation will witness the return of Christ? Thirty-eight years of careful study of Bible prophecies have convinced me of the overwhelming evidence that Jesus Christ will likely return in our generation.

Each of the prophecies that we will examine in this chapter refers to a unique event that was never fulfilled in any past generation. And due to their unique nature, many of these predictions could not be fulfilled again in another generation. These events have to come to pass in our lifetime. Our Lord Jesus Christ warned, "And when these things begin to come to pass, then look up, and lift up your heads; for your redemption draweth nigh" (Luke 21:28). Jesus' words will never fail, as we have seen in the astounding developments of the mid-twentieth century, which were foretold thousands of years ago. In this chapter we will look at the fulfillment of prophecy in our day and additional prophecies that soon will be fulfilled in our generation.

The Rebirth of Israel

Israel's rebirth as a nation is one of the most extraordinary and unlikely of all biblical prophecies. Ezekiel predicted with marvelous precision that Israel would be reborn in the spring of 1948. Jesus also prophesied about the rebirth of Israel.

> Now learn a parable of the fig tree; When his branch is yet tender, and putteth forth leaves, ye know that summer is nigh: so likewise ye, when ye shall see all these things, know that it is near, even at the doors. Verily I say unto you, This generation shall not pass, till all these things be fulfilled. Heaven and earth shall pass away, but my words shall not pass away. (Matthew 24:32–35)

In the Scriptures, the images of figs and the fig tree are used as symbols for Israel. The Bible uses these images in five different passages as an exclusive symbol of the nation Israel (see Judges 9:8–15; Jeremiah 24:1–10; Hosea 9:10; Matthew 21:18–20; 24:32–

34). Israel is unique in a number of ways. God created Israel as a people for Himself, long before the Jews had a homeland. The Lord made a covenant with Abraham, and He was true to His word. He protected His chosen people when they were slaves in Egypt, and He preserved their identity when both the northern kingdom and the southern kingdom were taken into captivity.

God gave His people the Promised Land, and after Solomon built the Temple in Jerusalem, His presence was in the Holy of Holies. But after the Roman legions destroyed Jerusalem in AD 70, the Jews were scattered around the world. They lived in exile for two thousand years, and then God fulfilled one of His most remarkable prophecies.

In 1948, God worked a miracle that defies the human imagination. He again created a homeland for His people and brought the Jews back to Israel. No other ancient nation ever ceased to exist for a period of centuries and then returned to take its place on the stage of world history. "Who hath heard such a thing? who hath seen such things? Shall the earth be made to bring forth in one day? or shall a nation be born at once? for as soon as Zion travailed, she brought forth her children" (Isaiah 66:8).

Most nations evolved gradually over the centuries, such as Egypt or France. In the time of the ancient prophets, no one had ever witnessed a nation being created in a day. Yet the prophet Isaiah predicted that Israel would come into existence just that quickly—*in "one day."* The prophecies of Isaiah and Ezekiel were fulfilled precisely as predicted on a date that stands out in history: May 15, 1948.

Predictions About the Arab-Israeli Conflict

The fulfillment of prophecies surrounding the rebirth of Israel did not end with the declaration of Israel's independence in 1948. Three thousand years ago God inspired David to predict that the reborn nation of Israel would be immediately surrounded by enemies, including the Arab nations of Jordan, Egypt, Saudi Arabia, and Syria.

> For, lo, thine enemies make a tumult: and they that hate thee have lifted up the head. They have taken crafty counsel

against thy people, and consulted against thy hidden ones. They have said, Come, and let us cut them off from being a nation; that the name of Israel may be no more in remembrance. For they have consulted together with one consent: they are confederate against thee: the tabernacles of Edom, and the Ishmaelites; of Moab, and the Hagarenes; Gebal, and Ammon, and Amalek; the Philistines with the inhabitants of Tyre; Assur also is joined with them: they have holpen the children of Lot. Selah. (Psalm 83:2–8)

Incredibly, David was describing the modern states of the Middle East by naming the ancient nations that joined with the Palestinians in their attempt to destroy the Jewish state.

The Miraculous Restoration of the Hebrew Language

Zephaniah predicted something just as improbable—many would say impossible—as the rebirth of Israel. God inspired Zephaniah to reveal that He would restore the ancient dead language of Hebrew as the living, spoken language of the nation of Israel: "For then will I turn to the people a pure language, that they may all call upon the name of the LORD, to serve him with one consent" (Zephaniah 3:9). This prophecy is all the more amazing when you consider that Hebrew ceased to be the common language of the Jews long before the life of Christ.

No other nation has ever lost its language and later recovered it. No one is speaking ancient Egyptian or Chaldee today. A Jewish scholar, Eliezer ben Yehuda, began working to revive the dead language of Hebrew with its original seven thousand words related to Temple worship as used by the priests.[1] Ben Yehuda invented thousands of new Hebrew words to stand for things that were not known in ancient Israel, objects such as fountain pens, aircraft, and so forth. He created a fourteen-volume dictionary for the new living language of Hebrew.

Ultimately, ben Yehuda re-created modern Hebrew as the living language of five million Israelis. As the Jews began to return from seventy different nations in 1948, following two thousand years of exile, the government and army began to unify these widely divergent peoples through teaching them Hebrew. The

Jews of Israel will someday fulfill the prophecy of Zephaniah by calling "upon the name of the LORD, to serve him with one consent" when they see their Messiah (Zephaniah 3:9).

The Return of Ethiopian Jews to Israel

Zephaniah made another seemingly impossible prophecy when he declared that God would return the Ethiopian Jews to the land of Israel after almost three thousand years. In the days of King Solomon, a group of Jews from each of the twelve tribes immigrated to Ethiopia with Prince Menelik, Solomon's son, and the queen of Sheba, as detailed in my book *Armageddon: Appointment with Destiny.*[2]

Numerous Old Testament prophecies foretold the final return of the Jewish exiles to the Holy Land. "Thus saith the Lord GOD; Behold, I will take the children of Israel from among the heathen, whither they be gone, and will gather them on every side, and bring them into their own land" (Ezekiel 37:21). The prophet Zephaniah foretold the return of a specific group of Jews to the Promised Land in the last days: "From beyond the rivers of Ethiopia my suppliants, even the daughter of my dispersed, shall bring mine offering" (Zephaniah 3:10).

Isaiah confirmed the prediction of Zephaniah: "I will say to the north, Give up; and to the south, Keep not back: bring my sons from far, and my daughters from the ends of the earth" (Isaiah 43:6). Isaiah was predicting the miraculous return of the Jews from Russia (the north) as well as Ethiopia (the south). In the latter part of the 1980s and especially in the spring of 1991, more than twenty-five thousand Jews returned to Israel from Ethiopia.[3]

The Astonishing Fertility of Israel

Israel, in addition to recovering her homeland, her lost language, and millions of Jewish exiles, was destined to become fertile again: "He shall cause them that come of Jacob to take root: Israel shall blossom and bud, and fill the face of the world with fruit" (Isaiah 27:6). The Jews have transformed the previously deserted and desolate land into the most agriculturally efficient land on earth. Some 90 percent of Israel's flower production is now exported, mostly to Europe. Israel supplies more than 90 percent of the citrus fruit consumed by hundreds of millions of Europeans. The kibbutzim (collective settlements) and moshavim (cooperative settlements) account for 79 percent of Israel's agricultural produce.[4]

The prophet Joel declared that the desert nation would experience tremendous increases of rain in the last days: "Be glad then, ye children of Zion, and rejoice in the LORD your God: for he hath given you the former rain moderately, and he will cause to come down for you the rain, the former rain, and the latter rain in the first month" (Joel 2:23). Rainfall did in fact increase in Israel, and the returning Jews planted more than two hundred million trees and transformed the environment of the Promised Land. "And the parched ground shall become a pool, and the thirsty land springs of water: in the habitation of dragons, where each lay, shall be grass with reeds and rushes" (Isaiah 35:7).

Another curious prediction found in Ezekiel 38 claimed that Israel would dwell "without walls...nor gates" in the last days. In the ancient past even small villages depended on walls for defense against invading armies. Yet God inspired Ezekiel to record the following in reference to the coming Russian-Arab invasion of Israel: "And thou shalt say, I will go up to the land of unwalled villages; I will go to them that are at rest, that dwell safely, all of them dwelling without walls, and having neither bars nor gates" (Ezekiel 38:11). How could Ezekiel have known twenty-five centuries ago that the development of modern weapons of war would make city walls and gates irrelevant for defensive purposes? Even army bases and residential settlements have no walls today.

Plans to Rebuild the Temple

The Bible tells us that Israel will rebuild the Temple in Jerusalem in the last days. Isaiah wrote, "And it shall come to pass in the last days, that the mountain of the LORD's house shall be established in the top of the mountains, and shall be exalted above the hills; and all nations shall flow unto it" (Isaiah 2:2). In the book of Revelation (11:1–2), John tells us that the angel took him into the future to measure the Temple that will exist during the seven-year Tribulation period. Paul confirms this future event in his prophecy about the Antichrist occupying the rebuilt Temple:

Let no man deceive you by any means: for that day shall not come, except there come a falling away first, and that man of sin be revealed, the son of perdition; who opposeth and exalteth himself above all that is called God, or that is worshipped; so that he as God sitteth in the temple of God, shewing himself that he is God. (2 Thessalonians 2:3–4)

Ezekiel described his vision of the future Temple with Levites and priests worshiping God: "And thou shalt give to the priests the Levites that be of the seed of Zadok, which approach unto me, to minister unto me, saith the Lord GoD, a young bullock for a sin offering" (Ezekiel 43:19).[5]

The Oil of Anointing

One of the most unusual aspects of the ancient Tabernacle and Temple was the oil of anointing that was specially prepared using five specific ingredients. The oil was used to anoint the Temple and the high priests. Moses described God's command to Israel: "And thou shalt make it an oil of holy ointment, an ointment compound after the art of the apothecary: it shall be an holy anointing oil. And thou shalt anoint the tabernacle of the congregation therewith, and the ark of the testimony" (Exodus 30:25–26). However, the oil and its ingredients were lost, seemingly forever, when the Romans destroyed the Temple in AD 70. One of the five ingredients required for the oil of anointing was afars'mon. And the Romans burned the only two groves where afars'mon trees grew. Without this special ingredient, God's command to anoint the rebuilt Temple with oil could not be fulfilled.

In addition, Daniel foretold that, when the Messiah returns, He will be anointed with this same oil.

Seventy weeks are determined upon thy people and upon thy holy city, to finish the transgression, and to make an end of sins, and to make reconciliation for iniquity, and to bring in everlasting righteousness, and to seal up the vision and prophecy, and to anoint the most Holy. (Daniel 9:24)

How could these prophecies be fulfilled when one of the key ingredients was lost forever? Incredibly, archaeologists led by Dr.

Joseph Patrich of Hebrew University found a clay flask buried in a cave near the Dead Sea caves.[6] The flask was filled with the ancient oil of anointing and was discovered after archaeologists followed directions listed in the Copper Scroll. Jewish priests in the first century AD had hidden various treasures of the Second Temple to keep the Roman legions from stealing or destroying the Temple treasures and worship vessels. Scientists from Hebrew University confirmed with carbon-14 dating that the oil discovered near the Dead Sea was two thousand years old and is composed of the five ingredients described in Exodus 30:25–26.[7]

The ancient oil of anointing is in the possession of the two chief rabbis of Israel. Someday, when Israel's Messiah returns to the rebuilt Temple, I believe Daniel's prophecy will be fulfilled. Christ will be anointed with the sacred oil as God's anointed King.

Vessels for Future Temple Worship

Ezekiel foretold that the sacred vessels and linen robes would be prepared for use in the Temple during the Millennium.

> They shall enter into my sanctuary, and they shall come near to my table, to minister unto me, and they shall keep my charge.

> And it shall come to pass, that when they enter in at the gates of the inner court, they shall be clothed with linen garments; and no wool shall come upon them, whiles they minister in the gates of the inner court, and within. (Ezekiel 44:16–17)

The Temple Institute is one Israeli group that is actively preparing for the rebuilding of the Temple. The organization has constructed more than seventy-five Temple objects and vessels for worship, as well as priestly garments required for future Temple services.

The yeshivas, or Jewish Bible colleges, have trained more than five hundred young men from the tribe of Levi to fulfill their future duties related to Temple worship, music, and sacrifice. The prophecies describe the resumption of the sacrifice of the ashes of the Red Heifer to produce the waters of purification (see Numbers 19). This will be needed to cleanse the defiled Temple objects, the priests, and the defiled stones on the Temple Mount. Ezekiel confirmed that the waters of purification will be used to cleanse the future Temple and the Jewish people: "Then will I sprinkle clean water upon you, and ye shall be clean: from all your filthiness, and from all your idols, will I cleanse you" (Ezekiel 36:25).

The Revival of the Roman Empire

The Bible foretold the revival of the Roman Empire in the final generation when the Messiah will return:

> And the fourth kingdom [the revived Roman Empire] shall be strong as iron: forasmuch as iron breaketh in pieces and subdueth all things: and as iron that breaketh all these, shall it break in pieces and bruise. And whereas thou sawest the feet and toes, part of potters' clay, and part of iron, the kingdom shall be divided; but there shall be in it of the strength of the iron, forasmuch as thou sawest the iron mixed with miry clay. And as the toes of the feet were part of iron, and part of clay, so the kingdom shall be partly strong, and partly broken. And whereas thou sawest iron mixed with miry clay, they shall mingle themselves with the seed of men: but they shall not cleave one to another, even as iron is not mixed with clay. And in the days of these kings shall the God of heaven set up a kingdom [the Millennial Kingdom of Jesus Christ], which shall never be destroyed: and the kingdom shall not be left to other people, but it shall break in pieces and consume all these kingdoms, and it shall stand for ever. (Daniel 2:40–44)

Other prophecies in Daniel 7 and Revelation 13 and 17 confirm the revival of the Roman Empire as a ten-nation superstate. Following the devastation of two world wars, the leadership of Europe came together to create a confederate form of superstate to bring the major nations of Europe together. Europe had not been united in such a way since the days of ancient Rome. In 1957, six countries signed the Treaty of Rome, which laid the foundation for the future United States of Europe. Henri Spaak, the former secretary-general of NATO, admitted in a BBC documentary that "we felt like Romans on that day.... We were consciously re-creating the Roman Empire once more."[8] The European Union is an economic, political, and, potentially, a military colossus that will dominate world events in the near future.

The Rebuilding of Babylon

One of the most unusual prophecies in the Bible reveals that the city of Babylon will be rebuilt and later destroyed by God at the time of Armageddon. The city will be consumed by supernatural fire from heaven. The prophet Isaiah foretold this destruction: "Howl ye; for the day of the LORD is at hand; it shall come as a destruction from the Almighty.... And Babylon, the glory of kingdoms, the beauty of the Chaldees' excellency, shall be as when God overthrew Sodom and Gomorrah" (Isaiah 13:6, 19). He declared that Babylon will not only exist again but it will be destroyed on the Great Day of the Lord.

When Saddam Hussein ruled Iraq with an iron fist, the Iraqi government spent more than $2.5 billion rebuilding Babylon. Hussein wanted the rebuilt city to become the center of a renewed Babylonian Empire that would rule the Middle East as a regional superpower. He spent decades rebuilding the ruined city and its magnificent palaces. Many of the sixty million clay bricks manufactured to rebuild the walls, which extend fifty-six miles in circumference, contain the following inscription: "In the era of President Saddam Hussein all Babylon was constructed in three stages. From Nebuchadnezzar to Saddam Hussein, Babylon is rising again."[9]

The ancient city of Babylon was built over an underground lake of asphalt and oil. In this way God has already provided the fuel needed for the city's final destruction. In another prophecy God foretold through Isaiah that the wicked city would burn forever:

> For it is the day of the LORD's vengeance, and the year of recompenses for the controversy of Zion. And the streams thereof shall be turned into pitch, and the dust thereof into brimstone,

and the land thereof shall become burning pitch. It shall not be quenched night nor day; the smoke thereof shall go up for ever: from generation to generation it shall lie waste; none shall pass through it for ever and ever. (Isaiah 34:8–10)

One-World Government

More than two thousand years ago, John described a future global government led by the coming dictator, the Antichrist.

And it was given unto him to make war with the saints, and to overcome them: and power was given him over all kindreds, and tongues, and nations. And all that dwell upon the earth shall worship him. (Revelation 13:7–8)

There has never before been a world government. However, as I outlined in my book *Shadow Government,* the world's elite are moving behind the scenes to install a world government as quickly as possible.[10]

Deadly Pestilence

The Bible describes terrible plagues and horrible sores occurring throughout the world during the Great Tribulation. The plagues that will destroy hundreds of millions of lives in the last days may include the effects of biological and chemical weapons. The prophet Zechariah also described terrible plagues at the Battle of Armageddon:

And this shall be the plague wherewith the LORD will smite all the people that have fought against Jerusalem; Their flesh shall consume away while they stand upon their feet, and their eyes shall consume away in their holes, and their tongue shall consume away in their mouth. (Zechariah 14:12)

The apostle John as well provided a horrifying description of plagues in the last days:

So I looked, and behold, an ashy pale horse…and its rider's name was Death, and Hades…followed him closely. And they were given authority and power over a fourth part of the earth to kill with the sword and with famine and with plague (pestilence, disease) and with wild beasts of the earth. (Revelation 6:8, AMP)

In our time fully one-fourth of the human population will be killed by plague and pestilence, famine, warfare, and "wild beasts." Tragically, the AIDS epidemic that rages in many parts of the world, as well as the specter of a new viral pandemic, demonstrate how new plagues could come about as part of the fulfillment of this prophecy in our generation.

Jesus warned about plagues in the last days: "For nation shall rise against nation, and kingdom against kingdom: and there shall be famines, and *pestilences*, and earthquakes, in divers places" (Matthew 24:7). The combination of high levels of promiscuity, a virtual absence of effective sanitation, minimal health education, and a lack of antibiotics or condom protection has produced an epidemic of all forms of sexually transmitted diseases, including HIV/AIDS, throughout most of the third world. The only practical solution to the spread of HIV/AIDS is to return to God's laws regarding a monogamous marriage relationship between a faithful husband and wife.

The Central Intelligence Agency produced a report on the AIDS epidemic in Africa that was staggering in its conclusions. The report predicted that, at worst, as much as 75 percent of the population of sub-Saharan Africa might become infected. This would mean the ultimate infection and eventual death by AIDS of up to three hundred million people on the African continent alone. The mind can scarcely imagine death on this massive scale. The life expectancy for people living in southern Africa already has dropped from over age sixty to less than age forty. The prognosis for Asia and parts of South America is tragically similar.

In an MSNBC report, Charlene Laino stated, "For the first time since the Black Plague of the 14th century, the population of some African countries is expected to drop as AIDS continues to sweep through rural and urban communities alike.... And in regions hardest hit by the fatal scourge, life expectancy will plummet to age 30 by the end of the decade—the lowest level in 100 years."[11]

Worldwide Famine

The apostle John described his vision of the horrible famine in the last days: "And I beheld, and lo a black horse; and he that sat on him had a pair of balances in his hand" (Revelation 6:5). The scales represent famine, and the prophet explains that a day's wages at that time would buy only enough wheat or barley to feed a workman, not his family.

Despite advances in food production and food storage, more people are suffering from malnutrition than at any other time in history. Hundreds of millions of people are in danger of starvation, while another billion people lack proper nutrition and access to clean water. Civil wars, which force huge numbers of people to leave their homes, fuel huge decreases in food production. Warfare also produces refugee populations that have little access to food, medical care, or sanitation.

In 2002 the Rome-based UN Food and Agriculture Organization warned that more than four million people in southern Africa faced severe food shortages because of bad weather and a reduction in the land area planted with crops. The aggregate output of southern Africa's main staple, maize, was 25 percent below 2000 levels, at 13.4 million tons, and "well below the average of the past five years." Serious food shortages affected rural and urban areas of Malawi, Zambia, and Zimbabwe.[12] In light of the massive changes in world weather patterns, we could easily witness terrible famine in the future even in countries that so far have felt themselves immune to hunger.

The Bible predicts devastating global famine affecting one-quarter of the Earth during the seven years of the Tribulation period. Famine conditions will be compounded by the destruction caused by weapons of mass destruction used in horrific wars, together with the drop in world agricultural production in response to the cataclysmic divine judgments of great heat, frightening darkness, global plague, disruptive earthquakes, and poisoned waters.

Preparations for the Mark of the Beast

The apostle John in the book of Revelation describes the creation of a cashless society in the last days. At that time, possession of a predetermined number, 666, will be essential to enable you to obtain goods and to transact business in any economy.

> And he causeth all, both small and great, rich and poor, free and bond, to receive a mark in their right hand, or in their foreheads: and that no man might buy or sell, save he that had the mark, or the name of the beast, or the number of his name. Here is wisdom. Let him that hath understanding count the number of the beast: for it is the number of a man; and his number is Six hundred threescore and six. (Revelation 13:16–18)

We already live in a 95 percent cashless society. Less than 5 percent of our money exists as paper currency or coins. John in Revelation describes a time when the number 666 will be placed beneath the skin on one's right hand or forehead to control people in the Antichrist's empire. For the first time in history we are developing technology that would allow tiny computer chips holding your complete medical and financial records to be placed beneath the skin of your right hand or forehead.

Already a tiny computer chip can hold as much information as is contained in thirty sets of the *Encyclopaedia Britannica*. This chip can be configured in a shape the size of two grains of rice, which means it could easily be injected beneath the skin.[13] How could the apostle John have known that the future would hold such incredible technology unless God inspired him to write the words?

Worldwide Mass Communications

John prophesied that during the Tribulation the Antichrist will kill two of God's witnesses who will stop the rain from falling for three and a half years. The prophet declared that people around the world will see the deaths of the two witnesses and will observe their bodies lying unburied in Jerusalem for three and a half days. The whole world will hold a party, exchanging gifts in their relief that their tormentors are dead. Then the human population will watch, astonished, as God resurrects His two witnesses to heaven (see Revelation 11:3–12).

How could the news that these men were killed travel instantaneously around the world in any generation before today's? Only seventy years ago it would have taken a week for the news to travel from Israel to Japan or New York. However, today more than one billion people around the world can watch Olympic events live on television. For the first time in history, John's prophecy about the whole world watching an event in Jerusalem can be fulfilled.

The Gospel Will Be Preached in All the World

One of the most wonderful of the Bible's last-days prophecies concerns the prediction of Jesus Christ that "this gospel of the kingdom shall be preached in all the world for a witness unto all nations; and then shall the end come" (Matthew 24:14). Portions of the Bible have been translated into more than 3,850 languages covering 98 percent of the world's population. Electronic communication transmits the message of hope in Jesus Christ worldwide.

According to the *World Christian Encyclopedia*, those who research the growth of religions throughout the globe have determined that every day more than 115,000 people accept Jesus Christ as their Savior.[14] Muslim authorities often boast that their religion is growing faster than any other. However, while Islam is rapidly expanding (primarily through biological growth), studies reveal that Christianity (especially evangelical Christianity) is growing even more rapidly. Evangelical Christianity is the only religious group in the world with significant growth through conversion, at a rate almost double that of Islam.[15]

Despite the pessimistic analysis of some writers that the population of the Earth is growing faster than the growth of the Church, the truth is that the gospel is being preached in all the world with astonishing success. The meticulous research reported in the *World Christian Encyclopedia* reveals that almost seventeen million people accept Jesus Christ every year, in addition to the fifty-three million who are born into Christian homes and are raised as Christians. When we subtract the number of Christians who die each year (about twenty-one million annually), we are left with a minimum growth of forty-nine million new Christian believers every year.

Approximately two billion people throughout the world claim to be Christians, with probably one-third of them (650 million) personally committed to Christ's Great Commission. In addition, it is fascinating to note that the annual growth rate of Christianity, at 4.7 percent, is almost twice as great as the growth of Islam (2.6 percent annually).[16]

We have never witnessed such a great explosion in numbers of those following the Christian faith from the first days of the Church until today. There were only one million Christians in China in 1949 even after a century of faithful missionary work. However, the Church in China has grown astronomically despite tremendous persecution and the killings of untold millions of believers. Today, the lowest estimates calculate that there are more than one hundred million true followers of Christ in Communist China.

A fascinating study by the Lausanne Statistics Task Force examined the progress of evangelism during the last five centuries. The researchers concluded that the growth of the Church throughout the globe is far greater than previously reported. The number of born-again Christians grew three times faster than the rate of growth of the world's population in the seventeen years between 1980 and 1997. The historically verifiable records of the Lausanne Statistics Task Force reveal an incredible growth in the number of Christians worldwide.[17]

The Explosive Growth of Christian Faith in Our Generation
In 1430, one in ninety-nine of the world's population was Christian.

In 1790, one in forty-nine of the world's population was Christian.

In 1940, one in thirty-two of the world's population was Christian.

In 1970, one in nineteen of the world's population was Christian.

In 1980, one in sixteen of the world's population was Christian.

In 1983, one in thirteen of the world's population was Christian.

In 1986, one in eleven of the world's population was Christian.

In 1997, one in ten of the world's population was Christian.[18]

In only sixty years the number of Christians throughout the world has grown by an astonishing 1,000 percent. The evangelical Church is growing almost three times faster than the expanding world population.[19] The number of adherents to evangelical Christianity grew worldwide in six decades from only 40 million dedicated evangelical believers in 1934 to more than 540 million born-again Christians by the mid-1990s. This happened during a period in which the world's population grew by 400 percent.

Christian radio broadcasts are now reaching almost half of the world's 360 "mega-languages," covering 78 percent of the earth's population, according to the broadcasting group World by 2000. Evangelical broadcasters are preaching the gospel to every language group throughout the globe. The combination of tremendous evangelism efforts by mission organizations, the dedication of more than one million national pastors, and the work of Christian broadcasters are helping to fulfill the Great Commission of Jesus Christ in our lifetime.

The Growth of Pentecostal and Charismatic Christianity

The remarkable growth of Pentecostal and charismatic Christianity was the single most significant spiritual development in the twentieth century. In 1900, there were approximately 900,000 Pentecostal and charismatic Christians. By 1970 the number had grown to 72 million (accounting for 6.4 percent of Christians globally). In one century, the number of Pentecostals and charismatics had exploded to 523.7 million people (making up 27.7 percent of the entire Christian population of the world). At the beginning of the twenty-first century, there were 141.43 million from Latin America, 134.9 million from Asia, 126 million from Africa, and 37.6 million from Europe, with another 83.8 million Pentecostals and charismatics from North America.[20]

Dramatic Increases in Knowledge and Travel

Twenty-five centuries ago the book of Daniel predicted that there would be an explosion of knowledge and a huge increase in travel in the last days: "But thou, O Daniel, shut up the words, and seal the book, even to the time of the end: many shall run to and fro, and knowledge shall be increased" (12:4). Throughout thousands of years of history, the level of knowledge increased only incrementally. In some generations the level of general knowledge actually *decreased*. Yet in the last century and a half there has been an unprecedented explosion of knowledge. More scientists are alive and working today than have lived in all of the rest of history.

Human knowledge doubles every twenty-four months. This is staggering in light of Daniel's inspired prediction from the ancient past. In addition, Daniel stated that a characteristic of the last days would be an awesome increase in mobility. The speed of transportation has exploded in the last century. Throughout history most people never traveled faster than the speed of a galloping horse. Today, men and women travel at nearly eighteen thousand miles an hour in the space shuttle. In addition, while most people in past centuries never traveled more than twenty miles from the place they were born, millions of people now travel the globe as part of their normal course of business or on international vacations.

Preparations for the Battle of Armageddon

Numerous prophecies deal with the climactic battle at the end of this age. The Battle of Armageddon will bring about the defeat of the Antichrist's armies and the ultimate victory of Jesus Christ. He will establish His kingdom on earth for one thousand years. The apostle John identified the location of the battlefield: "And he gathered them together into a place called in the Hebrew tongue Armageddon" (Revelation 16:16). John also stated that the army of the eastern nations (the forces of the "kings of the east," verse 12) would consist of an astonishing two hundred million soldiers.

> And the four angels were loosed, which were prepared for an hour, and a day, and a month, and a year, for to slay the third part of men. And the number of the army of the horsemen were two hundred thousand thousand: and I heard the number of them. (Revelation 9:15–16)

An army this size was unheard of in the first century. Consider that the population of the entire Roman Empire in the days of John was only two hundred million. Even today, trying to picture an army that size boggles the mind.

However, the population of the nations of Asia are growing so quickly that an army containing almost two hundred million soldiers could be amassed in the next few years. Years ago, reports issued by various human rights organizations revealed that China, India, and North Korea were involved in the selective abortion of female unborn infants. In addition, many in these nations kill young girls who are not wanted by their parents. As a result, Chinese officials have admitted that their country has a staggering imbalance in the numbers of boys and girls. This gender imbalance has resulted in an excess of more than seventy million young men compared to the number of young women in China.[21] This growing imbalance in the male and female population throughout Asia will produce up to two hundred million young men who will not be able to find unmarried women in their age group. These men will be of military age.

Strategic Military Developments

Another prophecy in the book of Revelation declares that the Euphrates River will be dried up to allow the enormous army of the "kings of the east," the vast army numbering two hundred million soldiers, to cross from Asia to invade Israel: "And the sixth angel poured out his vial upon the great river Euphrates; and the water thereof was dried up, that the way of the kings of the east might be prepared" (Revelation 16:12). Throughout history the Euphrates River has been an impenetrable military barrier between East and West. However, after the government of Turkey constructed the Ataturk Dam, it became possible for the Euphrates to be dammed up.

John foretold a second development that would assist the huge army of the kings of the east in its march to Israel. A military highway across Asia would allow the two-hundred-million man force to reach the final battle in Israel. John describes the building of this highway: "The way of the kings of the east might be prepared" (Revelation 16:12).

The Chinese government has spent enormous sums building

a military superhighway across Asia. China sent its laborers to work side by side with Pakistani laborers in building the highway through the Karakorum Mountains. The route parallels the ancient Silk Road followed by Marco Polo.[22] This highway has no economic purpose, and no foreigners are allowed to travel anywhere near it. The highway has been completed through the south of China, Tibet, and Pakistan. This curious prophecy about "the way of the kings of the east" is being fulfilled, setting the stage for the final battle of this age.

The Odds Against Prophecies Being Fulfilled in Our Generation

Almost two thousand years have passed from the time of Jesus Christ until our generation. As we consider the many prophecies that have been fulfilled in our generation, we have to ask: what are the odds that even ten of the prophecies would be fulfilled *by chance* during our lifetime? If these prophecies could not have come to pass by chance, then their fulfillment is proof that God inspired the writers of the Bible.

In the Bible there are several types of generations. One generation is defined as the length of life of the average person, say, seventy or eighty years. However, a generation of governing is usually defined as forty years, as indicated in the forty-year reigns of Gideon, David, Solomon, and others. During the last two thousand years since the days of Jesus Christ, there were fifty such forty-year generations. Therefore, the odds are one in fifty that any one of the prophecies might happen by chance in a particular generation. That same number represents the odds that one prophecy could be fulfilled in our generation rather than during some other generation.

Let's use the prophecy about the rebirth of Israel as one example. There was only one chance in fifty that Israel would become a nation in our lifetime rather than in one of the other forty-nine generations since the time of Christ.

According to the laws of combined probability, the chance that two or more events will occur in a given time period is equal to the chance that one event will occur multiplied by the chance that the second event would occur. So if the odds are fifty to one against Israel being reborn by chance in our lifetime, and the odds are also fifty to one against the revival of the Roman Empire taking place in our generation, then the combined probability is fifty times fifty. So the odds against even two of these prophecies being fulfilled in our generation, by pure chance, is one in twenty-five hundred.

To calculate the probability of even ten of these prophecies occurring in our generation by chance, use this calculation:

There are forty years to a generation.

There are fifty generations from the time of Jesus Christ until today.

The odds are one in fifty that any one of these prophecies might occur in our lifetime.

To calculate the chances that more than one prophecy might be fulfilled in our generation, the odds are multiplied as follows:

1 event = 1 × 50 (1 in 50)

2 events = 50 × 50 (1 in 2,500)

3 events = 50 × 50 × 50 (1 in 125,000)

4 events = 50 × 50 × 50 × 50 (1 in 6.25 million)

5 events = 50 × 50 × 50 × 50 × 50 (1 in 312.5 million)

6 events = 50 × 50 × 50 × 50 × 50 × 50 (1 in 15.6 billion)

7 events = 50 × 50 × 50 × 50 × 50 × 50 × 50 (1 in 781.25 billion)

8 events = 50 × 50 × 50 × 50 × 50 × 50 × 50 × 50 (1 in 39 trillion)

9 events = 50 × 50 × 50 × 50 × 50 × 50 × 50 × 50 × 50 (1 in 1,953 trillion)

10 events = 50 × 50 × 50 × 50 × 50 × 50 × 50 × 50 × 50 × 50 (1 in 97,656 trillion)

The odds against even ten prophecies occurring by random chance in one generation are staggering—only 1 chance in 97,656 trillion. Another way of looking at this is that the chance that the prophets correctly guessed these prophecies, simply by thinking them up out of thin air, is also 1 chance in 97,656 trillion. It is mathematically impossible that men making predictions about the future could have written the prophetic books of the Bible without the supernatural assistance and inspiration of God.

The Scriptures teach that the final generation of this age will witness the fulfillment of a staggering number of prophecies pointing to the imminent return of the Messiah. It is appropriate that Christian believers today are intensely interested not only in the prophecies themselves, but also in signs that indicate this age is coming to a close.

Jesus' earliest disciples asked him a legitimate question. We read in Matthew that as Jesus "sat upon the mount of Olives, the disciples came unto him privately, saying, Tell us, when shall these things be? and what shall be the sign of thy coming, and of the end of the world?" (24:3). Two thousand years ago followers of Jesus already were eager to know about the time of His return to earth.

Those who love and follow Jesus Christ today share the same longing for Him to come back. I am convinced that these words of Jesus speak especially to our generation:

> And when these things begin to come to pass, then look up, and lift up your heads; for your redemption draweth nigh. (Luke 21:28)

Notes

1. For more on this, see Robert St. John, *Tongue of the Prophets: The Life Story of Eliezer Ben Yehuda* (Garden City, NY: Doubleday, 1952).
2. For more on this, see Grant R. Jeffrey, *Armageddon: Appointment with Destiny* (Colorado Springs: WaterBrook, 1997).
3. Found at www.us-israel.org/jsource/Judaism/ejhist.html (accessed February 10, 2010).
4. Found at www.agron.co.il/english/agrocult.asp (site now discontinued).
5. For more on the ongoing developments in preparation for rebuilding the Temple in Jerusalem, see Grant R. Jeffrey, *The New Temple and the Second Coming: The Prophecy That Points to Christ's Return in Your Generation* (Colorado Springs: WaterBrook, 2007).
6. The Associated Press, February 16, 1989. Joseph Patrich, "Hideouts in the Judean Wilderness: Jewish Revolutionaries and Christian Ascetics Sought Shelter and Protection in Cliffside Caves," *Biblical Archaeological Review* 15, no. 5 (September–October 1989): 32–42. Joel Brinkley, "Balsam Oil of Judah's Kings Found in Cave Near Dead Sea," *New York Times,* February 16, 1989.
7. To read the complete story of the Copper Scroll and the search for the lost treasures of the Temple, including the oil of anointing, see Jeffrey, *The New Temple and the Second Coming.*
8. Found at http://europa.eu.int/abc/obj/chrono/40years/3testim/coll-en.htm (site now discontinued).
9. Inscription found at www.zionministry.com/index.html (site now discontinued).
10. For more on this, see Grant R. Jeffrey, *Shadow Government: How the Secret Global Elite Is Using Surveillance Against You* (Colorado Springs: WaterBrook, 2009).
11. Charlene Laino of MSNBC, reporting from the Thirteenth International AIDS Conference held in Durban, South Africa, July 10, 2002, www.msnbc.com/news/430295.asp?cp1=1 (accessed November 25, 2009).

12. For more on this, see "Poor Harvests Raise Fears of African Famine," Agence France Press, February 20, 2002, www.globalpolicy.org/component/content/article/211/44497.html.
13. For more on this development, see *Business Week,* June 3, 1996, 123.
14. See David B. Barrett, *World Christian Encyclopedia,* 2nd ed. (Oxford: Oxford University Press, 2001).
15. Barrett, *World Christian Encyclopedia.*
16. Barrett, *World Christian Encyclopedia.*
17. These numbers were supplied by the Lausanne Statistics Task Force on Evangelism; data found at www.adherents .com/Na_170.html (site now discontinued).
18. These numbers were supplied by the Lausanne Statistics Task Force on Evangelism; data found at www.adherents .com/Na_170.html (site now discontinued).
19. Barrett, *World Christian Encyclopedia.*
20. Barrett, *World Christian Encyclopedia.*
21. For more on this, see David Rennie, "Girls Lost as Chinese Reach 1.2 Billion," *Daily Telegraph* (London), March 29, 2001.
22. Found at www.atimes.com/ind-pak/DE25Df02.html (site now discontinued).

9

The Mysterious Bible Codes

"It is the glory of God to conceal a matter, but the glory of kings is to search out a matter." (Proverbs 25:2)

Several years ago researchers in Israel discovered a staggering phenomenon of hidden codes within the Hebrew text of the Old Testament that reveal a remarkable knowledge about future events and personalities that cannot be explained unless God supernaturally inspired the writers to record His precise words. The material in this chapter is possibly the most intriguing evidence presented in this book that will point to the truth that the Scriptures are truly inspired by God.

During the last few years, millions of people have heard about this phenomenon known as the Bible Codes. However, there are many questions that must be answered. Is it possible that God has actually hidden a series of encoded words within the Hebrew text of the Bible that reveal His supernatural knowledge of historical and current events? But, is this phenomenon genuine? Are the claims about the Bible Codes true?

If this information is accurate, this Bible Codes phenomenon provides powerful new evidence that the Scriptures must truly be the inspired Word of God. However, if this discovery is false, it could easily cause great confusion to millions of interested people, as well as to the Church itself. Numerous articles about the Bible Codes have appeared in major newspapers and magazines throughout the world, including *Time* and *Newsweek*. Millions of people have read several best selling books that explore the Bible Code phenomenon, including my 1996 book, *The Signature of God*, that first introduced the intriguing subject to the North American audience.[1]

Many radio and television shows have discussed this impressive discovery. When I first heard about the codes during a trip to Israel in the late 1980s, I was naturally quite skeptical. However, after more than fifteen years of careful evaluation of the phenomenon, I believe that there is powerful evidence that the code is genuine. Additional research during the last six years has provided more evidence that God placed these codes in the Scriptures. They provide fascinating details about historical events that have come to pass thousands of years after the biblical text was written. The Bible Codes provide a new type of evidence that supplements the many other types of evidence that prove the Scriptures are supernatural. This discovery may provide a last measure of incontrovertible evidence to our skeptical generation that the Bible is the inspired Word of God.

I trust that this in-depth study of the mysterious Bible Codes will help you to understand this phenomenon from a balanced Christian perspective. This book will explore many of the issues raised by this remarkable discovery as well as the numerous legitimate questions and criticisms that have been raised by atheistic, Jewish, and Christian critics who doubt that the Bible Code phenomenon is genuine. I understand the natural reluctance of those who have not spent time exploring this phenomenon to accept the reality of the codes without a detailed examination.

There is no question that the Bible Codes represent an astonishing new claim that demands a high level of validation before we should accept it. By nature I am a skeptic. When I first heard about this, I thought that the claims of the code research-ers seemed unbelievable. That is why I am not offended in the slightest when someone tells me that they cannot accept the Bible Codes as genuine. However, after almost a dozen years of research, I am more convinced than ever that God placed the Bible Codes within the text of the Bible to prove to this skeptical generation through this remarkable new evidence that He inspired the human writers to record His revelation to humanity in the Word of God.

A group of mathematicians and computer researchers in both Israel and North America have discovered a series of intriguing Bible Codes about Adolf Hitler and the Holocaust, the Oklahoma City Bombing, the assassination of Yitzchak Rabin, the War in the Gulf, and much more. This book will reveal exactly how Israeli computer scientists recently redis-covered the Bible Codes, which were hidden within the Bible for over three thousand years. In addition, you will learn how Bible students around the world are discovering new codes for themselves, using sophisticated computer programs.

Some of the most fascinating Bible Code research for Christians involves the marvelous discovery by Yacov Rambsel of forty-one encoded words naming Jesus and His disciples, Mary, Joseph, Pilate, and many other people in the life of Christ including King Herod and the High Priest Caiaphas. These names were found encoded in the well known "suffer-ing Messiah" prophecy of Isaiah 53, which predicted the trial, crucifixion, and burial of Jesus Christ more than seven centuries before He was born. This will be explored in detail in chapter 10 of this book.

Many readers will be intrigued by the discovery of remark-able 9/11 Bible Codes that name Osama bin Laden, al Qaeda, the World Trade Center, New York, as well as numerous addi-tional names connected to the tragic Islamic terrorist attack on September 11, 2001, which are fully explored in this chapter.

This chapter will answer your questions about the nature and validity of the Bible Codes and the fascinating scientific evidence that proves the Bible is truly the inspired Word of God. In addition, I will attempt to provide comprehensive answers to the legitimate questions and objections to the Bible Codes raised over the last few years by atheists, Christians, and Jews. It does not surprise me that most people are initially quite skeptical about the codes. As someone who tends to be a skeptic, I waited more than ten years from the time that I first began to gather evidence about this remarkable research before I felt that it was appropriate to write a chapter in my book in 1996 to share the astonishing code discoveries of the Israeli scientists with my readers.

It was vital that I be absolutely convinced of the reliability of this information and that these ELS codes would provide credible evidence supporting the supernatural origin of the Bible. In my opinion, the discovery of the Yeshua Codes about Jesus Christ in the Hebrew Bible provided God's "seal of approval" on this remarkable phenomenon. The new codes revealed Jesus of Nazareth as the true Messiah and acknowledge that He came in the flesh. The codes identifying Jesus as the Son of God provide compelling evidence that God placed these hidden codes within the Bible to be widely shared with this modern generation of skeptics.

The Bible has been studied extensively by hundreds of millions of Jews and Christians over the last thirty-five hundred years. Therefore, some readers have naturally asked how anyone in our generation could possibly discover something new that was not previously known. This is a legitimate question. However, many new archeological, scientific and medical discoveries during the last one hundred and fifty years have provided convincing new evidence regarding the reliability of the ancient biblical text.

Dr. William Albright, the greatest Christian archeologist of the past century, spent his life exploring the land of Israel and the surrounding nations in his search for archeological artifacts. As a result of his and other archeologists' numerous discoveries, Dr. Albright concluded that the Bible was totally accurate in every area where he had examined the archeological evidence. When he summarized the final results of the thousands of archeological discoveries made during the last century, Dr. Albright concluded: "There can be no doubt that archeology has confirmed the substantial historicity of Old Testament tradition."[2]

With powerful apologetic evidence, Christians can challenge the skeptics in our generation to seriously consider the claims of the Bible that it is the supernatural Word of God. The Lord commands Christians, in the words of 1 Peter, to be prepared to explain and defend the reasonableness of our faith in the Bible and in Jesus Christ. We need to be prepared to persuade men and women to turn from their unbelief to seriously consider the claims of Jesus Christ. "But sanctify the Lord God in your hearts: and be ready always to give an answer to every man that asketh you a reason of the hope that is in you with meekness and fear" (1 Peter 3:15). In light of God's command to defend our faith to our generation of unbelievers, I find it natural that we should from time to time discover new types of evidence in both the text of the Scriptures as well as in the world of science and archeology. I found an interesting quotation from the Christian writer, Joseph Butler, in his *The Analogy of Religion* that illustrates this point. "Nor is it at all incredible that a book which has been so long in the possession of mankind, should contain many truths as yet undiscovered."[3]

The Original Discovery of the Bible Codes

Rabbi Michael Dov Weissmandl was a brilliant Czechoslovakian Jewish scholar in astronomy, mathematics, and Judaic studies. In the years before World War I, he found an obscure but intriguing reference to the Bible Codes in a rare book written by a fourteenth-century rabbi known as Rabbeynu Bachayah. The book described a curious pattern of letters encoded within the Torah by skipping an equal number of letters. This discovery inspired Rabbi Weissmandl to begin exploring to see if he could detect other examples of similar codes hidden within the Torah. During the following years, Weissmandl found that he could locate certain meaningful and related words or phrases, such as "hammer" and "anvil" if he examined the letters at sequences that were equally spaced in the Hebrew text. In other words, if he found the first letter of a significant word such as "Torah," and then, by skipping forward seven letters he found the second

Hebrew Alphabet Chart

Hebrew Letter		*Phonetics*
א		Aleph
ב		Bet
ג		Gimmel
ד		Dalet
ה		Heh
ו		Vav
ז		Za'yin
ח		Chet
ט		Tet
י		Yod
כ	ך	Kaf
ל		Lamed
מ	ם	Mem
נ	ן	Nun
ס		Sa'mek
ע		Ayin
פ	ף	Peh
צ		Tzadai
ק		Qoph
ר		Resh
שׂ	שׁ	Sin Shin
ת		Tav

The second Hebrew letter is the final form.
Hebrew is written and read from right to left

letter of the same word, he would continue to skip forward the same number of letters to see whether or not the complete word "Torah" was spelled out in the text at equally spaced intervals. Rabbi Weissmandl described this unusual phenomenon as "equidistant letter sequences" (ELS).

Weissmandl was amazed to find that numerous examples of significant words were hidden within the Hebrew text of the Torah at equally spaced intervals. These spaced intervals between significant letters varied from every two letters, every seven letters, and numerous other intervals. However, once they found a particular word spelled out at, say every twenty-second letter, the balance of the letters in the encoded words in this group were often spaced at an interval of every twenty-second letter.

Initially, Rabbi Weissmandl could not be certain if this phenomenon was truly significant or whether it was simply due to the great number of possible combinations of words and phrases that could occur by random chance by skipping forward various intervals of letters in the Hebrew text. The proof that this phenomenon was evidence of a supernatural intelligence and design was confirmed almost forty years later in Israel. The invention of sophisticated computers and statistical analysis was finally able to analyze the text of the Bible to prove that these codes could not have been produced by random chance.

Although Rabbi Weissmandl found many coded names by simply manually counting the letters in the text, he did not record his discoveries in writing. Fortunately, some of his students did record several examples of his code discoveries. Over the following decades, students in Israel who had heard about his research began searching the Torah for themselves to ascertain whether or not such codes actually existed. Their discoveries ultimately resulted in the research studies at Hebrew University that have proven the validity of this research. The introduction of high-speed computers allowed Jewish scholars at Hebrew University to explore the text of the Torah in ways that previous generations could only dream about.

Equidistant Letter Sequences

A group of dedicated Jewish scholars in Israel, following up on Rabbi Weissmandl's research, found many additional hidden codes embedded within the text of the Torah. A paper called "Equidistant Letter Sequences in the Book of Genesis" was published in August 1994 in the scholarly journal *Statistical Science*. This academic publication is one of the most prominent mathematical and scientific journals in the world. The study was completed by three eminent Israeli mathematicians Doron Witztum, Yoav Rosenberg, and Eliyahu Rips at the world-renowned Hebrew University and the Jerusalem College of Technology. This study has been republished in several other respected scholarly journals, including *Bible Review*, October 1995, as well as on the Internet. Their discoveries of complex Hebrew codes that reveal supernatural and prophetic knowledge about the future is causing tremendous consternation in the academic community because it challenges the long-held beliefs of liberal scholars who generally reject verbal inspiration of the Bible.

This scientific discovery of the ELS code phenomenon is earthshaking in its potential consequences because it reveals a staggering level of mathematical design and intelligence that could only have been produced by a supernatural mind. This discovery provides compelling mathematical proof that the Bible was inspired by God. The data demolishes the false claim by liberal scholars and skeptics that the Bible was written and edited by uninspired men and that it is full of errors and contradictions. Despite the fact that numerous scholars and scientists have attempted to challenge the validity of this Bible Code research, the evidence for the existence of this phenomenon has not been successfully refuted.

Every Jot and Tittle

Jesus Christ Himself affirmed that the actual letters composing the Scriptures were directly inspired by God and were preserved in their precise order throughout eternity. "For verily I say unto you, Till heaven and earth pass, one jot or one tittle shall in no wise pass from the law, till all be fulfilled" (Matthew 5:18). The English word *jot* is our translation of the Greek word *iota*, the Greek letter *i*. This *iota* is the Greek equivalent of the Hebrew letter *yod*, the smallest letter in the Hebrew alphabet. The word *tittle* is the Greek word *keraia*, derived from the smallest Hebrew grammatical symbol. Jesus Christ stated that even the smallest of the letters and grammatical marks in the original text of the Bible were directly inspired by God.

This intriguing statement by Jesus about the Scriptures has been confirmed two thousand years later by means of an intricate analysis of the Hebrew text of the Bible by mathematicians and computer scientists in Israel. To their total surprise, these researchers discovered that every single letter of the Torah fits into a complicated tapestry of staggering mathematical precision. In this regard, we should remember the provocative words found in Proverbs 25:2, "It is the glory of God to conceal a thing: but the honour of kings is to search out a matter."

This phenomenon of the Bible Codes was placed within the text of the Word of God thousands of years ago; however, God has hidden it successfully until our generation. Many of these codes could not have been discovered by manual examination of the text. The invention of high-speed computers enabled the researchers to examine every possible combination occurring in any of hundreds of possible skip distances (from every second letter to every five hundredth letter, for example) throughout the millions of Hebrew letters in the Old Testament. However, once a meaningful ELS pattern has been detected by the computer program, anyone can personally verify the existence of that particular Bible Code by manually counting out the Hebrew letters to verify that a particular ELS word is spelled out by skipping the appropriate number of letters.

How Do the Bible Codes Work?

The Bible Codes are meaningful Hebrew words spelled out in the biblical text by skipping an equal number of letters. The researchers called this equal skipping of letters "Equidistant Letter Sequence" (ELS). The hidden message is spelled out within the normal surface text by skipping an equal number of letters (say every seventh letter). For example, they discovered that the Hebrew word for Israel, יִשְׂרָאֵל, was spelled out in the opening passage of Genesis by skipping every seven letters and once again by skipping every fifty letters within a short passage of only five verses (Genesis 1:30–2:3). It is interesting to note that these verses where we find "Israel" encoded are known as the *Kiddush* and are recited by Jews around the world every Sabbath.

The practice of hiding an encoded word within a surface text by skipping every tenth, forty-eighth, etc. letter has been used by spies for centuries to send secret messages. For example, an American spy working in a British fort during the Revolutionary War might have written an innocent sounding letter to his mother in which he wrote about his health, the weather, and such. However, the spy created a secret message by encoding his message using every twelfth letter. This requires the spy to carefully choose the words of his surface text to conceal his secret message. When his commander intercepted the letter, he would circle every twelfth letter he found and read the secret message, which might have been: "Four hundred soldiers and twenty-two cannons in fort."

The Central Intelligence Agency would use their computers to create a chemistry professor's treatise that they knew the Russian spies would steal and then distribute to Russian scientists at their secret labs. According to a pre-arranged code, a Russian lab worker who was secretly spying for the CIA would ignore everything else in the treatise, but he would look for the secret message by selecting every seventy-seventh letter to find out which documents he should photograph for the CIA.

Some Jewish rabbis have always known that there were some ELS patterns and words encoded in the Bible, which had been found in the past. Later in this chapter we will examine some of the historical quotes that reveal knowledge of this curious phenomenon long before the creation of computers that could demonstrate the remarkable code patterns running through the Hebrew text of the Bible. However, until the development of high-speed computers, it was impossible to systematically search the biblical text to see if any other coded words might be hidden within the Scriptures.

Almost twenty-five years ago, a group of Israeli researchers developed a computer search program and placed the Hebrew text of the Bible into the computer. Using the ancient Hebrew *Textus Receptus* (the "received text," the ancient Masoretic Hebrew text used by the King James translators) of the Torah, Professors Doron Witztum, Eliyahu Rips, and Yoav Rosenberg began by placing the Hebrew text of the first five books of the Bible into their computers.

The mathematicians initially chose three hundred arbitrary Hebrew word pairs that were logically related in meaning, such as "hammer" and "anvil," or "man" and "woman." They asked the computer program to locate any such word pairs in close proximity within the text of Genesis. Once the computer found the first letter in Hebrew of "hammer," it would search for the second letter at various intervals or spaces between letters (say skipping every second, third, or seventeenth letters). If the program couldn't locate the second letter of the target word "hammer" following the first letter at a two-space interval, it would then search at a three-space interval, then a four-space interval, etc. Once it located the second letter at, say, the twelve-space interval, it would then look forward in the text for the third letter at the same twelve-space interval, and so on through the entire 78,064 Hebrew letters in Genesis. The computer also looked for encoded words by checking in reverse order.

After the program had examined the text for each of the three hundred word pairs, the researchers were astonished to realize that every single word pair had been located in Genesis in close proximity to each other word. As statisticians, they were naturally astounded because they knew it was humanly impossible to construct such an intricate and complicated pattern within a surface text, such as Genesis, which recorded the history of the Jewish people. After calculating the probabilities of this phenomenon occurring randomly by chance alone, they published their conclusions in 1988 as part of another scientist's paper in a highly respected British scientific journal, the *Journal of the Royal Statistical Society*.[4] The odds against the three hundred word pairs occurring by chance in the text of Genesis were phenomenal. The bottom line is that if the phenomenal results reported by the Israeli scientists were genuine, only a supernatural intelligence far beyond our human capacity could have produced the extraordinarily intricate pattern of encoded words they discovered within the Hebrew text of the Bible.

The term "interval" or "skip distance" indicates the number of Hebrew letters that are skipped in the original biblical passage to spell out the encoded word in equally spaced intervals (ELS). If the interval number in brackets is positive (22), then the encoded word begins at the indicated passage and reads right to left (the same direction in which we read a Hebrew text), skipping the indicated number of Hebrew letters. However, if the interval number in brackets is preceded by a minus sign (−13), the encoded word begins at the indicated passage and reads left to right, skipping the indicated number of Hebrew letters.

These ELS word pairs were found compacted together much more closely in the biblical text than random chance would suggest was probable. As they studied these curious patterns further, the scientists discovered that many of the ELS-encoded words related to events and personalities in human history that occurred from ancient times until today. These coded words are interlaced in intricate patterns at evenly spaced intervals in the text, reading both forward and backward. The scientists realized that these ELS-encoded letters formed words and associations of such complexity and design that it was impossible that the letter patterns could have occurred by random chance alone.

Their initial experiment was reported in their contribution to a 1988 paper entitled "Probability, Statistics and Theology" by the mathematician D. J. Bartholomew, which was published by the British *Journal of the Royal Statistical Society*. This article by Bartholomew included the paper on the ELS codes discovered by Doron Witztum, Eliyahu Rips, and Yoav Rosenberg that was read before the Royal Statistical Society on November 11th, 1987.[5]

The Word *Torah*, תורה, Encoded in the Bible

When the researchers looked at the string of Hebrew letters beginning in Genesis 1:1, they counted forward fifty letters from the first appearance of the letter ת, the first letter (tav) of the Hebrew word *Torah* and found the second letter in the word *Torah*, ו. Skipping forward another fifty letters, they found the third letter of the word *Torah*, ר. The last skip forward of fifty letters revealed the fourth letter in the word *Torah*, ה. The Hebrew word תורה, *Torah*, the Law, was spelled out using every fiftieth letter of the text.

To their surprise, they found that in the first verse of Exodus, the second book in the Bible, the same word תורה, *Torah*, was once again spelled out at the same fifty-letter intervals beginning with the first appearance of the letter ת. However, when they examined the opening verses of Leviticus, the third book of the Bible, the ELS word *Torah* was not encoded. The word *God* was spelled out when they skipped forward every eighth letter from the first letter yod, י, that appeared in the book.

When they examined the initial verses of Numbers and Deuteronomy, the fourth and fifth books of the Bible, the scientists again found that the word *Torah* was encoded. In the Book of Numbers, *Torah* was spelled out in reverse at a fifty-letter interval. However, in the Book of Deuteronomy, it appeared in reverse order at a forty-nine-letter interval beginning in the fifth verse of the book.

The mathematician Dr. Daniel Michelson calculated that the odds were more than three million to one against the word *Torah* being encoded four times by chance alone within the opening verses within the first five books of the Bible.[6] Bible students know that the number fifty is very significant in Scripture. For example, God commanded Israel to free their slaves, to cancel all debts, and to return family lands that had been pledged to a lender on the fiftieth Year of Jubilee. In addition, the Bible reveals that God presented Law itself, the Torah, to the Jewish people at Mount Sinai precisely fifty days after their miraculous Exodus from Egypt.

Eden Encoded in Genesis

Israeli Professor Eliyahu Rips discovered that the key word *Eden* was encoded repeatedly sixteen times within the relatively short Genesis 2:4-10 passage (only 379 Hebrew letters) dealing with the Garden of Eden. Professor Michelson calculated that while you would expect to find the ELS word *Eden* five times by random chance, the odds against finding sixteen *Eden*s occurring in ELS codes by random chance in such a short passage were only one chance in ten thousand.[7]

Another fascinating feature of this phenomenon was found by Dr. Doron Witztum in the Genesis 2 passage that deals with the Garden of Eden. Twenty-five different ELS Hebrew names of trees were found encoded within the text of this one chapter in Genesis that records God's creation of vegetation. The mathematicians calculated that the laws of probability suggest the odds against this occurring by chance alone are a hundred thousand to one.[8]

Thousands of detailed and precise ELS patterns and codes such as these were discovered hidden in the Hebrew text of the ancient Scriptures. Mathematicians and statisticians, after exhaustive statistical analysis, concluded that this pattern of coded words could not have occurred by chance, nor could a human writer have purposely produced this complex phenomenon. Their conclusion was that only a divine intelligence could have directed Moses to record this precise Hebrew biblical text containing such complex codes thousands of years ago.

Other Codes Reveal God's Prophetic Foreknowledge

The researchers discovered that some of the words encoded in the text of the Torah concerned events and personalities that occurred thousands of years after Moses wrote the Torah. Naturally, many academics rejected out of hand the very possibility that this Bible Codes phenomenon could be real. However, despite many attempts to deny its validity and numerous false claims that you could find these same complex ELS patterns in other non-biblical texts, no one has successfully refuted the reported ELS data or the Bible Codes phenomenon. The critics

have simply denied that the ELS codes are statistically meaningful or they have claimed you could find the same phenomenon
in other non-biblical texts. In the following chapters we will
address these arguments by the code critics and demonstrate
that their arguments are not valid.

The Ancestors of King David Named
Centuries Before They Were Born

One of the most interesting of the experiments examined the
text of Genesis 38, which recorded the history of the great
Jewish patriarch Judah and his relationship with his widowed
daughter-in-law Tamar, who gave birth as a result of this illicit
intercourse to two sons, Pharez and Zerah. The Book of Ruth tells
us that King David, the greatest king of Israel, was descended
from Pharez, the son of the patriarch Judah as follows: Pharez
was the ancestor of Boaz, who married his kinsman Ruth, who
gave birth to Obed (*Oved*), who was the father of Jesse (*Yishai*),
who was the father of King David. Each of the five Hebrew
names of the key ancestors of King David were found encoded
at forty-nine-letter intervals, reading left to right, within this
Genesis 38 text. Incredibly, these five names (Boaz, Ruth, Oved,
Yishai, and David) were encoded at the same forty-nine-letter
ELS interval in the precise chronological order they were born,
as recorded in the Bible. According to Dr. Moshe Katz, the odds
were calculated as only one chance in 800,000 that the five
names of David's ancestors would occur in this particular passage and that they would be found in the exact, chronological
order in which they lived.[9]

They examined Genesis 28, Jacob's vision of the ladder
to heaven, which he received at Mount Moriah, the "place
of God." The key words *Temple* and *Torah* were encoded at
twenty-six-letter intervals in a continuous sequence of nine
Hebrew letters beginning with the מ letter in the word *place*
(Genesis 28:16). The occurrence of these two significant words
Temple and *Torah* in sequence within a biblical passage declaring
that "this is none other but the house of God, and this is the
gate of heaven" is extraordinary. The researchers calculated the

probability of these two key words occurring by random chance in that particular passage at about one chance in 17 billion.[10]

Aaron, Israel's High Priest, Encoded in Leviticus

In another analysis, Israeli mathematician Dr. Eliyahu Rips searched an eleven-verse section of Leviticus chapter 1, which records God's laws of worship concerning the priesthood of the Kohanien, the "sons of Aaron," Israel's High Priest. They found the Hebrew name אהרן, *Aaron,* encoded twenty-five times in this one small section of Leviticus (716 Hebrew letters) instead of eight times, as the laws of probability would suggest. Statisticians calculated that the odds against *Aaron* occurring twenty-five times by chance in this small passage were approximately 400,000 to one.[11]

The Feast of Hanukkah and the Hasmoneans

The wicked Syrian king Antiochus IV slaughtered tens of thousands of Jews who refused to worship him when he conquered Jerusalem. Antiochus IV stopped the Temple sacrifice in 168 B.C. He then defiled the altar by sacrificing a pig upon it, provoking a Jewish rebellion, led by a courageous old man named Mattathias and his five sons. This triggered a spectacular war of religious independence. The Jews, led by is son Judas Maccabaeus ("the Hammer"), defeated the Syrian army against impossible odds in 165 B.C. The Jews reconquered the Temple site on the twenty-fourth day of the ninth month, exactly three years to the day after Antiochus IV had stopped the daily sacrifice.

The Jews cleansed the sacred Temple (1 Maccabees 4:52-54) and reinstituted Temple worship. The Jewish *Talmud* claims that a priest found a one-day supply of the sacred oil hidden in a wall of the Temple. When the oil was used to light the candelabra, it miraculously lasted for the full eight days of the celebration, until new sacred oil could be refined. The Feast of Dedication has been commemorated ever since by the annual eight-day Hanukkah celebration.

The Israeli researchers found the encoded ELS word *Hanukkah,* which refers to the festival (at a −261 interval) in Genesis 36:24-37. Incredibly, this was encoded near the ELS word

Hasmoneans (–524), the name of the family of great warriors led by Judas Maccabee who ruled Israel in the following century. The name *Mattathias*, who led the Jewish rebellion against Syria, was also encoded in Genesis 36:33-40 by skipping every sixty-two letters right to left. In addition, the name of the Jewish general *Maccabee* was found by Doron Witztum, encoded every second letter right to left in Genesis 36:31-32.

King Louis and the French Revolution

Another passage in Genesis reveals a remarkable cluster of encoded words about the French Revolution. The following words are included: *Mapecha HaSarfatit* ("the French Revolution"), "Louis," the name of the French king, and the word *Beit* (house of) *Bourbon*, his royal dynasty. In the same grouping were the following words: *Hamarseille* (the Hebrew name of the French national anthem) and the word *Bastillia* (the Hebrew name of the infamous French prison for political prisoners that was stormed by revolutionaries). Interestingly, this ELS cluster dealing with the French Revolution appears in Genesis 39–41, a passage which describes Joseph's imprisonment in Egypt. The Hebrew word for *Bastillia* is found encoded within the text in Genesis 39:20 that describes "the prison in which the king keeps his prisoners."

They discovered the ELS word *Zedekiah*, who was the last king of Judah when the Babylonian army conquered Jerusalem in 587 B.C. Intriguingly, the encoded name *Matanya* appeared in close proximity within the text. This was the original birth name of King Zedekiah before he ascended the throne (2 Kings 24:17).

The Assassination of Anwar Sadat

Possibly the most fascinating of the codes are those that reveal events that have occurred in our generation. The late Egyptian president Anwar Sadat courageously flew to Israel to meet with the Israeli leaders in an attempt to break the circle of continuous warfare between Egypt and Israel. Tragically, President Sadat was assassinated during a military parade on October 6, 1981, by Islamic fundamentalists from the Moslem Brotherhood who remain bitterly opposed to the peace process. The Israeli researchers found the encoded names *Anwar* and *Sadat* together with *Chaled Islambooli*, חאלד אסלמבלי, the leader of the Moslem Brotherhood assassination team, encoded in Genesis 18. The assassin's name, חאלד, Chaled, appears in ELS code at an interval of six letters, right to left, in Genesis 18:4 beginning with the second letter of the eighth word in that verse. The same code sequence also contained the date *8 Tishri* (October 6) and the year of his assassination, *1981*, together with these encoded words: *president, gunfire, shot, murder,* and *parade.*

Hitler and the Holocaust Bible Codes

One of the most curious of all the hidden ELS codes is the discovery of the words *Hitler, Nazis,* and the names of several of the Holocaust death camps embedded within the text of Deuteronomy. The Israeli researchers naturally wondered if the Bible Codes might reveal anything about the Holocaust, the greatest tragedy in the history of the Jewish people. When they asked the program to search for the target words *Hitler, Nazis,* and *Holocaust,* the computer found that every one of these target words was encoded in a cluster of codes within a small passage in Deuteronomy 10:17–22:

> For the Lord your God is God of gods, and Lord of lords, a great God, a mighty, and a terrible, which regardeth not persons, nor taketh reward: He doth execute the judgment of the fatherless and widow, and loveth the stranger, in giving him food and raiment. Love ye therefore the stranger: for ye were strangers in the land of Egypt. Thou shalt fear the Lord thy God; him shalt thou serve, and to him shalt thou cleave, and swear by his name. He is thy praise, and he is thy God, that hath done for thee these great and terrible things, which thine eyes have seen. Thy fathers went down into Egypt with threescore and ten persons; and now the Lord thy God hath made thee as the stars of heaven for multitude. (Deuteronomy 10:17-22)

They found the word *Hitler,* היטלר, spelled out at a twenty-two-letter interval. Several of the names of concentration death camps were found embedded within this same text, beginning with the second to last appearance of the Hebrew letter bet, ב, in this passage. Counting every thirteenth letter from left to right the coded letters spelled the phrase *b'yam marah Auschwitz*, which means "in the bitter sea of Auschwitz." As they skipped forward another thirteen letters, they came to the letter resh, ר. From the resh they counted every twenty-second letter from left to right and connected to the word *Hitler*, היטלר. Hitler's Nazis ultimately slaughtered over six million Jews and another six million Poles and Russians in the death camps in Eastern Europe. The names of two of the Nazi concentration camps, *Auschwitz* and *Belsen*, were found encoded close to *Hitler* and *Berlin* in a cluster of encoded ELS words: *Germany*, *Poland*, *genocide*, *plagues*, *cremetoria*, *an evil house*, *Fuhrer*, and *Mein Kampf*.

Deuteronomy 33:16 also contained a hidden code about the Nazi Holocaust. Beginning with the first Hebrew letter mem, מ, they counted every 246th letter from left to right and found the encoded word *Melek Natzim*, which means "King of the Nazis." This same passage contained the phrase *kemi bait rah*, "an evil house rose up." In Deuteronomy 32:52, beginning with the letter aleph, א, and counting from left to right every 670 letters spells the name *Aik'man*, a Hebrew variant of the name *Eichmann*. Adolf Eichmann was the Nazi official who designed the Final Solution, the system of concentration death camps used in the Holocaust. He was finally captured after the war in Argentina, abducted to Israel, tried, and executed as a mass murderer.

The series of hidden codes dealing with Nazi Germany and the Holocaust concluded in Deuteronomy 33:21 with a final significant code. Beginning with the letter resh, ר, that appeared in the word *Yisrael*, researchers counted every twenty-second letter from left to right and found the tragic phrase *re'tzach alm*, which means "a people cry murder, slaughter."

Many Jews have asked why the prophecies of the Bible say nothing about the Holocaust, the worst tragedy in the history of God's Chosen People. The discovery of the Bible Codes provides evidence that God encoded prophetic words about the Holocaust within the text of the Bible.

Hitler, the Nazis, and the Death Camps
Were Prophesied in the Bible

Encoded ELS Word	Hebrew	Interval	Begins at:
Hitler	היטלר	(22)	Deut. 10:17
Auschwitz	אושוריץ	(−13)	Deut. 10:21
Holocaust	שׁואה	(13)	Deut. 10:20
Germany	גרמניה	(−933)	Deut. 33:28
Crematorium for my sons	כבשׁן לבני	(134)	Deut. 31:28
The Holocaust	השׁואה	(50)	Deut. 31:16
Plagues	מגפות	(−134)	Deut. 32:32
Eichmann	אייכמן	(9670)	Deut. 32:52
Auschwitz	אושׁוריץ	(−536)	Deut. 33:24
In Poland	בפולין	(−107)	Deut. 32:22
King of the Nazis	מלך נאצים	(−246)	Deut. 33:16
Genocide	רצח עם	(−22)	Deut. 33:21
The Fuhrer	הפירר	(5)	Deut. 32:50
Hitler	היטלר	(−3)	Num. 19:13
Mein Kampf	מין קאמפ	(9832)	Num. 22:1

17כי י_וה א_היכם הוא א_הי הא_הים וא_ני הא_נים
הא_ הגדל הגבר והנורא אשר לא-ישא פנים ולא יקח
שחד: 18ועשה משפט יתום ואלמנה ואהב גר לתת לו
לחם ושמלה: 19ואהבתם את-הגר כי-גרים הייתם בארץ
מצרים: 20את-י_וה א_היך תירא אתו תעבד ובו תדבק
ובשמו תשבע: 21הוא תהלתך והוא א_היך אשר-עשה
אתך את-הגדלת ואת-הנוראת האלה אשר ראו עיניך:
22בשבעים נפש ירדו אבתיך מצרימה ועתה שמך י_וה
א_היך ככוכבי השמים לרב:

Hebrew Text of Deuteronomy 10:17-22 Passage.

Mathematicians Confirm Their ELS Findings

In 1994 the Israeli scientists wrote a follow-up paper on their word-pair ELS experiment using the 66 Famous Rabbis (discussed later in this chapter) for submission to *Statistical Science*, a scientific journal that insisted that a group of opposing scholars review and challenge their data and examine their computer program before publication. Despite the fact that all of the reviewers held previous beliefs against the inspiration of the Scriptures, the overwhelming evidence and the integrity of the data forced the editors to approve the study's scientific accuracy and reluctantly publish the article. Robert Kass, the editor of *Statistical Science*, wrote this comment about the study that was published in August 1994: "Our referees were baffled: their prior beliefs made them think the Book of Genesis could not possibly contain meaningful references to modern day individuals, yet when the authors carried out additional analysis and checks the effect persisted The paper is thus offered to *Statistical Science* readers as a challenging puzzle."[12]

The study concluded that the peculiar sequences of Hebrew letters appearing in the biblical text at equal spaces from each other forming significant words could not possibly have occurred by simple coincidence or random chance.

The Response from Recognized Experts

I realize that this information about the Bible Code phenomenon will sound almost unbelievable to many readers. However, the well-respected mathematician Professor David Kazhdan, chairman of the Department of Mathematics at Harvard University, and fellow scientists from other universities including Yale and Hebrew University in Jerusalem confirmed that this is "serious research carried out by serious investigators." These recognized experts in mathematics wrote a letter confirming the value of this research in the introduction to a recent Israeli book about this phenomenon called *Maymad HaNosaf* (*The Added Dimension*), written by Professor Doron Witztum of the Jerusalem College of Technology.[13] Dr. David Kazhdan made the following statement during an interview with a newspaper in 1996: "The phenomenon is real; what it means is up to the individual."

Professor Witztum is the leading researcher on these Bible Codes. Realizing that this discovery is extremely controversial in today's academic world, these scientists encouraged additional research on the phenomenon and declared that "the results are sufficiently striking to deserve a wide audience." In light of their known attitude of rejection of the Bible's divine inspiration and the supernatural, their statement is a powerful endorsement that the phenomenon is legitimate and is worthy of continued study.

Scientists who have studied these results state that it would be extremely difficult to create such a Hebrew document containing hundreds of encoded ELS words. They concluded that it would be virtually impossible to reproduce this phenomenon in a Hebrew text, even if they had the help of a group of brilliant linguists or the assistance of the world's most sophisticated supercomputers. In addition, it is impossible to account for the prophetic knowledge regarding future personalities and events found in these codes. The evidence suggests that God inspired Moses to record the precise Hebrew words including the ELS spelled codes in the words of the Torah.

In addition to demonstrating that God inspired the text of the Torah, the evidence of this marvelous design destroys the Documentary Hypothesis, the theory of liberal skeptics that several different "editors" interwove different texts centuries after the death of Moses creating the Book of Genesis. The fact that researchers have found a number of very long ELS patterns extending throughout the first five books of the Bible suggests that only one supernatural mind could have imposed this marvelously complex design upon the Torah. The researchers have since discovered similar codes throughout the whole Old Testament.

The Famous Jewish Sages Experiment

In a 1994 follow-up paper published in the *Statistical Science* journal,[14] the Israeli team of researchers recorded the results of their search for pairs of encoded words that relate to people and events that occurred thousands of years after Moses wrote the Torah. They selected the names of thirty-four of the most prominent rabbis and Jewish sages during the thousand years leading up to A.D. 1900. Interestingly, the researchers simply selected the thirty-four Jewsh sages with the longest biographies in the *Encyclopedia of History of the Great Men in Israel.*[15] They asked the computer program to search the text of the Torah for close word pairs coded at equally spaced intervals that contained both the names of the famous rabbis paired with their date of birth or death, using the Hebrew month and day. (The Jewish people celebrate the memory of their famous sages by commemorating their date of death.) Incredibly, the computer program found every single one of the thirty-four names of these famous rabbis embedded in the text of Genesis paired at significantly close proximity with the actual dates of their birth or death.

Scholars at the *Statistical Science* journal who reviewed this experimental data were naturally amazed. They demanded that the scientists run the computer test program again on a second sample searching for the next thirty-two most prominent Jewish sages listed in a major Jewish encyclopedia. To the astonishment of the skeptical reviewers, the results on the second set of famous sages were equally successful. The staggering result of the combined test revealed that the names and dates of their birth or death of every one of the sixty-six most famous Jewish sages from A.D. 1000 to 1900 were encoded in close proximity within the text of Genesis. The odds against these particular rabbis' names and dates occurring in close proximity by random chance were calculated by the mathematicians as only one chance in 62,500.[16]

In the *Statistical Journal* article in August 1994 Robert Kass made the following statement: "It has been noted that when the book of Genesis is written as two-dimensional arrays, equidistant letter sequences spelling words with related meanings often appear in close proximity. Quantitative tools for measuring this phenomenon are developed. Randomization analysis shows that the effect is significant at the level of 0.00002 [one chance in 50,000]."[17]

Naturally, the researchers attempted to reproduce these results by running the computer program on other religious Hebrew texts outside the Bible. The researchers could not detect significant ELS codes beyond what you would normally find by random chance in any other Hebrew text outside the Bible.

When you carefully consider the ELS phenomenon, you can see that even a minor change of spelling or choice of words would destroy the precise sequence of Hebrew letters that reveals these hidden words encoded at evenly spaced distances throughout a particular text of the Torah. A critic insisted they

attempt to find similar complex ELS codes in a Hebrew translation of Tolstoy's famous novel *War and Peace* because it was the
same length as the Book of Genesis. However, the phenomenon
was not present in *War and Peace,* nor any other modern Hebrew
writing. In fact, an exhaustive analysis reveals that no other
Hebrew text outside the Old Testament contains these mysterious codes, not even the Hebrew apocryphal books written
during the four hundred years before the birth of Christ.

Following the 1994 appearance of the article on the Bible
Codes in *Bible Review,* there was a virtual onslaught of letters to
the editor in the following monthly issues attacking the article
in the strongest terms. Most of the critical letters dismissed
the phenomenon without seriously considering the scientific
data that was presented. Several critics attacked the author's
argument and data in ways that revealed they either failed to
grasp the actual statistical method used to detect and analyze
the Hebrew codes or they didn't understand the rigorous methodology that eliminated the possibility that this phenomenon
had occurred by pure random chance.

After his research was published in *Bible Review* in November 1995, Dr. Jeffrey Satinover responded to the critics who
had challenged his assertion that a pattern of elaborate and
significant words was encoded within the Torah. Dr. Satinover
replied to his critics as follows:

> The robustness of the Torah codes findings derives from
> the rigor of the research. To be published in a journal
> such as *Statistical Science,* it had to run, without stum-
> bling, an unusually long gauntlet manned by some of
> the world's most eminent statisticians. The results were
> thus triply unusual: in the extraordinariness of what
> was found; in the strict scrutiny the findings had to hold
> up under; and in the unusually small odds (less than 1
> in 62,500) that they were due to chance. Other amazing
> claims about the Bible, Shakespeare, etc., have never
> even remotely approached this kind of rigor, and have
> therefore never come at all close to publication in a peer-
> reviewed, hard-science venue. The editor of *Statistical*

Science, himself a skeptic, has challenged readers to find a flaw: though many have tried, none has succeeded. All the 'First Crack' questions asked by *Bible Review* readers—and many more sophisticated ones—have therefore already been asked by professional critics and exhaustively answered by the Israeli researchers. Complete and convincing responses to even these initial criticisms can get fairly technical.[18]

Some critics have suggested that the Israeli scientists simply played with the computer program long enough, that by chance alone "they got lucky." This objection raises the relevant objection that there might be numerous unreported "hidden failures," a common problem in most scientific research today. To prevent this from occurring, editorial observers from the *Statistical Journal* demanded that the Israeli scientists analyze their data by examining a completely new group of personalities that were chosen solely by the *Statistical Journal's* editorial judges, namely the sixty-six most famous Jewish sages. The results I quoted earlier in this chapter were based on this group of individuals chosen by these judges. In addition, the judges appointed by the *Statistical Journal* analyzed the computer programs to determine that they were both valid and neutral in their design.

We need to keep in mind that the standard text of the five books of the Torah was electronically published years ago in widely available computer programs and printed texts. These texts cannot be modified. In fact, as a result of the production and sale of numerous "Bible Code" computer programs that are now available in North America, anyone with a computer and lots of time can personally verify the existence of these codes within the Hebrew text of the Scriptures. I have personally verified the presence of these fascinating patterns of hidden codes during long hours of examination using the computer programs I acquired several years ago in Jerusalem when this research was just beginning.

Professor Harold Gans, a senior researcher who examined sophisticated foreign government intelligence codes for the U.S. Army, has publicly confirmed the existence of these codes as reported in *Statistical Journal* through the use of advanced analytic techniques and his own sophisticated computer program. Dr. Gans is a brilliant mathematician who has published 180 technical papers. When Gans learned of this discovery by Professor Doron Witztum, as a skeptic and a non-religious Jew, he initially thought that the claims were "ridiculous." Unlike many readers, as an intelligence specialist dealing with complex codes and computers, Gans had the technical ability to test the claims and data for himself. In 1989, he created a complex and original computer program on his computer to check Witztum's data. For nineteen straight days and nights, Gans let his program examine all possible variations and combinations in the 78,064 Hebrew letters in the Book of Genesis. Dr. Gans's computer program checked through hundreds of thousands of possible letter combinations at many different spaced intervals. Finally, Gans was forced to conclude that these codes actually existed and that they could not have occurred by random chance or human design. He had confirmed the absolute accuracy of Professor Witztum's conclusions. As a result of his discoveries, Professor Gans now teaches classes in synagogues throughout the world about the extraordinary evidence proving divine authorship of the Bible.

Dr. Gans's follow-up study found that the text of Genesis also revealed the encoded names of the actual cities where each of these sixty-six sages was born. Gans calculated that the odds against this occurring by chance was one chance in two hundred thousand as recorded in his paper "Coincidence of Equidistant Letter Sequenced Pairs in the Book of Genesis."[19]

Many scientists from other universities and laboratories are now conducting careful investigations that examine the remarkable nature of the phenomenon. After seven years, the critics of the codes finally published an article in *Statistical Science* that attempts to critique the original experiment by the Israeli scientists concerning the methodology used in the experiment concerning the sixty-six great Jewish sages that was first published in 1994 in *Statistical Science*.

Are the Bible Codes Meaningful or Are They Accidental?

Regardless of the relative merits of the statistical analysis of the presence of the sixty-six rabbis and their dates of death as well as birth cities, the basic phenomenon of the Bible Codes exists as anyone in possession of a Hebrew Bible can confirm. The question that always remains to be answered: Does this phenomenon provide evidence that it was placed there by some supernatural design, or is the presence of these numerous codes regarding future events and people simply the result of random chance? The decision is ultimately a value judgment that each person must make for himself. The mathematician will examine his calculations of statistical probability to determine his answer. The average reader will arrive at his or her own logical and common sense conclusion based on their assessment of the probability or improbability that the ancient Hebrew text of the Bible could contain these ELS patterns naming all of these people, places, and events by random chance as opposed to the supernatural design of God. The decision is yours.

The 9/11 Terrorist Attack Bible Codes

When the tragic, horrific Islamic terrorist attacks took place on September 11, 2001 millions of people throughout the civilized world were stunned to witness such appalling hatred, evil, and the sudden death of over three thousand innocent lives. As people everywhere attempted to process the devastating news that America had been attacked without warning, naturally those students of the Word of God who study the Bible Codes were motivated to begin a rigorous computer search of the Bible to determine if there were any ELS codes that related to this terrible event.

My friends at Bible Code Digest have developed an excellent Web site that seriously examines and explores the existence and significance of the ELS code phenomenon. Dave Swaney of Bible Code Digest has graciously given me permission to use the excellent research completed by his team of code researchers regarding these ELS code discoveries related to the World Trade

Center terrorist attack. I encourage anyone who is interested in exploring the Bible Code phenomenon in more detail to examine their fascinating web site: www.biblecodedigest.com. The following code discoveries relating to the tragic 9/11 terror attack were discovered and reported on their Web site. A statistical analysis of the probabilities of these particular ELS codes occurring in any Hebrew text can be examined in the pages of their site.

In the days following September 11, their team found numerous ELS codes in a very significant passage of the Old Testament—Ezekiel 37, the prophetic passage where Ezekiel saw a vision of "the valley of dry bones" that represented the exiled nation of Israel being reborn in the last days in response to the command of God. Virtually all of the Islamic terrorist proclamations identify America's support for the existence and security of the State of Israel as one of the major reasons they have dedicated themselves to the destruction of the United States of America, the "Great Satan" in their propaganda pronouncements. It is fascinating that this remarkable cluster of significant ELS encoded words related to the 9/11 terrorist attack should be found within this vital prophecy about the rebirth of Israel as a nation in our generation after almost two thousand years of exile.

After a great deal of research, the Bible Code Digest team found the following words that were grouped around the prophecy of Ezekiel 37. While many of these ELS codes have large skip distances, the fact that they cross over each other in close proximity within this key prophecy is quite significant. Where two numbers are given in the ELS skip distance column, that word is encoded twice in this prophecy. Further details are available for your analysis at www.biblecodedigest.com.

Bible Codes About the
September 11, 2001 Terrorist Attack

ELS Encoded Word	ELS Skip Distance
Manhattan	698
World Trade Center	78
Tower Destroyed Toward the Mountain, Oh God	904

Pentagon	65626
Hijackers	29
Ignite the Airliner	267
Terror Hot in me	430
Where are They?	37
And let God not strike Terror	37
Terror of the Sea is There in Them	448
Jihad	210
Arafat	904
Philistines	1406
Bin Laden, Blood of the Poor	93
You will spit at Tradition, Al Kada	1430
Muhammed Omar	37
Taliban	81
Fire from the Heart	267
Saddam Hussein	150684
Saddam	87, 942
Hussein	3714, 3985
This is the King of Babylon	5564
Iraq	195

This list enumerates only the most prominent of the Bible Codes that make reference to events related to the attacks made on the Pentagon and the twin towers of the World Trade Center.[20]

In my book *War on Terror—Unfolding Bible Prophecy*,[21] I documented compelling evidence that the late President Saddam Hussein of Iraq supported Osama bin Laden's terrorist attacks on American targets on September 11, 2001. Hussein had vowed to wage a "war of vengeance" against the United States following the Gulf War in 1991. Hussein rebuilt the city of Babylon and proclaimed that his destiny was to conquer Israel and her allies, just as King Nebuchadnezzar had done twenty-six centuries earlier.

The September 11 Terrorist Attack
Bible Code: Ezekiel 7:2-8

In the first part of Ezekiel chapter 7 the Bible Code Digest researchers found another large group of interesting ELS code words that crossed through or appeared in close proximity to this key Ezekiel prophecy that relate to the terrible events of September 11, 2001.

More Bible Codes Found in Ezekiel 7:2-8
Related to the Sept. 11 Attack

New York
U.S.
An Unheard of Disaster
In the Morning
September 11
2001
bin Laden
Afghan
Taliban
Airliner
Firemen
Saddam
Iraq
Conspiracy
Devastation
Cruelty
Terror
Horrible
Death
Destruction
Butchery[22]

The full list of ELS codes and the analysis of their statistical probability can be downloaded for examination at Bible Codes Digest's Web site. These fascinating ELS codes were found in a very powerful prophecy, Ezekiel 7:2-8, that God proclaimed to the unrepentant people of Israel before the final destruction of their nation, city, and Temple at the hands of the invading Babylonian army of King Nebuchadnezzar in 587 B.C.

Also, thou son of man, thus saith the Lord God unto the land of Israel; An end, the end is come upon the four corners of the land. Now is the end come upon thee, and I will send mine anger upon thee, and will judge thee according to thy ways, and will recompense upon thee all thine abominations. And mine eye shall not spare thee, neither will I have pity: but I will recompense thy ways upon thee, and thine abominations shall be in the midst of thee: and ye shall know that I am the Lord. Thus saith the Lord God; An evil, an only evil, behold, is come. An end is come, the end is come: it watcheth for thee; behold, it is come. The morning is come unto thee, O thou that dwellest in the land: the time is come, the day of trouble is near, and not the sounding again of the mountains. Now will I shortly pour out my fury upon thee, and accomplish mine anger upon thee: and I will judge thee according to thy ways, and will recompense thee for all thine abominations. (Ezekiel 7:2-8)

When God judges an unrepentant nation as He did with ancient Israel, He normally uses an evil nation such as the pagan Babylonian empire as His instrument of judgment. However, God will ultimately deliver His righteous judgment upon the pagan nation of Babylon as prophesied numerous times in Isaiah 13:1, 6, 19 and Revelation 18.

Strong Cautions Regarding the Bible Codes

While I believe that many of these ELS codes in the Bible are significant, there are numerous accidental and meaningless ELS words that can be found as well. I also strongly warn readers to consider these vital biblical principles that will keep us from misusing these ELS Bible Codes.

Bible Codes Are Found Only in the Orthodox Hebrew Text of the Old Testament

No one has been able to locate multiple, detailed, and meaningful Bible codes in clusters within any other Hebrew literature outside the Bible. Experimenters have carefully examined other Hebrew writings for the existence of codes including the Jewish *Talmud*, the *Mishnah*, the apocryphal writings of *Tobit* and *Maccabees*, etc. They even examined modern Hebrew literature such as translations of *War and Peace*. However, the scientists found no significant complex patterns of ELS codes similar to the ones recorded in this book in any other Hebrew literature outside the Old Testament. Several researchers have also found Bible Codes in the Greek text of the New Testament as detailed in my book *The Mysterious Bible Codes*.[23] However, much work remains to be done to verify this phenomenon in the New Testament.

Bible Codes Cannot Accurately Prophesy Future Events

One cannot discover meaningful encoded information about a future event until the event occurs. Obviously, it is impossible to know what target words to ask the program to search for until after an event has happened. However, once an event occurs, such as the Gulf War, we can ask the computer to look in the Bible text for such target words as *Saddam Hussein* or *General Schwarzkopf*. The encoded words related to a future event cannot be discovered in the biblical text in advance of the event because you wouldn't know what ELS words to ask the computer to look for. After a terrible event such as the Sept. 11, 2001, World Trade Center bombing occurs, the Bible Codes can confirm that the Scriptures contain encoded data about that historical event that occurred long after the Scriptures were written.

However, the codes cannot be used to foretell future events. Even if you correctly guessed at the right target words before a future event, such as the assassination of a prominent politician, and you found the name of the person (say, *Peters*) and the word *killed*, you would still not know anything meaningful about the future. Until the event occurs, any suggestion that the occurrence of these two code words means that the politician would be killed would be merely a meaningless guess. The appearance of the words *Peters* and *killed* might suggest an assassination. However, these words without a context might be simply accidental or they might relate to the fact that Peters killed someone else. Since we find ELS words, not sentences, there is no way to determine the meaning of an ELS pattern until the event occurs. Only then can we understand the context and the meaning.

The Bible prohibits us from engaging in foretelling the future. A recent book called *The Bible Code* by agnostic writer Michael

Drosnin claims that he himself discovered codes that allowed him to predict future events. However, a careful examination of his claims reveals that the encoded information he discovered is insufficient to allow anyone to confidently predict any future event. Michael Drosnin may have made a guess about a particular, tragic future event based on his discovery of the encoded name *Yitzchak Rabin*. However, it was simply a guess. There was not enough information in the code he discovered to allow him to confidently affirm that a particular future event, namely the assassination of Yitzchak Rabin, would actually occur. Michael Drosnin claims that he warned the prime minister of Israel about the danger of assassination based on the fact that he found that one of the eight letters of the encoded words *Yitzchak Rabin* happened to appear in the surface text of Deuteronomy 4:42, which reads in Hebrew "assassin that will assassinate."

However, it was impossible to know in advance of the tragic event what this particular combination actually meant. It could easily have meant that Prime Minister Rabin might order the assassination of some terrorist in the future, or an assassination attempt would fail, or it could easily have meant nothing at all. The point is that the limited information from the encoded individual words can only be accurately interpreted after the fulfillment of an historical event, such as the Holocaust, the Gulf War, or the 9/11 attacks. God did not place these ELS codes within the Bible to enable men to play at becoming prophets of future events. The Bible repeatedly forbids fortune-telling.

The major Israeli code researchers, including Professor Eli Rips, and all of the serious Christian code researchers, including Yacov Rambsel and myself, deny that the Bible Codes can be used to accurately predict future events. The information encoded in the Bible can only be accurately interpreted after a historical event has actually occurred. Then we can compare the details of the historical event with the encoded information in the Bible to determine whether or not God had encoded these prophetic details centuries before the events occurred. In this manner, the Bible Codes give God the glory, not the human researcher. The prophet Isaiah declared these words of God, "I will not give my glory unto another" (Isaiah 48:11).

Bible Codes Do *Not* Reveal Any Hidden Sentences, Teachings, or Doctrines

There are no secret sentences, detailed messages, or theological statements to be found in the encoded ELS words. God's message of salvation and His commandments for holy living are to be found only in the normal, surface text of the Scriptures. The Bible Codes can only reveal key words, such as people's names, places, and occasionally dates (using the Hebrew calendar) that provide confirmation of the supernatural inspiration and origin of the Scriptures. The fact that the ELS patterns reveal words, not complex sentences, prevents anyone from claiming they have found a hidden theological message or making a definite prediction about a future event. Significantly, no one has claimed to discover any new teaching or doctrine in the Bible Codes because there are no sentences; only ELS words.

The Bible Codes have Nothing to Do with Numerology

The phenomenon of the Bible Codes has nothing to do with occult numerology. Numerology is connected with divination or foretelling the future and is clearly forbidden by the Bible. There is nothing occult or secret about the codes. This ELS phenomenon was openly published in scientific and mathematical journals, taught, and broadcast widely since it was first discovered twenty years ago.

The particular interval between the Hebrew letters, the actual number of letters to be skipped, has no importance or significance. The codes have nothing to do with "the occult significance of numbers," as Webster's defines numerology. Obviously, the coded words are found at various intervals (i.e., by skipping two, seven, sixty-one, or more letters). However, the significance or meaning of the encoded ELS word does not relate to the particular interval (the number of letters skipped). Either a particular word is spelled out in Hebrew letters at equal intervals or it is not. Anyone with a Hebrew-English Interlinear Bible can examine a particular encoded word and verify that these words are truly spelled out at ELS intervals. Computer programs such as Bible Codes 2000 are widely available to allow anyone to verify these codes for themselves. The program Bible Code 2000 can be purchased using the order form at the back of the book if you wish to personally research the Bible Codes.

Why Did God Place These Hidden Codes in the Bible?

For almost seventeen centuries, from the time of Emperor Constantine's conversion in A.D. 312 until the beginning of the last century, the Bible was generally accepted by the majority of Western culture as the inspired and authoritative Word of God. However, we have witnessed an unrelenting assault on the authority of the Bible by the intellectual elite, the academic community, liberal theologians, and the secular media during the last one hundred years. Most people in our culture have been exposed to countless attacks on the authority and accuracy of the Scriptures throughout high school, college, and from the mass media. I believe that God has provided this extraordinary new evidence to prove to this generation of skeptics that the Bible is truly the Word of God. The complex nature of these codes means that the phenomenal discovery of many of these encoded words could not have occurred until the development of high-speed computers during the last twenty years.

In a sense, God secretly hid these fascinating codes within the text of the Bible thousands of years ago with a time lock that could not be opened until the arrival of our generation and the development of sophisticated computers. In His prophetic foreknowledge, God knew that our generation would be characterized by an unrelenting attack on the authority of the Scriptures. No previous generation needed the additional scientific evidence provided by the discovery of these codes as much as our present skeptical generation.

Hundreds of years ago, a famous rabbi known as the Vilna Gaon lived and taught in the city of Vilna, Latvia, near the Baltic Sea in northern Europe. This brilliant and mystical Jewish sage taught his students that God had hidden a vast amount of information secretly encoded within the Hebrew letters of the

Torah. Consider the intriguing and suggestive statement about the hidden codes by this famous Jewish sage.

> The rule is that all that was, is, and will be unto the end of time is included in Torah from first word to the last word. And not merely in a general sense, but including the details of every species and of each person individually and the most minute details of everything that happened to him from the day of his birth until his death; likewise of every kind of animal and beast and living thing that exists, and of herbage, and of all that grows or is inert. (Vilna Gaon, Introduction to *Sifra Ditzniut*)

There is a strong tradition that a number of codes were discovered in past centuries by various Jewish sages, including Rabbeinu Bachya, Moses Maimonides, and the Vilna Gaon. Since World War I, Rabbi Michael Weissmandl and others have taught about these codes. There is an interesting statement suggesting knowledge of the codes in the Jewish mystical writing known as the *Zohar*. "The entire Torah is replete with Divine Names. Divine Names run through every single word in the Torah."[24] In approximately A.D. 1200, the brilliant Jewish sage Moses Maimonides, known as Rambam, made a curious comment about this statement in the *Zohar* that indicated he understood that there were complex codes hidden in the Torah. He said that the hidden codes provided another reason why a Torah scroll should be considered as unfit for use if even one single letter was missing from the text. The removal or addition of a single letter from the Hebrew text would eliminate the codes found hidden within that section of text. Also, there is a suggestive statement in the *Talmud* that refers to the codes: "Everything is alluded to in the Torah."[25]

A group called the Discovery Seminar, sponsored by the Aish HaTorah College of Jewish Studies, presents the phenomenon of the Bible Codes to Jewish groups and synagogues throughout the world. This group was created in Israel by a number of scientists, mathematicians, and Judaic scholars. In addition to giving presentations in Israel, Aish HaTorah has adapted the material to English, enabling their teams to share this fascinating information with Jewish audiences throughout the world showing the divine inspiration and authority of the Torah. Numerous agnostic Jews have reportedly returned to their religious roots in Orthodox Judaism as a result of their exposure to the Bible Codes.

The discovery of the Bible Codes revealing information about the life, death, and ministry of Jesus of Nazareth in the prophetic passages of the Old Testament, written centuries before His birth, provides powerful new evidence that Jesus is the true Messiah and the Son of God. The discovery in our generation of the hidden Bible Codes has fascinated millions of Jews, Christians, unbelievers, and skeptics during the last several years. However, a number of Christians have wondered why God would have placed a series of hidden codes within the Hebrew Bible text and not have placed a similar code within the New Testament. Research has been conducted regarding the possibility that the Bible Code phenomenon might be found in the Greek text of the New Testament. I have funded a small team of computer specialists who have developed a computer software program to search the Greek text of the Scriptures. They recently discovered a significant series of Bible Codes about Jesus Christ and various historical events within the Greek New Testament but this is not available for sale. The discovery of the ELS codes in the Greek New Testament is documented in my book *The Mysterious Bible Codes*.[26]

After studying and thinking about the Bible Code phenomenon for many years, I have come to a personal conclusion. The Bible Codes proclaim one message to humanity and have only one purpose: They provide compelling evidence to our generation that the Bible is truly the inspired Word of God.

The Implications of Bible Code Research

Many scholars who are philosophically opposed to the existence of God and the inspiration of the Bible are stunned by this research. Despite many arguments and challenges the data still stands. Several secular scientific journals have declared that the ELS phenomenon in the Bible is real and not a result of fraud or computer error. The simple truth is that this phenomenon could not have occurred by random chance alone. Nor could any group of brilliant human beings, even with supercomputers at their disposal, produce this awesome result of encoding a huge number of significant names about future events within the surface text of the Torah.

Since all scholars agree that the five books of Moses were written thousands of years ago, we have compelling evidence that this ELS Bible Code phenomenon is another clearly authenticated signature of God upon the pages of Scripture. The evidence in the next chapter will reveal that God has encoded the name of His Son, the Messiah, *Yeshua,* throughout the key messianic prophecies in the Hebrew text of the Old Testament.

Notes

1. Grant R. Jeffrey, *The Signature of God* Toronto: Frontier Research Publications, 1996.

2. William F. Albright, *Archeology and the Religions of Israel* (Baltimore: John Hopkins University Press, 1956) 176.

3. Joseph Butler, *The Analogy of Religion, Natural and Revealed* (1736), II, iii.

4. D. J. Bartholomew, "Probability, Statistics and Theology" *Journal of the Royal Statistical Society—A* (1988) 151, Part 1, pp. 137-178.

5. D. J. Bartholomew, "Probability, Statistics and Theology" *Journal of the Royal Statistical Society—A* (1988) 151, Part 1, pp. 137-178.

6. Daniel Michelson, "Codes in the Torah" *B'Or Ha'Torah*, No. 6 (1987), Jerusalem: Shamir.

7. Daniel Michelson, "Codes in the Torah" *B'Or Ha'Torah*, No. 6 (1987), Jerusalem: Shamir.

8. Daniel Michelson, "Codes in the Torah" *B'Or Ha'Torah*, No. 6 (1987), Jerusalem: Shamir.

9. Moshe Katz, *Computorah—Hidden Codes in the Torah*. Jerusalem: Computorah, 1996, p. 120.

10. Daniel Michelson, "Codes in the Torah" *B'Or Ha'Torah*, No. 6 (1987), Jerusalem: Shamir.

11. Daniel Michelson, "Codes in the Torah" *B'Or HaTorah*, No. 6 (1987), p. 7-39. Jerusalem: Shamir.

12. Robert Kass, "Equidistant Letter Sequences in the Book of Genesis," *Statistical Science*, August 1994.

13. Doron Witztum, *HaMeimad HaNosaf* (*The Additional Dimension*) Jerusalem: 1989.

14. Robert Kass, "Equidistant Letter Sequences in the Book of Genesis," *Statistical Science*, August 1994.

15. *Encyclopedia of the History of the Great Men in Israel* Jerusalem: Y. Chachik Publishers, 1940.

16. Robert Kass, "Equidistant Letter Sequences in the Book of Genesis," *Statistical Science*, August 1994.

17. Robert Kass, "Equidistant Letter Sequences in the Book of Genesis," *Statistical Science*, August 1994.

18. Jeffrey Satinover, *Bible Review,* November 1995.
19. Jeffrey Satinover, *Cracking the Bible Code* New York: William Morrow, 1997, p. 224.
20. Internet site: http.www.biblecodedigest.com.
21. Grant R. Jeffrey, *War On Terror – Unfolding Bible Prophecy* Toronto: Frontier Research Publications, 2002.
22. Internet site: http.www.biblecodedigest.com.
23. Grant R. Jeffrey. *The Mysterious Bible Codes* Nashville: Word Publishing, 1998.
24. *Zohar* II, 87a.
25. *Talmud Tan'anis* 9a.
26. Grant R. Jeffrey. *The Mysterious Bible Codes* Nashville: Word Publishing, 1998.

10

Bible Codes Reveal the Name of Yeshua in the Old Testament

Of all the codes that I have researched, the following are the most fascinating discoveries that I could share with you. Not only has God included thousands of hidden ELS codes within the text of the Bible, but He has actually placed the encoded name *Yeshua,* ישוע (the Hebrew name of Jesus), in numerous significant prophetic passages from Genesis to Malachi throughout the Old Testament. God has also placed the significant ELS code *Yeshua is My Name,* ישוע שמי, within a key messianic prophecy, Isaiah 53:8-10.

The research conducted during the last several years on the Bible Codes within the text of the Scriptures has given us the strongest possible evidence that the Bible was truly inspired by God. However, once I fully appreciated that the ELS codes revealed significant information about historical events such as Hitler's death camps, the War in the Gulf, and the French

Revolution, I naturally wondered if God had secretly encoded the name of Jesus Christ in the text of the Old Testament.

Providentially, several years ago I received a request from Yacov Rambsel, asking if he could quote from the research material I had written on the laws of probability regarding the messianic prophecies fulfilled in the life, death, and resurrection of Jesus from my 1988 book *Armageddon—Appointment with Destiny*.[1] In discussing this material with Yacov, I realized that he had a real passion for the study of the Hebrew Scriptures and for Jesus Christ as his Messiah. After I completed my chapter on the Bible Codes in the first edition of *The Signature of God* in April 1996, I called Yacov to ask him to review the Hebrew text for accuracy.

Yacov told me that he had just completed his own manuscript on the Bible Codes that focused on a series of extraordinary discoveries about the name of Jesus – Yeshua encoded throughout the Old Testament. His research provided the answer to my question about whether God had encoded the name of Jesus within the Hebrew Scriptures. With Yacov Rambsel's permission, I will share a portion of the phenomenal research that he has completed during thousands of hours of painstaking analysis of the hidden ELS codes. As I mentioned earlier, the Israeli researchers used complex computer programs to explore these codes, and I purchased three Bible Code computer search programs in Jerusalem in 1991 that I used on my Macintosh computer to verify the code research at Hebrew University. However, Yacov completed his detailed analysis by patiently examining the Hebrew text of the Old Testament manually letter by letter and then individually counting the equally spaced intervals between the letters. The amount of work and dedication involved to complete his analysis is staggering. I highly recommend to anyone who is fascinated by this research that they acquire a copy of Yacov Rambsel's book, *Yeshua—The Name of Jesus Revealed in the Old Testament*[2] and his sequel *His Name is Jesus*[3] published by Frontier Research Publications, Inc. You can purchase these books in Christian bookstores; by using the order form at the back of this book; or through our website: www.grantjeffrey.com.

Yacov Rambsel discovered the original Hebrew name of Jesus, *Yeshua*, יֵשׁוּעַ, encoded in Genesis beginning with the very first verse Genesis 1:1, "In the beginning God created the heaven and the earth." Starting with the very first word in the Bible, beginning with the Hebrew letter *yod*, י, the fifth letter in the word, *B'raisheet*, בְּרֵאשִׁית, "In the beginning," the name יֵשׁוּעַ *Yeshua* was found encoded by counting forward every 521st letter. He found the letters that spell *Yeshua Yakhol*, which translates, as "Jesus is able." Some of the Jewish critics who attacked the Yeshua Codes have wrongly claimed that *Yeshua* is *not* the correct Hebrew name of Jesus of Nazareth. However, at the end of this chapter I provide strong historical evidence that *Yeshua*, יֵשׁוּעַ, is the correct Hebrew name of Jesus of Nazareth as used in His lifetime in ancient Israel.

One of the most interesting features is that virtually every one of the major Messianic passages of the Old Testament contains the name *Yeshua*, יֵשׁוּעַ, encoded within the Hebrew text of the ancient prophecies about the coming of the Messiah. As an example, Yacov found the name *Yeshua* embedded in the key messianic prophecy in Isaiah 53:10 that described the trial, death, and burial of Christ. "Yet it pleased the Lord to bruise him; he hath put him to grief: when thou shalt make his soul an offering for sin, he shall see his seed, he shall prolong his days, and the pleasure of the Lord shall prosper in his hand" (Isaiah 53:10).

Yeshua Is My Name

Beginning with the second Hebrew letter *yod*, י, that occurs in the phrase *He shall prolong, ya'arik Kyray*, Yacov counted forward right to left every 20th letter and discovered the Hebrew phrase יֵשׁוּעַ שְׁמִי, *Yeshua Shmi*. "Yeshua [Jesus] is My Name" was encoded in this powerful prophecy that teaches us about the suffering Messiah who died to atone for our sins. The probability that this fascinating ELS combination "Yeshua [Jesus] is My Name" would appear by random chance in this key Messianic prophecy in Isaiah is simply staggering!

A passage in the Book of Genesis declared that the God provided "coats of skin" for Adam and Eve to cover their nakedness after they sinned: "Unto Adam also and to his wife did the Lord God make coats of skins, and clothed them" (Genesis 3:21). This verse revealed that God killed the first animal in history as a blood sacrifice to provide a covering for the sins and nakedness of Adam and Eve. This was a prophetic sign of the Passover Lamb that would be slain in the future as a symbol of the salvation of the Jews every Passover as they annually celebrated their Exodus from Egypt. This also symbolized the perfect sacrifice of the Lamb of God to atone for the sins of all those who would confess their sins and ask Christ to forgive them.

However, this important passage also contains an ELS pattern about Jesus as the true "Lamb of God." Beginning with the last Hebrew letter *heh*, ה, in Genesis 3:20 and counting forward every ninth letter, we find the word *Yoshiah*, meaning "He will save." The name Joshua, *Yoshiah* is a Hebrew equivalent name for *Yeshua* (Jesus). This encoded name *Yoshiah* found in the first few chapters of the Old Testament reminds us of the parallel message given to the young virgin Mary by the angel that declared, "Thou shalt call his name JESUS: for he shall save his people from their sins" (Matthew 1:21).

The Betrayal of Yeshua by Judas Iscariot

One of the most startling of all the Messianic codes Yacov found was hidden within Psalm 41:7-10 which predicted the betrayal of Jesus by His disciple Judas Iscariot: "An evil disease, say they, cleaveth fast unto him: and now that he lieth he shall rise up no more. Yea, mine own familiar friend, in whom I trusted, which did eat of my bread, hath lifted up his heel against me" (Psalm 41:8-9). Yacov noted that verse 8 contained the phrase "they plot evil," *yach' shvu rah'ah*. However, he noticed that beginning with the letter *yod*, י, when he skipped forward right to left every second letter he found it spelled out the word ישוע, *Yeshua*. In other words, in the exact verse where King David prophesied the tragic betrayal of Jesus the Messiah over one thousand years before it occurred, we also find the name of the person who was betrayed encoded by skipping only two letters at a time within this prophetic passage.

One of the most well known of the messianic prophecies in

the Old Testament describes the exact price of Christ's betrayal, thirty pieces of silver. Over five hundred years before the birth of Jesus, the prophet Zechariah wrote this prediction: "And I said unto them, If ye think good, give me my price; and if not, forbear. So they weighed for my price thirty pieces of silver" (Zechariah 11:12). The phrase reading "my price" is *se'kari*. Beginning with the letter *yod*, ׳, Yacov counted forward every twenty-fourth letter and found the word *Yeshua*, ישׁוע. The Lord must have inspired Zechariah to choose these specific Hebrew words and this precise spelling to create this remarkable Bible Code. Here, in this key prophecy written five hundred years before Christ's birth, where the prophet described the precise price of our Lord's betrayal, God included a hidden Bible Code to His Chosen People that identified the name of their promised Messiah, *Yeshua*, Jesus.

In the verses that followed this prediction of Christ's first coming, the prophet Zechariah looked forward twenty-five centuries into the future to describe the tremendous emotional upheaval and mourning that will occur when the Jewish people's spiritual eyes will finally be opened to see that the Messiah Jesus of Nazareth whom they have rejected for twenty centuries, is in fact, their Messiah, *Yeshua*, who was crucified two thousand years ago. Zechariah prophetically saw Jesus' Second Coming to save Israel from the Antichrist's armies following the battle of Armageddon. Then the Jewish remnant will see Jesus Christ as their true Messiah: "And I will pour upon the house of David, and upon the inhabitants of Jerusalem, the spirit of grace and of supplications: and they shall look upon me whom they have pierced, and they shall mourn for him, as one mourneth for his only son, and shall be in bitterness for him, as one that is in bitterness for his firstborn" (Zechariah 12:10). Beginning with the letter *chet*, ה, found in the phrase, "an only son," היחיד, Yacov discovered that the word *Mashiach*, משׁיח, meaning "Messiah" was encoded by counting forward every thirty-eighth letter.

Leviticus reveals a fascinating hidden ELS concerning the blood of Jesus Christ that was shed for our sins. We are taught throughout the Scriptures that Jesus Christ is our great High

Priest. "But Christ being come an high priest of good things to come, by a greater and more perfect tabernacle, not made with hands, that is to say, not of this building" (Hebrews 9:11). In Leviticus, Moses revealed God's detailed instructions regarding the rules for the use of the oil of anointing by the holy priest-hood and the sacrifices for the sins of the Chosen People.

> And he that is the high priest among his brethren, upon whose head the anointing oil was poured, and that is consecrated to put on the garments, shall not uncover his head, nor rend his clothes; neither shall he go in to any dead body, nor defile himself for his father, or for his mother; neither shall he go out of the sanctuary, nor profane the sanctuary of his God; for the crown of the anointing oil of his God is upon him: I Am the Lord. (Leviticus 21:10-12).

This passage about the anointing of the High Priest prophetically speaks to us of the greater High Priest Jesus the Messiah, who has completed the sacrifice for our sins through His sacrificial death on the Cross once and forever. The anointing of the High Priest of Israel prophetically symbolizes the long awaited anointing of Jesus Christ at His Second Coming, which will be accomplished when the anointing oil (recently found hidden near Qumran by the Dead Sea) as described in Exodus 30:25-35, will be used to anoint Yeshua when He appears as Israel's Messiah-King to usher in the Millennial Kingdom.

Yacov examined this passage and found that, beginning with the first *heh*, ה, in Leviticus 21:10 and counting forward every third letter, it spelled out the phrase *hain dam Yeshua*, which means "Behold! The blood of Yeshua." It is awesome to realize that God secretly encoded these profound words about His Son Jesus in these key messianic prophetic passages throughout the Old Testament over a thousand years before the birth of Jesus.

The study *Statistical Significance Discovered in the Yeshua Codes*[4] was published on the Internet in 1997. This study calculated the probability of this phrase "Behold! The blood of Yeshua" appearing at an ELS interval of every three letters by random chance in a book the size of Leviticus. Their conclusion was that the odds against this happening were so great that you would have to search through 69,711 books the size of Leviticus to expect to discover this phrase appearing only one time at an interval of every three letters.

Another key messianic prophecy, Psalm 72:13-15, includes significant words revealing that Jesus "shall save the souls of the needy. He shall redeem their soul." This significant prophetic passage also contains the ELS encoded word *Yeshua*, יֵשׁוּעַ, which was encoded by skipping every nineteen letters, revealing Jesus Christ as the source of our personal salvation from sin and guilt.

The prophet Isaiah prophesied more than seven centuries before the birth of Jesus Christ that He would come as the great liberator to mankind. Isaiah's prophecy (61:1-2) of the Great Jubilee at the end of this age reminded Israel that their Messiah would finally cancel all their debts and proclaim liberty to all of those who are captives to sin. "The Spirit of the Lord God is on me; because the Lord hath anointed me to preach good tidings unto the meek; he hath sent me to bind up the brokenhearted, to proclaim liberty to the captives, and the opening of the prison to them that are bound; to proclaim the acceptable year of the Lord, and the day of vengeance of our God; to comfort all that mourn" (Isaiah 61:1-2). Starting with the *yod*, י, in the phrase "The Spirit of the Lord God," *Ruach Adonai Yehovah*, and skipping every nine letters from left to right spells *Yeshua*. In addition, Yacov discovered that the word Joshua *Oshiyah*, אוֹשִׁיעַ, was also encoded beginning with the last letter aleph, א, in the second verse and counting every thirty-sixth letter from left to right. This word *Oshiyah* means "I will Save" and is a variation of the word *Yeshua* as we saw earlier in Genesis 3:20.

Yeshua Revealed in Daniel's Vision of the Seventy Weeks

Of the many discoveries made by Yacov Rambsel, one of the most significant findings concerns Daniel's great prophecy of his vision of the seventy weeks recorded in Daniel 9:25-27.

Yeshua Coded in the Old Testament Prophecies

יֵשׁוּעַ

גִּילִי מְאֹד בַּת־צִיּוֹן הָרִיעִי בַּת יְרוּשָׁלַם
הִנֵּה מַלְכֵּךְ יָבוֹא לָךְ צַדִּיק וְנוֹשָׁע הוּא
עָנִי וְרֹכֵב עַל־חֲמוֹר וְעַל עַיִר בֶּן־אֲתֹנוֹת:

Rejoice greatly, O daughter of Zion; shout, O daughter of Jerusalem

Behold, thy King cometh unto thee: he is just, and having salvation;

lowly, and riding upon an ass, and upon a colt the foal of an ass.   Zechariah 9:9

יֵשׁוּעַ

כַּמַּיִם נִשְׁפַּכְתִּי וְהִתְפָּרְדוּ כָּל־עַצְמוֹתָי
הָיָה לִבִּי כַּדּוֹנָג נָמֵס בְּתוֹךְ מֵעָי
יָבֵשׁ כַּחֶרֶשׂ ׀ כֹּחִי וּלְשׁוֹנִי מֻדְבָּק מַלְקוֹחָי
וְלַעֲפַר־מָוֶת תִּשְׁפְּתֵנִי כִּי סְבָבוּנִי כְּלָבִים
עֲדַת מְרֵעִים הִקִּיפוּנִי כָּאֲרִי יָדַי וְרַגְלָי:

My strength is dried up like a potsherd; and my tongue cleaveth

to my jaws; and thou hast brought me into the dust of death.

For dogs have compassed me: the assembly of the wicked have

enclosed me: they pierced my hands and my feet.

I may tell all my bones: they look and stare upon me.   Psalms 22:15-17

יֵשׁוּעַ

וְתֵדַע וְתַשְׂכֵּל מִן־מֹצָא דָבָר לְהָשִׁיב וְלִבְנוֹת יְרוּשָׁלַם
עַד־מָשִׁיחַ נָגִיד שָׁבֻעִים שִׁבְעָה וְשָׁבֻעִים שִׁשִּׁים וּשְׁנַיִם
תָּשׁוּב וְנִבְנְתָה רְחוֹב וְחָרוּץ וּבְצוֹק הָעִתִּים וְאַחֲרֵי
הַשָּׁבֻעִים שִׁשִּׁים וּשְׁנַיִם יִכָּרֵת מָשִׁיחַ וְאֵין לוֹ וְהָעִיר
וְהַקֹּדֶשׁ יַשְׁחִית עַם נָגִיד הַבָּא וְקִצּוֹ בַשֶּׁטֶף וְעַד
קֵץ מִלְחָמָה נֶחֱרֶצֶת שֹׁמֵמוֹת:

Know therefore and understand, that from the going forth of the commandment to

restore and to build Jerusalem unto the Messiah the Prince shall be seven weeks,

and threescore and two weeks: the street shall be built again, and the wall, even

in troublous times. And after threescore and two weeks shall Messiah be cut off,

but not for himself: and the people of the prince that shall come shall destroy the

city and the sanctuary.   Daniel 9:25,26

Yeshua Coded in the Old Testament Prophecies

יֵשׁוּעַ

מֵעֹצֶר וּמִמִּשְׁפָּט לֻקָּח וְאֶת־דּוֹרוֹ מִי יְשׂוֹחֵחַ כִּי נִגְזַר

מֵאֶרֶץ חַיִּים מִפֶּשַׁע עַמִּי נֶגַע לָמוֹ: וַיִּתֵּן אֶת־רְשָׁעִים

קִבְרוֹ וְאֶת־עָשִׁיר בְּמֹתָיו עַל לֹא־חָמָס עָשָׂה וְלֹא מִרְמָה

בְּפִיו וַיהוָה חָפֵץ דַּכְּאוֹ הֶחֱלִי אִם־תָּשִׂים אָשָׁם נַפְשׁוֹ

יִרְאֶה זֶרַע יַאֲרִיךְ יָמִים וְחֵפֶץ יְהוָה בְּיָדוֹ יִצְלָח:

He was taken from prison and from judgment: and who shall declare his generation?

for he was cut off out of the land of the living: for the transgression of my people was

he stricken. And he made his grave with the wicked, and with the rich in his death

because he had done no violence, neither was any deceit in his mouth.

Yet it pleased the Lord to bruise him; he hath put him to grief: when thou shalt make

his soul an offering for sin, he shall see his seed, he shall prolong his days, and the

pleasure of the Lord shall prosper in his hand. Isaiah 53:8-10

יֵשׁוּעַ

לָכֵן יִתֵּן אֲדֹנָי הוּא לָכֶם אוֹת הִנֵּה הָעַלְמָה   7:14

הָרָה וְיֹלֶדֶת בֵּן וְקָרָאת שְׁמוֹ עִמָּנוּ אֵל:

חֶמְאָה וּדְבַשׁ יֹאכֵל לְדַעְתּוֹ מָאוֹס בָּרָע וּבָחוֹר בַּטּוֹב: 7:15

Therefore the Lord himself shall give you a sign;

Behold, a virgin shall conceive, and bear a son,

and shall call his name Immanuel.

Butter and honey shall he eat, that he may know

to refuse the evil, and choose the good. Isaiah 7:14, 15

יֵשׁוּעַ

יַחַד עָלַי יִתְלַחֲשׁוּ כָּל־שֹׂנְאָי עָלַי | יַחְשְׁבוּ רָעָה לִי: 41:8

דְּבַר־בְּלִיַּעַל יָצוּק בּוֹ וַאֲשֶׁר שָׁכַב לֹא־יוֹסִיף לָקוּם: 41:9

An evil disease, say they, cleaveth fast unto him:

and now that he lieth he shall rise up no more.

Yea, mine own familiar friend, in whom I trusted,

which did eat of my bread, hath lifted up his heel against me Psalms 41:8, 9

Know therefore and understand, that from the going forth of the commandment to restore and to build Jerusalem unto the Messiah the Prince shall be seven weeks, and threescore and two weeks: the street shall be built again, and the wall, even in troublous times. And after threescore and two weeks shall Messiah be cut off, but not for himself: and the people of the prince that shall come shall destroy the city and the sanctuary; and the end thereof shall be with a flood, and unto the end of the war desolations are determined. And he shall confirm the covenant with many for one week: and in the midst of the week he shall cause the sacrifice and the oblation to cease, and for the overspreading of abominations he shall make it desolate, even until the consummation, and that determined shall be poured upon the desolate. (Daniel 9:25-27)

Serious students of the Bible are familiar with the controversy during the last century among theologians about the correct identity of the "Messiah the Prince" referred to in Daniel 9:25. Those who deny that Daniel's prophecy prophesies Jesus Christ's first coming have claimed that "Messiah the Prince" was a reference to King Hezekiah or some other historical individual. However, Yacov Rambsel made a wonderful discovery when he found the name ישוע, *Yeshua*, in Daniel 9:26 starting with the letter *yod*, י, in the phrase "the city," *v'ha'iry*, by counting left to right every twenty-sixth letter. In addition, he found the name *Nazarene*, נצרת, encoded every 112 letters together with the encoded words: *King*, מלך (46), *Branch*, נצר (50), *Jesse*, ישי (10), and *Messiah*, משיח (52), all found within Daniel's prophecy of the seventy weeks.

Word	Hebrew	Interval	Reference begins
Yeshua	ישוע	(−26)	Dan. 9:26
Nazarene	נצרת	(112)	Dan. 9:23-27
King	מלך	(46)	Dan. 9:24-25
Branch	נצר	(50)	Dan. 9:24-25
Jesse	ישי	(10)	Dan. 9:25
Messiah	משיח	(52)	Dan. 9:25-26

King David's Psalm 22 Prophecy:
Yeshua, the Crucified Messiah

A thousand years before Jesus of Nazareth was born, King David wrote his prophetic Psalm 22, which clearly predicted the death of Jesus by crucifixion in these key words "they pierced my hands and my feet." The method of execution known as crucifixion was not even invented when King David made his remarkable prediction. In addition, David's prophecy revealed that the soldiers would gamble for the garments of Jesus of Nazareth in these words, "For dogs have compassed me: the assembly of the wicked have enclosed me: they pierced my hands and my feet. I may tell all my bones: they look and stare upon me. They part my garments among them, and cast lots upon my vesture" (Psalm 22:16-18). The clear fulfillment of David's prophetic psalm in the death of Jesus of Nazareth on the Cross is confirmed by an intriguing group of ELS words found clustered together in this important prophetic passage about the crucified Messiah.

The word *Yeshua*, ישׁוע, was found encoded right to left beginning with the letters of the first verse of this psalm, which contains one of the most important messianic prophecies in the whole of the Old Testament. The following words are encoded within this significant messianic and prophetic Psalm 22. In addition to revealing the name *Yeshua* connected to the one who would fulfill the prophecy; it reveals that He would be the "anointed" one, descended from "Jesse," and that He would be the "King of the Jews." Jesus of Nazareth fulfilled the prophecies of the "Branch" and was named *Yeshua* by the angel Gabriel's pronouncement to Mary because "He will save His people from their sins."

Word	Hebrew	Interval	Reference begins
Yeshua	ישׁוע	(50)	Ps. 22:1
King	מלך	(8)	Ps. 22:10-11
Branch	נצר	(3)	Ps. 22:11
Jesse	ישׁי	(14)	Ps. 22:12-13
Messiah	משׁיח	(8)	Ps. 22:14-15
Salvation	ישׁע	(49)	Ps. 22:24-26

Jesus' Life and Death in the Bible Codes

Naturally, the Orthodox Jewish researchers from Israeli strongly reject the significance of the Yeshua Codes discovered by Yacov Rambsel. In their public criticism against these codes they are forced by the evidence to admit that these ELS word patterns do exist, but they reject our conclusion that these ELS patterns are genuine and meaningful ELS codes because they are clustered together in such prophetically significant passages. However, the recent *Statistical Significance Discoveries in the Yeshua Codes* proves that some of these Yeshua codes cannot be explained by random chance.[5] Several of our critics challenged us to find a complex series of ELS words revealing the name of Yeshua together with His apostles in one location in the Hebrew text. The next section will reveal the results of our experiment, which we believe validates that these ELS Yeshua codes are purposeful.

Yeshua Found in Isaiah's Prophecy about the "Suffering Messiah"

One of the most interesting subjects mentioned in the first edition of my book *The Signature of God* was Yacov Rambsel's incredible discovery of the name of *Yeshua* Jesus encoded in the major messianic prophetic passages throughout the Old Testament. I verified by my computer and through manual examination of my Hebrew-English Interlinear Bible that Yacov had found the name *Yeshua* encoded in Isaiah 53:10. This famous messianic prophecy foretold the grief of the suffering Messiah and His atoning sacrifice when He offered Himself as the Lamb of God, a perfect sacrifice for our sins through His death on the Cross: "Yet it pleased the Lord to bruise him; he hath put him to grief: when thou shalt make his soul an offering for sin, he shall see his seed, he shall prolong his days, and the pleasure of the Lord shall prosper in his hand" (Isaiah 53:10).

The words *Yeshua Shmi* (Yeshua [Jesus] is My Name), שְׁמִי יֵשׁוּעַ, are encoded in this messianic verse beginning with the second Hebrew letter yod (י) beginning in the phrase "He shall prolong," *ya'arik*, יַאֲרִיךְ, and counting every twentieth letter left to right. Yacov's discovery of the name *Yeshua* encoded in

Isaiah 53 and in dozens of other well-known messianic prophecies has thrilled thousands of readers of my book *The Signature of God* as well as Yacov's bestselling book *Yeshua*.[6]

However, I challenged Yacov to continue his code research and complete an in-depth investigation of possible additional codes related to the life of Jesus in the text of Isaiah 53. As a result of hundreds of hours of further detailed research, I would like to share his additional discoveries. Over forty ELS names of individuals and places associated with the crucifixion of Jesus of Nazareth were found encoded in Isaiah's "Suffering Servant" passage, which was written seven centuries before the birth of Jesus. I hope that you will be as thrilled with this astonishing discovery as I am. Yacov's complete research on this project is documented in his book *His Name Is Jesus*, published by Frontier Research Publications Inc. I highly recommend his book to anyone who is interested by the phenomenon of the Bible Codes. With Yacov's permission, I will share a portion of his research on the incredible codes found in Isaiah 53.

Within these key chapters of Isaiah, God has secretly encoded the names of the people, the locations, and key events in the life of Jesus Christ that were historically recorded in the New Testament seven centuries later. God clearly is in charge of human history. The Lord has revealed His supernatural prophetic knowledge of future events to our generation through the extraordinary discovery of the Bible Codes. This unprecedented phenomenon is a forceful reminder of the words recorded by Moses thousands of years ago: "The secret things belong unto the Lord our God: but those things which are revealed belong unto us and to our children for ever, that we may do all the words of this law" (Deuteronomy 29:29). Let us examine the details of this remarkable series of Bible Codes about Jesus Christ and His crucifixion found in the prophecy of Isaiah.

First, we need to review the words of Isaiah's remarkable prophecy about the coming Messiah who would suffer for the sins of mankind. The full passage from Isaiah 52:13 through chapter 53 reads as follows:

Behold, my Servant shall deal prudently, he shall be

exalted and extolled, and be very high. As many were astonied at thee; his visage was so marred more than any man, and his form more than the sons of men: So shall he sprinkle many nations; the kings shall shut their mouths at him: for that which had not been told them shall they see; and that which they had not heard shall they consider.

Who hath believed our report? and to whom is the arm of the Lord revealed? For he shall grow up before him as a tender plant, and as a root out of a dry ground: he hath no form nor comeliness; and when we shall see him, there is no beauty that we should desire him. He is despised and rejected of men; a man of sorrows, and acquainted with grief: and we hid as it were our faces from him; he was despised, and we esteemed him not. Surely he hath borne our griefs, and carried our sorrows: yet we did esteem him stricken, smitten of God, and afflicted. But he was wounded for our transgressions, he was bruised for our iniquities: the chastisement of our peace was upon him; and with his stripes we are healed.

All we like sheep have gone astray; we have turned every one to his own way; and the Lord hath laid on him the iniquity of us all. He was oppressed, and he was afflicted, yet he opened not his mouth: he is brought as a lamb to the slaughter, and as a sheep before her shearers is dumb, so he openeth not his mouth. He was taken from prison and from judgment: and who shall declare his generation? for he was cut off out of the land of the living: for the transgression of my people was he stricken. And he made his grave with the wicked, and with the rich in his death; because he had done no violence, neither was any deceit in his mouth.

Yet it pleased the Lord to bruise him; he hath put him to grief: when thou shalt make his soul an offering for sin, he shall see his seed, he shall prolong his days, and the pleasure of the Lord shall prosper in his hand. He shall see of the travail of his soul, and shall be satisfied: by his knowledge shall my righteous servant justify many; for he shall bear their iniquities. Therefore will I divide him a portion with the great, and he shall divide the spoil with the strong; because he hath poured out his soul unto death: and he was numbered with the transgressors; and he bare the sin of many, and made intercession for the transgressors. (Isaiah 52:13–53:1–12)

Some of the critics of the Yeshua Codes have challenged our conclusion that the name *Yeshua* is purposely encoded in Isaiah 53 and that this ELS actually refers to the historical Jesus of Nazareth. However, if the critics examine the encoded ELS words discovered in this messianic prophecy, they will find over forty encoded names identifying virtually everyone who was present at the crucifixion of Jesus Christ. The mathematical odds against finding forty words naming each of these key individuals, places, and events in the life and death of Jesus of Nazareth by random chance alone in a similar sized non-biblical Hebrew text are simply astronomical. The following section will reveal remarkable ELS code words found encoded in Isaiah's prophecy about the Suffering Messiah (Isaiah 52:12 to 53:13).

Yeshua the Nazarene

In Isaiah 53:6, starting with the third letter in the eleventh word and counting every forty-seventh letter from right to left, we find the word *Nazarene,* רזזנ, near the name *Yeshua,* ישׁוע, in the same messianic prophecy. Jesus lived with his family in the town of Nazareth in northern Galilee where Joseph, the husband of Jesus' mother Mary, pursued his occupation as a carpenter. The word "Nazarene" was also used to describe a special person who was chosen for a sacred purpose and dedicated at birth to the service of God. A Nazarite was totally dedicated when born to the worship of the Lord and was willing to take the serious vow of the Nazarene.

Another vital identification of Jesus with the word Nazarene appears in the life of Jesus the Nazarene, as described in the Gospel of Matthew: "And [Jesus] came and dwelt in a city called Nazareth: that it might be fulfilled which was spoken by the prophets, He shall be called a Nazarene [נזרי]" (Matthew 2:23).

Galilee

The codes reveal the place where Jesus lived for most of his life — Galilee. In Isaiah 53:7, starting with the second letter in the first word and counting every thirty-second letter from left to right spells "Galilee" גליל. There are two ways to spell "Galilee" in Hebrew. The first is with the hen ה at the end of the word, and the second is without the hen ה letter. Jesus was raised in Nazareth, in a region of northern Israel called Galilee, as confirmed in Matthew 21:11: "And the multitude said, this is Jesus [Yeshua] the prophet of Nazareth of Galilee." In addition, much of His ministry was conducted at various locations surrounding the beautiful Sea of Galilee.

Three Marys and the Disciple John at the Cross

The Gospel of John records that three women named Mary (*Miryam,* מרים) were present at the crucifixion of Jesus, together with His beloved disciple, John (*Yochanan,* יוחנן). The gospel of John says:

> Now there stood by the cross of Jesus his mother, and his mother's sister, Mary the wife of Cleophas, and Mary Magdalene. When Jesus therefore saw his mother, and the disciple [John] standing by, whom he loved, he saith unto his mother, Woman, behold thy son! Then saith He to the disciple [John], Behold thy mother! And from that hour that disciple took her unto his own home. (John 19:25–27)

This moving passage reveals the profound love of Jesus for His mother Mary and His loyal friend John. We find that the names of the three Marys and the disciple John are encoded beside the name Jesus (*Yeshua,* ישוע), which is spelled out at a twenty-letter interval reading left to right beginning in Isaiah 53:10.

In Isaiah 53:11, starting with the fifth letter in the ninth word and counting every twentieth letter from left to right spells *Ma 'al Yeshua Shmee ohz*, מעל ישוע שמי עז, a phrase which means "exceedingly high, Yeshua is my strong name." From the *yod*, י, in Yeshua's name, counting in reverse every twenty-eighth letter spells *John*, יוחנן. Isaiah 52:13 says, "Behold, my Servant [Yeshua] shall deal prudently, he shall be exalted and extolled, and be very high." In Isaiah 53:11, starting with the first letter in the first word and counting every forty-second letter from left to right spells "Messiah," *Mashiach*, משיח. From the *mem*, מ, in the word "Messiah," counting every twenty-third letter from left to right spells "Mary," מרים.

Remarkably, in Isaiah 53:10, all three of the ELS names of Mary use the same letter *yod*, י, in the word *ya'arik*, יאריך. This is the same letter that forms the first letter in the encoded names *Yeshua* and John. In Isaiah 53:10, starting with the third letter in the seventh word and counting every sixth letter from right to left spells "Mary," *Miryam*, מרים. In Isaiah 53:12, starting with the fifth letter in the fourth word and counting every forty-fourth letter from left to right again spells Mary מרים. It is interesting to find the names of three Marys encoded in these verses beside the encoded names *Yeshua* and John when we remember that John's Gospel records that these four individuals were all present at the crucifixion of Jesus Christ. In addition to naming Mary, the mother of Jesus, we also find in Isaiah 53: 2, starting with the second letter in the first word and counting every 210th letter from right to left spells "Joseph," *Yoseph*, יוסף, the name of Mary's husband.

"Disciples" Found in Isaiah 53

In Isaiah 53:12, starting with the third letter of the second word and counting every fifty-fifth letter from left to right spells *limmudim ahnan*, למדים אנן, which means "the disciples mourn." Sometimes, the letter *tav*, ת, precedes this word. In this same count of fifty-five, but adjacent to "disciples," we find the word "priest." In Isaiah 53:5, starting with the second letter in the first word and counting every fifty-fifth letter from left to right spells "the Kohanim" (the priestly tribe) *ha'kohain*, הכהן.

It is fascinating to discover that the names of almost every one of Jesus' disciples (Judas Iscariot is excluded) are encoded within Isaiah's messianic prophecy, written seven centuries before Jesus was born.

The disciple's names are encoded as follows:

1. *Peter.* In Isaiah 53:3, we find the name "Simon Peter," starting with the second letter in the fifth word and counting every nineteenth letter from right to left, the ELS code spells "Peter," *Kepha,* כפה.

2. *James,* the son of Zabbadai. In Isaiah 52:2, starting with the third letter in the ninth word and counting every thirty-fourth letter from left to right, the ELS code spells "James," *Ya'akov,* יעקב.

3. *John.* In Isaiah 53:10, starting with the fourth letter in the eleventh word and counting every twenty-eighth letter from left to right, the code spells "John," *Yochanan,* יוחנן.

4. *Andrew.* In Isaiah 53:4, starting with the first letter in the eleventh word, which is "God" *Elohim,* אלהים, and counting every forty-eighth letter from left to right, we find the encoded word "Andrew," *And'drai,* אנדרי.

5. *Philip.* In Isaiah 53:5, starting with the third letter in the tenth word and counting every 133rd letter from left to right spells "Philip," *Pilip,* פילך.

6. *Thomas.* In Isaiah 53:2, starting with the first letter in the eighth word and counting every thirty-fifth letter from right to left the encoded word spells "Thomas," *Toma,* תומא.

7. *Matthew.* There are three ways to spell the name of the disciple Matthew: *Mati,* מתי; *Mattai,* מתתי; and *Mattiyahu,* מתתיהו. The encoded word *Mattai,* מתתי, is an accepted abbreviated form of *Mattiyahu,* מתתיהו. In Isaiah 53:8, starting with the first letter in the twelfth word and counting every 295th letter from left to right we find the encoded word "Matthew," *Mattai,* מתתי.

8. *James,* son of Alphaeus. *Ben Chalipi Ya'akov,* חלפי יעקב בן. In Isaiah 52:2, starting with the fourth letter in the third word and counting every twentieth letter from left to right the encoded word spells the word *Ya'akov,* יעקב. Two of Christ's disciples were known by the name James. It is fascinating that

we found the name "James" *Ya'akov* יעקב encoded twice within Isaiah 53.

9. *Simon*, (Zelotes) the Canaanite. *Shimon hakanai* הקני שמעון. In Isaiah 52:14, starting with the first letter in the second word and counting every forty-seventh letter from right to left we find the encoded word "Simon," *Shimon*, שמעון.

10. *Thaddaeus*. In Isaiah 53:12, starting with the first letter of the eighth word and counting every fiftieth letter from left to right the encoded word spells the name "Thaddaeus," *Taddai*, תדי.

11. *Matthias*. In Isaiah 53:5, starting with the fourth letter in the seventh word and counting every eleventh letter from left to right spells "Matthias," *Mattiyah*, מתיה. It is fascinating to note that this name Matthias is the name of the last disciple who was chosen by lot by the elders of the early Church to replace the dead traitor Judas Iscariot, whose guilt in betraying Jesus Christ caused him to commit suicide. Luke, the writer of the book of Acts, records how Matthias, the replacement disciple, was chosen: "And they gave forth their lots; and the lot fell upon Matthias [מתיה]; and he was numbered with the eleven apostles" (Acts 1:26).

It is noteworthy that in the early Church an essential qualification for choosing a disciple to replace the deceased Judas Iscariot was that the person must have personally witnessed the three and one half year ministry of Jesus Christ as well as His resurrection (Acts 1:21–26). This eyewitness requirement was established to assure that Matthias could also personally testify to everyone about his personal, eyewitness experience of the life and ministry of Christ from His baptism to His death and resurrection from the dead, and finally, His ascension to heaven. It is interesting to note that the names of virtually every one of Christ's disciples were found encoded near the name *Yeshua* within Isaiah's prophecy. Significantly, the name of Judas Iscariot, the Lord's betrayer, was not found encoded in this passage.

Jesus' Trial and the Names of the Two High Priests

The codes reveal the names of Israel's two high priests at the time of Jesus' trial. Starting with the third letter in the seventh word in Isaiah 52:15 and counting every forty-first letter from right to left spells "Caiaphas," *Kayafa*, כיפה, the name of the high priest of Israel named in the Gospel account of the trial of Jesus. In Isaiah 53:3, starting with the fifth letter in the sixth word and counting every forty-fifth letter from right to left spells "Annas," *Ahnan*, ענך, who was the former high priest and the influential uncle of Caiaphas. The New Testament reveals the names of these high priests in Luke 3:2: "Annas and Caiaphas being the high priests, the word of God came unto John the son of Zacharias in the wilderness." The high (chief) priests were leaders in the Sanhedrin trial in the Temple that lead to Christ's crucifixion, according to John 19:15: "But they cried out, Away with him, away with him, crucify him. Pilate saith unto them, Shall I crucify your King? The chief priests answered, We have no king but Caesar."

The Pharisees, the Levites, King Herod, Rome, and Caesar

The Pharisees and King Herod were also involved in the crucifixion. We find their names encoded in Isaiah 53:9. Starting with the second letter in the fourteenth word and counting every sixty-fourth letter from left to right, we find the word "Pharisee," *pahrush*, פרוש. These Jewish religious leaders were a strong influence in both the Temple and in the broader Israeli society. They encouraged people to follow the strict religious laws of the Scriptures and the written and oral traditions based on the teachings of their rabbis over the centuries. In Isaiah 53:6, starting with the first letter in the fourth word and counting every twenty-ninth letter from left to right, we find the encoded words "the man Herod," *ish Herod*, איש הורד. The fact that both the names Pharisees and Herod are encoded in Isaiah's messianic prophecy is remarkable.

In Isaiah 53:11, starting with the first letter of the second word and counting every fourteenth letter from left to right, we find the Hebrew word "Levis," *Levim*, לוים, clearly identifying the Temple priests, chosen from the Jewish tribe of Levi, who joined in the conspiracy against Jesus. In addition, starting with the second letter in the thirteenth word in Isaiah 53:9 and counting every seventh letter from left to right, the encoded letters spell "the evil Roman city," *rah eer Romi*, רע עיר רומי, the power ruling the known world at that time that actually ordered the death of Jesus. The Jewish authorities did not possess the legal power to inflict a death sentence upon any offender found guilty in their Sanhedrin Court in the Temple. The only way a death sentence could be legally carried out by the Jewish authorities in Judea at that time was to find a Roman law that the prisoner had also broken and to then appeal to the Roman governor to sentence the person to death under the laws of Rome.

The Gentile soldiers of the Roman Empire who were present at the crucifixion spiritually represented the Roman emperor and the entire Gentile world who also rejected the claims of Jesus as Messiah, the Son of God, and thus spiritually the Gentiles shared the responsibility for the execution of God's Messiah. In this sense, all of humanity, Jews and Gentiles, was represented at the crucifixion of the Lamb of God, Jesus Christ. In Isaiah 53:11, starting with the fourth letter in the seventh word and counting every 194th letter from left to right, we find the encoded words *Kaisar ahmail ovaid*, קיסר עמל אבד, which mean "wicked, Caesar wretched [perish]," or alternatively phrased as "wicked Caesar, to perish." The wicked Roman emperor Tiberius died within five years following the death of Jesus Christ.

Jesus Christ: The Atonement Lamb and the Light of the World

The Gospel of John records that John the Baptist received a profound revelation of Jesus Christ as the Atonement Lamb of God when He came to be baptized in the Jordan River. "The next day John seeth Jesus coming unto him, and saith, Behold the Lamb of God, which taketh away the sin of the world" (John 1:29). In

Isaiah 52:12, starting with the second letter in the twelfth word and counting every nineteenth letter from left to right spells "from the Atonement Lamb," *me'kippur tela,* מכפר טלא.

In Isaiah 53:5, starting with the seventh letter in the fifth word and counting every twentieth letter from right to left, "lamp of the Lord" *ner Adonai,* נר יהוה, is spelled out. This encoded word is adjacent to *Yeshua,* ישוע, at a twenty-letter interval. The Gospel of John affirms repeatedly that Jesus Christ is the true light of the world. This is confirmed in the following passage: "Then spake Jesus again unto them, saying, I am the light of the world: he that followeth me shall not walk in darkness, but shall have the light of life" (John 8:12).

The Messianic Title "Shiloh," "Messiah" and "Passover"

In Isaiah 53:9, starting with the second letter in the eleventh word and counting every fifty-fourth letter from right to left spells *Shiloh,* שילה. Both Jewish and Christian scholars acknowledge that the word *Shiloh* is a clear prophetic title of the coming Messiah. In Genesis 49:10, Moses recorded the deathbed prophecy of the patriarch Jacob: "The sceptre shall not depart from Judah, nor a lawgiver from between his feet, until Shiloh come; and unto him [Yeshua] shall the gathering of the people be." This famous prophecy clearly identified the coming Messiah as "Shiloh." The discovery of the word *Shiloh* encoded beside the name *Yeshua* in the powerful messianic prophecy of Isaiah 53 provides compelling evidence of the identity of Jesus of Nazareth as God's Messiah in this passage.

In addition, the word *Yeshua* was found together with the word *Messiah* encoded in this key passage. In Isaiah 53:8, starting with the third letter in the second word and counting every sixty-fifth letter from left to right spells "Messiah," *Mashiach,* משיח. In this same count, but starting with the third letter in the tenth word of verse 10, which is the *ayin,* ע, and counting every sixty-fifth letter from left to right spells *Yeshua,* ישוע. It is fascinating that the words *Jesus* and *Messiah* are both encoded in this prophecy of Isaiah sharing the same 65-letter ELS interval. Also, the word *Passover* was found encoded in Isaiah 53:10.

Beginning at the third letter of the thirteenth word at an interval of every sixty-two letters in reverse spells "Passover," *Peh'sakh*, פסח.

The Bread and Wine

In Isaiah 53:1, starting with the fifth letter in the eighth word and counting every 210th letter from right to left spells "the bread," *ha'lachem*, הלחם, which may refer to the symbol of bread that Jesus used at the Last Supper to refer to His body, which was broken for our sins. Another group of Hebrew letters at the same 210-letter interval beginning with the second letter in the eleventh word spells the word "wine," *yeyin*, יין, which was the other key symbol used by Jesus at His last Passover Supper in the Upper Room to symbolize His blood, which was shed for our sins.

The names "Jonah" and "water" were also encoded close together in this passage. In Isaiah 52:4, starting with the fourth letter in the sixth word and counting every nineteenth letter from left to right spells "Jonah," יונה. A few verses later, in Isaiah 52: 7, starting with the first letter in the ninth word and counting every nineteenth letter from left to right spells "water," מים. The prophet Jonah was thrown in the water to awaken him to God's command to preach to his enemies, the Ninevites. These codes revealing "Jonah" and "water" remind us of the history of the prophet Jonah, who was "three days and three nights in the whale's belly." Jesus used Jonah's experience as a prophetic symbol of His own death and resurrection.

Those Who Watched the Crucifixion from Afar

Mark 15:40 says, "There were also women looking on afar off: among whom was Mary Magdalene, and Mary the mother of James the less and of Joses, and Salome." In Isaiah 52:15, starting with the third letter in the sixteenth word and counting every 113th letter from right to left spells "Salome," *Shalomit*, שלמית. In verse 13, starting with the fourth letter in the second word and counting every 149th letter from right to left spells "Joses," *Yosai*, יוסי. The man Joses was apparently another son of Mary, the mother of Jesus, and therefore was Jesus' half-brother. According to Mark 15:40, both Marys were weeping at the crucifixion of Jesus. Encoded in Isaiah 52:15, starting with the fifth letter in the eighteenth word and counting every thirteenth letter from left to right spells the words "the Marys weep bitterly," *na'ar Miryam be'ku abhor,* בכו מרים נאר. In Isaiah 53:9, starting with the first letter in the third word and counting every twenty-eighth letter from right to left spells "tremble Mary" *rahal Miryam,* מרים רעל. The letters adjacent to the above spell "the blessed" *habarucha,* הברוכה. Mary, the mother of Jesus, was called "blessed" in the Gospel of Luke: "And the angel came in unto her [Mary], and said, Hail, thou that art highly favoured, the Lord is with thee: blessed [הברוכה] art thou among women" (Luke 1:28).

Thus far, we have found ELS encoded words naming virtually every one of the people involved with the crucifixion of Jesus, in addition to many others who were present during His remarkable life of ministry.

The Cross and the Passover Feast

In Isaiah 53:10, starting with the third letter in the second word and counting every fifty-second letter from right to left spells "cross," צלב. From the same word, taking the first letter and counting every 104th letter from right to left spells "Passover," פסח, as mentioned earlier. In Isaiah 52:14, starting with the third letter in the sixth word and counting every twenty-sixth letter from left to right spells "My Feast (my sacrifice)," *Chaggai,* חגי. The Feast of Passover, the Chaggai, when Jesus was crucified, occurred the day following the evening Passover Supper, when the Last Supper occurred.

The Time and Place of Christ's Crucifixion

Jesus was crucified on the day of the Passover Feast, which took place annually on the fifteenth of the Jewish month Nisan (also known as the month of Aviv). Mount Moriah, the Temple Mount, is the place where God supernaturally provided a ram as a substitute sacrifice in the place of Abraham's son Isaac. This was also the place where God commanded King David to prepare the site for the building of the Temple, which was ultimately built by his son Solomon. However, Mount Moriah is a long mountain ridge that begins in the south of Jerusalem and continues northward past the northern city walls to the site of Golgotha, the "place of the skull," where Jesus was crucified outside the city walls, just north of the Damascus Gate. The Book of Hebrews confirms the Gospel account that Christ's death took place outside the city walls: "Wherefore Jesus also, that he might sanctify the people with his own blood, suffered without the gate" (Hebrews 13:12). In Isaiah 52:1, starting with the third letter in the eighth word and counting every twenty-seventh letter from right to left spells *aviv ve'moriah*, אביב ומריה, which means "Aviv of Mount Moriah." This is an intriguing Bible Code discovery naming the actual month of Passover, "Aviv," and "Mount Moriah," the place of Christ's sacrifice for our sins as written by Isaiah centuries before the event. The adjacent letters spell *rosh*, ראש, which means "the first" or "the head of the year" (the first month of the religious year was the month Nisan-Aviv, the month of Passover), when Jesus was crucified.

"Let Him Be Crucified"

Two thousand years ago, the Gentile Romans and the Jewish leaders joined together to crucify Jesus of Nazareth. Every human being on earth was morally represented by the Gentile Romans and the Jewish leadership because Jesus died on the Cross for all of our sins. Matthew records the terrible moment when the Roman governor agreed to Christ's death. "Pilate saith unto them, What shall I do then with Jesus which is called Christ? They all say unto him, Let him be crucified" (Matthew 27:22). The prophet Isaiah foretold this tragic series of events seven centuries earlier. "He was taken from prison and from judgment: and who shall declare his generation? for he was cut off out of the land of the living: for the transgression of my people was he stricken" (Isaiah 53:8). Perhaps the most interesting code discovery in this passage is the fact that this exact phrase was encoded in Isaiah's prophecy. Starting with the second letter in the sixth word of Isaiah 53:8 and counting every fifteenth letter right to left spells "let Him be crucified" *yitz'tzahlaiv,* יִצְלַב.

Over one thousand years before the birth of Jesus, the psalmist David wrote his prophetic Psalm 22, which foretold the tragic crucifixion of Christ. David wrote of the future death of the Messiah: "The assembly of the wicked have inclosed me: they pierced my hands and my feet" (Psalm 22:16). Incredibly in Isaiah 52:10, we find the word "pierce" encoded. Starting with the third letter in the fifteenth word, which is "in His hands" בְּיָדוֹ, and counting every ninety-two letters from left to right spells "pierce," *dahkar,* דקר in reverse.

Can any reader have any remaining doubt that the Bible Codes identify Jesus of Nazareth as the prophesied Messiah who died for our sins as the Son of God?

The following is a chart summarizing the most important codes found in Isaiah's prophecy that name virtually everyone associated with the crucifixion of Jesus. This summary list was prepared as a convenience for the reader and as an aid for those students of the Scripture who wish to check out these Bible Codes for themselves.

Jesus and His Disciples Found Encoded in Isaiah 53

ELS Word	Begins	Word	Letter	Interval
Yeshua Shmi –				
Jesus is My Name	Isa. 53:10	11	4	(–20)
Nazarene	Isa. 53:6	11	3	(47)
Messiah	Isa. 53:11	1	1	(–42)
Shiloh	Isa. 53:12	21	4	(19)
Passover	Isa. 53:10	13	3	(–62)
Galilee	Isa. 53:7	1	2	(–32)
Herod	Isa. 53:6	4	1	(–29)
Caesar	Isa. 53:11	7	4	(–194)
Evil Roman city	Isa. 53:9	13	2	(–7)
Caiaphas—High Priest	Isa. 52:15	7	3	(41)
Annas—High Priest	Isa. 53:3	6	5	(–45)
Mary	Isa. 53:11	1	1	(–23)
Mary	Isa. 53:10	7	3	(6)
Mary	Isa. 53:9	13	3	(44)

The Disciples	Isa. 53:12	2	3	(−55)
Peter	Isa. 53:10	11	5	(−14)
Matthew	Isa. 53:8	12	1	(−295)
John	Isa. 53:10	11	4	(−28)
Andrew	Isa. 53:4	11	1	(−48)
Philip	Isa. 53:5	10	3	(−133)
Thomas	Isa. 53:2	8	1	(35)
James	Isa. 52:2	9	3	(−34)
James	Isa. 52:2	3	4	(−20)
Simon	Isa. 52:14	2	1	(47)
Thaddaeus	Isa. 53:12	9	1	(−50)
Matthias	Isa. 53:5	7	4	(−11)
Let Him Be Crucified	Isa. 53:8	6	2	(15)
His Cross	Isa. 53:6	2	2	(−8)
Pierce	Isa. 52:10	15	3	(−92)
Lamp of the Lord	Isa. 53:5	5	7	(20)
His Signature	Isa. 52:7	8	4	(49)
Bread	Isa. 53:12	2	3	(26)
Wine	Isa. 53:5	11	2	(210)
From Zion	Isa. 52:14	6	1	(45)
Moriah	Isa. 52:7	4	5	(153)
Obed	Isa. 53:7	3	2	(−19)
Jesse	Isa. 52:9	3	1	(−19)
Seed	Isa. 52:15	2	2	(−19)
Water	Isa. 52:7	9	1	(−19)
Levites	Isa. 54:3	3	6	(19)
From the Atonement Lamb	Isa. 52:12	12	2	(−19)
Joseph	Isa. 53:2	1	2	(210)

When my book *The Signature of God* and Yacov Rambsel's book *Yeshua* were published in 1996, hundreds of thousands of readers were thrilled with this new discovery about the Bible Codes. Many students of the Scriptures were especially fascinated with Yacov's research that revealed the encoded name of Jesus found in well-known messianic prophecies. However, a number of Bible Code researchers in Israel and North America, as well as Orthodox Jewish rabbis, have disputed the significance of this discovery of Yeshua's name. They have pointed out that the name *Yeshua*, יֵשׁוּעַ, is a relatively small word with only four Hebrew letters.

Some of these critics have contemptuously rejected the significance of the Yeshua Codes and declared that one could find the name *Yeshua* יֵשׁוּעַ in virtually any passage in Hebrew literature (from a novel to the Israeli phone book). However, these critics ignore the fact that the name *Yeshua* appears at very small ELS intervals (i.e., every fifth, ninth, or twentieth letter, etc.) in dozens of well known messianic prophecies. No one has found significant names of any other historic personalities (such as Mohammed, Napoleon, Alexander the Great) encoded repeatedly at small ELS intervals within dozens of Old Testament messianic prophecies.

One critic claimed on the Internet that the name of a false messiah "Rev. Sung Yung Moon" appears by accident frequently in these same messianic prophecies where Yacov found the ELS *Yeshua*. However, this is not true. While the three letter Hebrew word for "moon" naturally appears by accident frequently including a few occasional places near some of these messianic prophecies, the ELS word "moon" does not identify the Rev. Sung Yung Moon of South Korea, who formed the Unification Church. The encoded words do not reveal "Rev. Sung Young Moon" as the critics falsely imply; it is only the three-letter Hebrew ELS word for "moon" that appears frequently by accident as you would expect with any three letter word. This particular criticism is without merit.

A Challenge to the Critics of the Yeshua Codes

Yacov's discovery of more than forty names of individuals and places associated with the crucifixion of Jesus of Nazareth in Isaiah's "Suffering Servant" messianic passage is unprecedented. In my 1997 book *The Handwriting of God*[8] I issued a challenge to the critics who reject the Yeshua Codes to find any other passage of similar length (only fifteen sentences as in Isaiah 52:13 to 53:12) in Hebrew literature outside the Bible that contains forty meaningful ELS codes, including the names of Jesus, the Nazarene, Messiah, Passover, Herod, Mary, and the names of Christ's disciples, etc. If they cannot discover these names encoded in any passage outside the Bible, and we believe it will be impossible, we will have additional evidence that these codes about *Yeshua* the Nazarene, and His disciples, are truly unprecedented. To make the task easier for our critics, we challenge them to find any fifteen-sentence passage in any language or literature outside the Bible that contains forty or more ELS words related to people, places, and events concerning a historical event. If our critics can accomplish this feat, I will be willing to admit that our discoveries in Isaiah 53 are not as significant as we claim. Over six years ago I made this challenge. I am still waiting for their answer.

Is the Hebrew Name of Jesus
Yeshua, יֵשׁוּעַ, or Yeshu, יֵשׁוּ?

Some Jewish critics have claimed that the name *Yeshua*, יֵשׁוּעַ, is not the true name that Jesus of Nazareth used during His lifetime. They have claimed that the three-letter name *Yeshu*, יֵשׁוּ, which is often used by Jews today when referring to Jesus is the correct Hebrew name. Several Israeli critics of the Yeshua Codes have claimed on the Internet, "Yeshua is a recent, manipulative invention used to facilitate the proselytization of Jews." Some readers have written, "Jews say *Yeshu* and Messianic Jews say *Yeshua*."

Obviously, it is vital that we determine the correct and authentic Hebrew name of Jesus as used in the first century by Jews in Israel. The Jewish linguist Eliezer Ben-Yehuda was the man who recreated the ancient Hebrew language in the last century in Palestine. He began with the ancient Hebrew words used in the Bible and Temple worship and began to expand the vocabulary with new, modern words based on biblical Hebrew forms and rules of grammar. It is interesting to note that Ben-Yehuda discusses the name Jesus in the prolegomena to his Thesaurus to the Hebrew language, *Thesaurus Totius Hebraitatis*. According to a study on this subject by Prof. Kai Kjoer-Hansen in the magazine *Mishkan*, Ben-Yehuda refers to Jesus eight times, using the spelling *Yeshua* every time. While most Hebrew writing today in Israel uses the shorter name

Yeshu, through centuries of long habit, the historical evidence strongly supports the claim that the original Hebrew name of Jesus was *Yeshua*, יֵשׁוּעַ.

The great Jewish rabbi Moses Maimonides, known as Rambam (A.D. 1200), wrote about Jesus using the name *Yeshua*, יֵשׁוּעַ, in his *Epistle to Yemen* as well as in his monumental fourteen-volume study *Mishnah Torah*, which codified all of the religious laws from the Torah. In his volume entitled *The Laws of Kings and Their Wars*, which deals with the qualifications of the true Messiah, Rabbi Maimonides wrote about Jesus of Nazareth and spelled His name twice as *Yeshua*, יֵשׁוּעַ. He wrote: "Jesus of Nazareth who aspired to be the Messiah and was executed by the court was also [alluded to] in Daniel's prophecies."[9] The Hebrew word "Jesus" was spelled as follows: *Yeshua* יֵשׁוּעַ. I acquired an uncensored edition of Rambam's *Mishnah Torah* in a Jewish bookstore in Jerusalem several years ago. Most editions of the *Mishnah Torah* have been censored during the last eight hundred years and have the relevant passages that deal with Jesus of Nazareth removed. However, when the Jews of Yemen flew back to Israel in the 1950s they carried with them their rare uncensored copies of the Mishnah Torah that dated back to the original eleventh-century writings of Maimonides. Rabbi Eliyahu Touger translated and edited this volume, which was published by the Maznaim Publishing Corporation in New York and Jerusalem in 1987. Rabbi Touger wrote this footnote: "Though most published texts of the *Mishnah Torah* conclude this chapter with this paragraph, a large portion of the Rambam's text was censored and left unpublished. We have included the original text, based on the Yemenite manuscripts of *Mishnah Torah* and early uncensored editions."[10]

In light of this overwhelming evidence I believe we can have confidence that the name *Yeshua*, יֵשׁוּעַ, is the genuine Hebrew name of Jesus of Nazareth. The name of Jesus of Nazareth found in the Bible Codes is also spelled with four letters יֵשׁוּעַ *Yeshua*. In conclusion, the Bible Codes are a fascinating discovery that points to the divine inspiration of the Holy Scriptures. They are worthy of further study.

Notes

1. Grant R. Jeffrey, *Armageddon—Appointment with Destiny*, Toronto: Frontier Research Publications, Inc., 1988.
2. Yacov Rambsel, *Yeshua—The Name of Jesus Revealed in the Old Testament*, Toronto: Frontier Research Publications, Inc. 1997.
3. Yacov Rambsel, *His Name Is Jesus*, Toronto: Frontier Research Publications, Inc. 1998.
4. Statistical Significance Discovered in the Yeshua Codes Internet site: http://www.yfiles.com/yeshuacodes.html.
5. Statistical Significance Discovered in the Yeshua Codes Internet site: http://www.yfiles.com/yeshuacodes.html.
6. Yacov Rambsel, *Yeshua—The Name of Jesus Revealed in the Old Testament*, Toronto: Frontier Research Publications, Inc. 1998.
7. Yacov Rambsel, *Yeshua— The Name of Jesus Revealed in the Old Testament*, Toronto: Frontier Research Publications, Inc. 1998.
8. Grant R. Jeffrey, *The Handwriting of God*, Toronto: Frontier Research Publications, Inc. 1997.
9. Moses Maimonides, *The Laws of Kings and Their Wars*, translated by Eliyahu Touger, New York: Maznaim Publishing Corp., 1987, pp. 234-235.
10. Moses Maimonides, *The Laws of Kings and Their Wars*, translated by Eliyahu Touger, New York: Maznaim Publishing Corp., 1987, p. 235.

11

The Phenomenon of "Undesigned Coincidences"

Compelling evidence that the Scriptures are absolutely reliable and inspired by God is revealed in the phenomenon known as "undesigned coincidences." This phenomenon cannot be explained unless the inspired writings of Scripture are completely true.

Evidence of undesigned coincidences was first noted in 1738 by Dr. Philip Doddridge in his book *Introduction to the First Epistle to the Thessalonians.* Doddridge wrote:

> Whoever reads over St. Paul's epistles with attention...will discern such intrinsic characters of their genuineness, and the divine authority of the doctrines they contain, as will perhaps produce in him a stronger conviction than all the external evidence with which they are attended. To which we may add, that the exact coincidence observable between the many allusions to particular facts, in this as well as in other epistles, and the account of the facts themselves, as

they are recorded in the history of the Acts, is a remarkable confirmation of the truth of each.[1]

Dr. William Paley, author of the noteworthy book *Horae Paulinae*, was the first writer to fully develop the evidence regarding undesigned coincidences. Paley presented his evidence as proof that no human could have created the epistles of Paul without the divine aid of God Himself.[2]

However, the greatest evidence of this type was researched by Rev. J. J. Blunt, as is detailed in his book *Undesigned Coincidences in the Writings of the Old and New Testament*. As Blunt declared in his fascinating manuscript, the evidence from "instances of coincidence without design" provide an incredibly strong proof that the Scriptures were inspired by God.[3]

The evidence from coincidence is so strong that juries often convict defendants of serious crimes based on the same category of evidence. When we consider the books of the Bible, the evidence establishes that the individual writers acted as independent witnesses to the facts they observed and recorded. Further, the coincidences could not have arisen as a result of deliberate plotting or any mutual understanding among the biblical writers. Often the facts and evidence that coincidentally prove the accuracy of the Bible's narrative are found in obscure passages not connected with the main passage or the theme of the story being told.

The Rebellion of Absalom

One of the most tragic stories found in the Scriptures concerns the revolt of David's son Absalom toward the end of David's reign. Absalom was the third son born to David as a result of his marriage with Maacah, the daughter of Talmai, king of Geshur. This story often has been preached from the pulpit to remind us of the consequences of pride and blind ambition. God judged Absalom's rebellion, which resulted in his death. Many preachers also have reminded parents about David's complacency in failing to discipline his favorite son as he grew to manhood full of pride and arrogance.

The Scriptures record that "Absalom prepared him chariots

and horses, and fifty men to run before him" (2 Samuel 15:1). He stirred rebellion against his father by promising the people that he would rule in their favor when he became king of Israel. David's unwillingness to deal with his son's growing rebellion set the stage for Absalom's revolt against his father's throne. It also led to David's flight from Jerusalem and the bitter war against the rebels. Finally, the tragic moment came when David heard of his loyal army's victory over the rebels. He cried out in anguish, "Is the young man Absalom safe?" (2 Samuel 18:29). When the servants of the king mustered the courage to tell the truth, they admitted that Absalom was dead. David wept bitterly for the loss of his beloved son, crying out, "O my son Absalom, my son, my son Absalom! would God I had died for thee, O Absalom, my son, my son!" (verse 33).

The Bible records that, in the midst of the rebellion, "Absalom sent for Ahithophel the Gilonite, David's counsellor, from his city, even from Giloh, while he offered sacrifices. And the conspiracy was strong; for the people increased continually with Absalom" (2 Samuel 15:12). Ahithophel had been King David's counselor or prime minister for many decades. The book of 2 Samuel tells us that Ahithophel was brilliant: "And the counsel of Ahithophel, which he counselled in those days, was as if a man had inquired at the oracle of God: so was all the counsel of Ahithophel both with David and with Absalom" (16:23). In fact, when David learned that his trusted friend and counselor had betrayed him, he was so afraid of the danger from Ahithophel that he prayed, "O LORD, I pray thee, turn the counsel of Ahithophel into foolishness" (15:31). (Years earlier David had prophesied a double prophecy that foresaw the betrayal by Ahithophel. However, David's words also predicted the ultimate betrayal a thousand years later of Jesus of Nazareth by His friend and disciple Judas Iscariot: "Yea, mine own familiar friend, in whom I trusted, which did eat of my bread, hath lifted up his heel against me" [Psalm 41:9].)

The question that has troubled many Bible students and writers of commentaries is this: Why did Ahithophel, David's trusted counselor, immediately join Absalom's rebellion after a lifetime of faithful service to the king? Further, why would Ahithophel ask the young prince to allow him to personally lead the army of rebels to attack before King David could escape? "Moreover Ahithophel said unto Absalom, Let me now choose out twelve thousand men, and I will arise and pursue after David this night:…and I will smite the king only" (2 Samuel 17:1–2). Finally, why would Ahithophel advise Absalom to openly have sexual relations with his father's wives on the roof of the palace?

> And Ahithophel said unto Absalom, Go in unto thy father's concubines, which he hath left to keep the house; and all Israel shall hear that thou art abhorred of thy father: then shall the hands of all that are with thee be strong. So they spread Absalom a tent upon the top of the house; and Absalom went in unto his father's concubines in the sight of all Israel. (2 Samuel 16:21–22)

The Bible does not specify the motivation for this incredible betrayal of David, as if the reason had been so obvious to people living in that day that there was no need to comment on it.

Solving the Mystery of Betrayal

The answer to this mystery is found in several passages in the Old Testament that often cause readers to skip forward because the list of names recorded in the chapter seems to have little relevance to us. However, the solution to the puzzle of Ahithophel's motive does exist in the Word of God, and it reveals an important lesson that every follower of Christ needs to learn. To solve the mystery, we need to go back almost thirty years to the incident when David committed adultery with Bathsheba, the beautiful wife of Uriah the Hittite. Most commentators and preachers have discussed the sin of David as if it was the result of a momentary weakness when he happened to observe the woman bathing. The truth is somewhat different.

When David should have been at war, leading his troops against the enemy, the Scriptures record that he stayed in his palace in Jerusalem.

> And it came to pass, after the year was expired, at the time when kings go forth to battle, that David sent Joab, and his

servants with him, and all Israel; and they destroyed the children of Ammon, and besieged Rabbah. But David tarried still at Jerusalem. (2 Samuel 11:1)

David's first mistake was that he was not in the place God had called him to be: leading his nation against her enemies. As the evidence unfolds, we also will find that Bathsheba was no stranger to the king.

When you read the Scriptures carefully you will note that the passage describing Bathsheba tells us that she was the "daughter of Eliam" and "the wife of Uriah the Hittite" (2 Samuel 11:3). Another passage lists the great military heroes that guarded King David throughout his many battles against Saul, the Philistines, and other enemy nations. This list of the thirty-seven "mighty men" of David records that "Eliam the son of Ahithophel the Gilonite" and "Uriah the Hittite" were part of this elite force (2 Samuel 23:34, 39).

Now we can begin to understand what was taking place behind the scenes. Uriah the Hittite, the husband of Bathsheba, and Eliam, the father of Bathsheba, were not strangers to David. They knew one another well. They were friends who had fought shoulder to shoulder against their enemies over many years. They had sat together around the campfire at night during many military campaigns.

Bathsheba was married to Uriah, David's bodyguard. She was the daughter of Eliam, another faithful bodyguard. David was able to spy on her as she was bathing because Uriah had a house close to the king's palace. This was most likely a reward for his years of loyal service. It is very likely that Bathsheba, Uriah, and her father, Eliam, had attended royal banquets in David's palace.

The story of David's sin with Bathsheba takes on a very different complexion in light of these facts, which went unnoticed by Bible students for centuries. When David committed adultery with Bathsheba, he took the wife of Uriah, a loyal friend, and the daughter of another friend. When she became pregnant, David tried to get Uriah to visit his wife to cause confusion over when and how she became pregnant. But Uriah refused to spend the night with his wife, and David conspired with his general,

Joab, to murder Uriah to cover up David's shameful betrayal and adultery. Later, the prophet Nathan came to David and proclaimed God's anger against David's sins of adultery and murder. Nathan warned that David would be afflicted by warfare the rest of his life. Further, the prophet foretold that "by this deed thou hast given great occasion to the enemies of the LORD to blaspheme, the child also that is born unto thee shall surely die" (2 Samuel 12:14). Throughout history this prophecy was fulfilled as skeptics attacked the Bible and David's character by referring to his great sin with Bathsheba.

The Rest of the Story
Note that 2 Samuel 23:34 told us that Eliam, the father of Bathsheba, was the son of Ahithophel, David's counselor. Ahithophel, the prime minister, was Bathsheba's grandfather. After David sinned with Bathsheba and killed Uriah, many people in the palace and the army would have realized that David was the father of the child born to Bathsheba. (At that time people knew the length of a woman's pregnancy was nine months.)

As David's counselor, Ahithophel must have burned with rage to know his king had betrayed his granddaughter's honor and killed Uriah, her husband, who was a fellow soldier with Ahithophel's son Eliam. However, there was nothing he could do at that time to exact his revenge. If he had risen in anger against the king he would have lost his life. So he remained silent, keeping his thoughts to himself all the years that followed. But then he saw an opportunity to destroy David. The Arabs have an expression that a man who "seeks his revenge before forty years has passed has moved in haste."

Finally, David's son Absalom revolted against his aged father. This was Ahithophel's chance to get revenge for the wrongs committed years earlier against his family. He joined Absalom's conspiracy and offered to kill David personally. Finally, we can understand Ahithophel's strange advice to Absalom to have sexual relations with David's wives "in the sight of all Israel." He was attempting to get his revenge by encouraging Absalom to do the same thing to David's wives that the king had done to his granddaughter.

Significantly, as David fled from Jerusalem, a man named Shimei cursed the king and cast stones at him saying, "Behold, thou art taken in thy mischief, because thou art a bloody man" (2 Samuel 16:8). When David's men wanted to kill the man who uttered the curse, the king stopped them. David stated that the man was right and that God had told him to curse the king. David knew very well, as did the people around him, why Ahithophel had joined Absalom's revolt.

These verses provide clues and evidence that enable serious students of the Bible to solve the mystery of Ahithophel's betrayal. More important, the clues scattered in passages throughout the Old Testament provide overwhelming evidence in support of the truthfulness of the Bible's account of the life of King David. No one writing a story like this as fiction would hide the clues so well that the mystery of Ahithophel's betrayal could not be discovered for thousands of years. However, someone who is accurately recording a contemporary series of events often will fail to call attention to the motive for a person's actions because the motive is so obvious to the writer. The presence of coincidental evidence such as we find in this analysis provides strong proof that the biblical record is a faithful and reliable account of the events in question.

David's Response to His Sin

There is one further detail that should not be overlooked. While Bathsheba's newborn son was sick, David fasted and prayed that God would allow the child to live. However, after the child died, David stopped fasting and said, "But now he is dead, wherefore should I fast? can I bring him back again? I shall go to him, but he shall not return to me" (2 Samuel 12:23). In this touching scene, where the Bible assures us that children who die will go to heaven, we can see the difference between the way a man thinks about his sin and the way God deals with our sins. David had sinned in his weakness. He sincerely repented of his sins, as witnessed by his touching words of deep repentance in the psalms. His son had died as God had warned him through Nathan. David stopped fasting and prepared to carry on with the rest of his life, believing that his sin and its consequences were over forever.

This is the way most Christians think about their sins, not realizing they are only half right. When convicted of our sin, we sincerely repent and ask God to forgive us. The Lord forgives our sin, and we wrongly believe, like David, that the consequences of our sins are removed. However, although God truly forgives our sins, the consequences of our choices and actions are not obliterated. God will not stop the natural consequences of our sin from affecting our lives and the lives of those around us.

When we sin, it is similar to throwing a pebble into a pond. The ripples on the surface of the water are like the effects of our sinful actions. Those consequences radiate out and affect many things in our lives and in the lives of the people we know. Often the consequences cause great problems many years later. David thought his sin with Bathsheba was dealt with forever, but the tragic consequences eventually caught up with him and almost caused him to lose his life and the throne. At a time when David should have been enjoying his victories and honors, the consequences of his sin from years earlier almost destroyed him. David was forced to flee from the royal city, escaping up the side of the Mount of Olives in fear after the betrayal of his son and his closest counselor. It was the worst moment in his long life.

Christians often underestimate the lasting consequences of their sins. Sometimes Christians, when they are tempted to sin, begin to think like David. They feel that they can sin, then ask God to forgive their sin, and He will make everything perfect—as if their sin had never occurred. But our sins have natural consequences that will continue to destroy our bodies, our friendships, our families, and our careers years after God has forgiven us. While God does forgive, He does not change the law of cause and effect.

David and Goliath

At the time when David faced Goliath on the battlefield, the Jews were under the brutal domination of the Philistines. The army of Israel faced the army of the Philistines, but King Saul could not find an Israelite brave enough to engage the Philistines' giant in hand-to-hand combat. The outcome would determine who would dominate the land. And then God raised up a hero to defeat Goliath, the Philistine warrior.

There are a number of coincidences in this story that provide strong proof that it describes an actual battlefield engagement. Consider that the Bible mentions that Goliath comes from the village of Gath: "And there went out a champion out of the camp of the Philistines, named Goliath, of Gath, whose height was six cubits and a span" (1 Samuel 17:4). This detail is significant because Gath was one of the villages where the giant race of Anakims lived. When the Israelite spies returned from Canaan, as Moses and the people waited for their report, all but two reported they were fearful of the giant races that lived in the land: "And they brought up an evil report of the land which they had searched unto the children of Israel, saying, The land, through which we have gone to search it, is a land that eateth up the inhabitants thereof; and all the people that we saw in it are men of a great stature" (Numbers 13:32).

The book of Joshua tells us that Gath was one of the few places where the giant race of Anakim still survived.

> And at that time came Joshua, and cut off the Anakims from the mountains, from Hebron, from Debir, from Anab, and from all the mountains of Judah, and from all the mountains of Israel: Joshua destroyed them utterly with their cities. There was none of the Anakims left in the land of the children of Israel: only in Gaza, in Gath, and in Ashdod, there remained. (11:21–22)

The remnants survived in only three cities in Israel. This coincidence that, four hundred years after the conquest of Canaan, we find Goliath living in Gath, one of those three villages, is a marvelous confirmation of the truthfulness of the biblical record. Three books of the Bible—Numbers, Joshua, and 1 Samuel—confirm the accuracy of one of the elements in this famous biblical account.

One other feature in the story always fascinated me as a young boy. Why did David pick up five smooth stones for his sling when he knew that God would guide his aim to kill the Philistine giant with only one stone? Did David lack faith in God's power to destroy Israel's great enemy? The answer appeared one night when I was reading 2 Samuel 21. I found that Goliath was not the only giant in his family. Goliath's father was a giant who had five sons, all of whom fought for the Philistines. Every one of Goliath's four brothers ultimately died in combat against the brave soldiers of Israel. Summarizing the story of their death in combat, Samuel recorded, "These four were born to the giant in Gath, and fell by the hand of David, and by the hand of his servants" (2 Samuel 21:22). When David picked up five smooth stones for his sling, he was being prudent in preparing for the possibility that Goliath's brothers might join the battle after Goliath was killed.

Why Did Israel Not Use Horses?

I grew up on a ranch in Canada where my family ran a western-style Christian summer camp, Frontier Ranch, where we raised more than one hundred quarter horses. Some of my fondest memories are of when I would ride my horse along the abandoned logging trails and camp out in the forest. As one who loves horses, I always thought it strange that the Israelites never used horses in their battles against the pagan armies in their conquest of the Holy Land.

Why did the armies of Israel, prior to Solomon, not use horses to defend the nation against the cavalries of enemy armies? There are 188 references to horses throughout the Old Testament, proving that the Jews were well aware of the animals. The book of Job describes the glory and bravery of horses:

> Hast thou given the horse strength? hast thou clothed his neck with thunder? Canst thou make him afraid as a grasshopper? the glory of his nostrils is terrible. He paweth in the valley, and rejoiceth in his strength: he goeth on to meet the armed men. He mocketh at fear, and is not affrighted; neither turneth he back from the sword. The quiver rattleth against him, the glittering spear and the shield. He swalloweth the ground with fierceness and rage: neither believeth he that it is the sound of the trumpet. (39:19–24)

Archaeology has revealed that horses were commonly used in the armies and societies of all the ancient nations of the Middle East, with the exception of Israel, until the reign of Solomon (approximately 970 BC). The Ten Commandments prohibited the Jews from coveting an ox or ass, but there was no mention of horses: "Thou shalt not covet thy neighbour's house, thou shalt not covet thy neighbour's wife, nor his manservant, nor his maidservant, nor his ox, nor his ass, nor any thing that is thy neighbour's" (Exodus 20:17). According to Joshua 15:18, when the daughter of Caleb, a leader of Israel, came to visit Othniel, she rode a donkey. Throughout the book of Judges, we find evidence that donkeys rather than horses were the normal mode of transportation for Israelites. It also reveals that the governors of Israel rode upon white asses.

Later, we read of Saul searching for the lost donkeys of his father. In the passages of the Old Testament dealing with the period before the reign of Solomon, although the Jewish state trained very effective armies and won numerous wars in their conquest of Canaan, they never used horses for cavalry nor to pull war chariots. The only horses mentioned were those of the enemies of Israel, such as the nine hundred chariots of King Jabin of Canaan (Judges 4:2–3). In the Bible's description of the battle with the Philistines, when the enemy seized the ark of God, Israel lost thirty thousand infantry, but there was no mention of horsemen (1 Samuel 4:10–11). In the Scriptures' description of Absalom's battle against David, Absalom was killed when he rode his mule under the branches of a tree, proving that even Israel's princes did not ride horses in that time (2 Samuel 18:9).

Why did Israel refuse to use horses for their cavalry when foreign armies had the advantage of horsemen in their cavalries? The answer is found in a single command of God in Deuteronomy 17:16 forbidding the use of horses.

But he [the king] shall not multiply horses to himself, nor cause the people to return to Egypt, to the end that he should multiply horses: forasmuch as the LORD hath said unto you, Ye shall henceforth return no more that way.

The primary reason for God's prohibition of horses was the fact that Egypt was the world's premier source of breeding farms to produce war-horses. God knew that Israel would be tempted to enter into alliances with Egypt to acquire horses for their army. Therefore, the Lord prohibited the use of horses to ensure that Israel would not depend on an alliance with Egypt. Just as the United States and Russia use the supply of advanced weapons they offer to client states to lock them into defensive treaties, ancient nations could purchase Egyptian war-horses only if they entered into defensive treaties with Egypt. If Israel had acquired horses from Egypt, she would have been entangled in a foreign alliance rather than trusting in the power of God.

However, there is another reason. Israel was a nation of valiant soldiers who won remarkable battles against more powerful armies through the power of God. When they acknowledged that they won such battles through God's miraculous intervention, the Lord received the glory. War chariots with horses and cavalry were the equivalent of modern tanks in terms of warfare. By forbidding the Jewish state to acquire horses, God assured that the Israelites would be forced to fight defensive battles to protect the territory of the Holy Land. If the aggressive armies of Israel had gone into battle with the heightened mobility of war-horses, they would have been tempted to conquer foreign lands and nations far beyond the borders of the Promised Land. The coincidence that Israel never used horses in battle until the apostasy that followed Solomon's reign, without the biblical writers ever explaining their motive, provides a strong indication that the narrative is genuine and accurate.

The coincidences discussed in this chapter form a subtle kind of proof for the inspiration of the Scriptures. I have touched on only the tip of the iceberg of the biblical coincidences that we could examine. However, if you think about this evidence carefully, you will appreciate that the undesigned coincidences are absolutely consistent with a belief in God's direct inspiration of the Bible.

Notes

1. Philip Doddridge, *Introduction to the First Epistle to the Thessalonians* (London: Matthew and Leigh, 1738).
2. For more on this, see William Paley, *Horae Paulinae, or, The Truth of the Scripture History of Paul* (London: Davis, 1790).
3. For more on this, see J. J. Blunt, *Undesigned Coincidences in the Writings of the Old and New Testament* (London: John Murray, 1876).

12

The Evidence of the Men Who Wrote the New Testament

The Bible itself is an astonishing miracle. Written fragment by fragment over fifteen centuries, under all different states of society and in different languages, by persons of opposite tempers, talents, and conditions, learned and unlearned, prince and peasant, bond and free. These writers produced such great works in such diverse categories—history, prophecy, poetry, allegory, emblematic representation, proverbs, epistle, sermon, prayer, precept, and example—all types of rational discourse. And consider the subjects that are treated—the most difficult subjects—still the writers are not found to contradict one another in even the slightest way.

THOMAS MACAULAY

Outside what we learn from the Scriptures, we know almost nothing about the lives of the Jewish patriarchs, priests, and prophets who recorded God's revelations to humanity in the Old Testament. However, one of the unusual features of the Scriptures that proves it was inspired by God is that the writers of the Bible wrote as no men have ever written before or since. The natural tendency of writers in literature is to protect their reputations by disguising or minimizing their weaknesses and failures. But in contrast to these normal human motivations, the writers of the Bible reveal themselves "warts and all" throughout their manuscripts. Rather than minimize their mistakes, these writers revealed their total character, both weaknesses and strengths. This characteristic of the Scriptures provides compelling evidence that these men were inspired by God to record the words for eternity. The writers of the Gospels admit to many human weaknesses and failures, yet they changed the world through the supernatural power of God's Spirit.

The Lives of the Apostles

When we examine the lives of the writers of the New Testament, we find a considerable amount of historical evidence about them. Jesus Christ chose the twelve apostles whose role was to confirm by their words and lives the reality of the life, death, and resurrection of Christ. As a new faith, Christianity needed reliable eyewitnesses who could verify the facts regarding the life of Jesus of Nazareth. He commanded these fishermen and tax collectors to abandon their previous lives and follow Him to a destiny that would go far beyond any other people in history. Two thousand years later, millions of parents still name their sons after the apostles who followed Jesus and turned their world upside-down.

Christ's choice of disciples was not based on their previous character or accomplishments. None of them had risen to prominence in the society of first-century Israel. Jesus did not choose the type of men most modern leaders would enlist to undertake the overwhelming task of preaching a revolutionary message to the world. None of the twelve disciples were religious scholars or professional men of distinction. None of the disciples were wealthy; none were leaders within Jewish society. None of them demonstrated personal qualities that suggested they would become great men of faith. However, after only three and a half years in the daily presence of Jesus, they were transformed into great men of God. They would stand unflinching against the imperial power of Rome, the greatest power on earth in their lifetime.

Jesus apparently chose His disciples in the same manner that the sculptor Michelangelo chose the rough marble material for his projects. The artist saw the possibilities hidden within an uncut stone. According to one story about Michelangelo, a young girl watched the sculptor at work in Rome. As he chiseled into the huge block of marble, she asked him how he knew the figure of David lay hidden inside. The answer, of course, was that Michelangelo saw in his imagination the possibility of what the marble could reveal. All he needed to do was to remove the unnecessary material that hid the beautiful sculpture from the eyes of anyone but the master artist.

Jesus Christ chose His band of disciples not for what they were before He met them but for what they could become after the touch of the Master's hand. The truth of this statement is found in the gospel of John, which recorded Christ's words: "And when Jesus beheld him, he said, Thou art Simon the son of Jona: thou shalt be called Cephas, which is by interpretation, A stone" (1:42). The transformation of the character of the apostles was possibly the greatest miracle performed by Jesus during His years of ministry. These simple men, after living in the presence of Christ, revolutionized the world.

When Jesus entered history, the Roman Empire held more than half of the world's population of slaves, each one subject to his or her master's vilest abuse. Most of humanity lived as slaves or serfs under the brutality of Rome's mighty legions. Yet the life and teachings of Jesus, as expressed in the lives of these twelve men and others who took up the cross to follow Him, transformed the empire. Followers of Jesus ultimately would transform the wicked Roman Empire into the first society in history that would uphold the rights of men and women to live in freedom. In a similar manner, Jesus is still transforming the lives and characters of countless men and women who are turning their world right side up with His teachings. When we encounter Jesus Christ, the most important thing is not our previous history of sinful rebellion but the transformation that Christ will produce in us. Through His grace He can transform every one of us into someone who can make a difference in our world as witnesses of His power to save and transform lives.

One of the criteria by which we can judge the trustworthiness of the testimony of the apostles is whether they held firmly and consistently throughout their lives to their testimony about Christ's miracles, His claims to be God, and His death and resurrection. The combined testimony of their teachings, the history of their lives, and their martyrdom provide the strongest witness to the truthfulness of their story. After the arrest, trial, and death of Jesus, these men initially fled in fear. However, their characters were transformed by the power of the Holy Spirit. Historical records of the first century prove that every one of these men faced a martyr's death without denying their faith in Jesus Christ as their Savior. What could possibly account for their transformation from defeated cowards to mighty men of God within just a few days of the death of their leader? The only answer that makes sense is that these men were transformed in their character and motivation by their personal knowledge of the facts surrounding the resurrection of Jesus.

Some atheists have suggested that the disciples, during the decades following Christ's death, simply invented their accounts of Jesus. These critics say the disciples, in an attempt to enhance Christ's authority, published the story that Jesus claimed to be God and rose from the dead. However, any fair-minded reader will carefully consider the historical evidence.

The apostles were continually threatened and pressured to deny their Lord, especially as they faced torture and martyrdom. However, none of them chose to save his life by denying his faith. Consider the following hypothetical situation. Suppose these men had conspired to form a new religion based on their imagination. How long would any of them continue to proclaim something they knew was a lie when they were faced with lengthy torture and a painful death? To escape martyrdom, all they had to do was to admit they had concocted a lie. It defies common sense and the evidence of history that any person, let alone a small group of men, would persist in proclaiming a lie when he could walk away unscathed by admitting that it was a fraud.

Yet history reveals that not one of these men who knew Jesus personally ever denied his testimony about Christ. This proves that these men possessed an absolute, unshakable personal knowledge about the truth of the life, death, and resurrection of Jesus Christ.

The Martyrdom of the Apostles

Most of our information about the deaths of the apostles and Jesus' closest early disciples is derived from Church traditions. While tradition is unreliable as to small details, it very seldom contains outright inventions. Eusebius, the most important of the early Church historians, wrote a history of the Church in AD 325 and said, "The apostles and disciples of the Savior scattered over the whole world, preached the Gospel everywhere." Church historian John N. Schumacher researched the lives of the apostles and earliest leading disciples and recounted the history of their martyrdoms.[1]

- Matthew suffered martyrdom in Ethiopia and was killed with a sword.
- Mark died in Alexandria, Egypt, after being dragged by horses through the streets until he was dead.
- Luke was hanged in Greece as a result of his tremendous preaching to the lost.
- John faced martyrdom when he was placed in a huge basin of boiling oil during a wave of persecution in Rome. However, he was miraculously delivered from death. John was then sentenced to the mines on the prison island of Patmos, where he wrote the prophetic book of Revelation. The apostle John was later freed and returned to serve as bishop of Edessa in modern Turkey. He died an old man, the only apostle to die peacefully.
- Peter was crucified upside down on an X-shaped cross. According to Church tradition, he told his tormentors that he felt unworthy to die in the same way that Jesus Christ had died.

- James the Just was the leader of the church in Jerusalem. He was thrown from the southeast pinnacle of the Temple—a drop exceeding one hundred feet—after he refused to deny his faith in Christ. When they discovered that he survived the fall, his enemies beat him to death with a fuller's club. This was the same pinnacle where Satan had taken Jesus during the temptation.
- James the Greater, a son of Zebedee, was a fisherman by trade when Jesus called him to a lifetime of ministry. As a strong leader of the Church, James was beheaded at Jerusalem. The Roman officer who guarded James watched in amazement as the apostle defended his faith at his trial. Later the officer walked beside James to the place of execution. Overcome by conviction, he declared his new faith to the judge and knelt beside James to be beheaded as a Christian.
- Bartholomew also was known as Nathanael. He preached about the life, death, and resurrection of our Lord in present-day Turkey. Bartholomew was martyred for his preaching in Armenia, where he was flayed to death with a whip.
- Andrew, the brother of Peter, was crucified on an X-shaped cross in Patras, Greece. After seven soldiers whipped him, they tied his body to the cross with cords to prolong his agony. His followers reported that, when he was led toward the cross, Andrew saluted it with these words: "I have long desired and expected this happy hour. The cross has been consecrated by the body of Christ hanging on it." He continued to preach to his tormentors for two days until he died.
- The apostle Thomas was stabbed with a spear in India during one of his missionary trips to establish the Church in the Indian subcontinent.
- Jude was killed with arrows when he refused to deny his faith in Jesus Christ.
- Matthias, the apostle chosen to replace the traitor Judas Iscariot, was stoned and then beheaded.

- Barnabas, one of the group of seventy disciples, wrote the epistle of Barnabas. He preached throughout Italy and Cyprus. Barnabas was stoned to death at Salonica.
- The apostle Paul was tortured and then beheaded by Emperor Nero at Rome in AD 67. Paul endured a lengthy imprisonment, which allowed him to write epistles to the churches. These letters, which teach many of the foundational doctrines of Christianity, form a large portion of the New Testament.

The details of the martyrdoms of the disciples and apostles are found in traditional early Church sources. These traditions were recounted in the writings of the Church fathers and the first official Church history, written by Eusebius. Although we cannot now verify every detail, the universal belief of the early Christian writers was that each of the apostles, except John, faced martyrdom faithfully, without denying his faith in the resurrection of Jesus Christ. (The apostle John would have died in an attempt on his life, but God protected him. He later died of old age.)

The Transformed Lives of Men and Women

J. W. Alexander wrote, "The study of God's Word for the purpose of discovering God's will is the secret discipline which has formed the greatest characters."[2] Some of the greatest evidence proving the truth of the Bible is found in the transformed lives of men and women who place their trust in Jesus Christ. An abiding faith in the revealed Word of God strengthens people to rely on God in the face of the greatest trials. An unshakable faith in the Bible's revelation will enable us to stand against the greatest persecutions, just as Hebrews 11 records.

The Scriptures have held the undying attention of the most brilliant men of each age. An anonymous writer stated, "He who teaches the Bible is never a scholar; he is always a student." Tertullian, an early Church father living in the second century, devoted his life to the study of Scripture each day and night. By the end of his life, Tertullian had memorized most of the Bible, including the punctuation! A profound love of the Scriptures motivated Christians in those early centuries of persecution to walk in obedience to their Savior.

The great Church historian Eusebius wrote about a Christian whose eyes were burned out during one of the ten great waves of persecution against the early Church. Despite the loss of his eyes, this saint could repeat from memory large portions of the Bible to assembled Christians. Thomas Beza, the brilliant translator of the Scriptures in 1585, had such a profound love of the words of his Savior that, at the age of eighty, he could still repeat from memory all of the New Testament epistles in the original Greek. Two of the leading Reformers during the Protestant Reformation, Thomas Cranmer and Nicholas Ridley, found their faith immeasurably strengthened as both memorized the entire New Testament during the time of their persecution.

Dr. A. T. Pierson suggested that we should approach spiritual discovery much as the ancient Jews approached the Temple. The outer Court of the Gentiles is analogous to the letter of Scripture. The inner Court of the Israelites, a much holier place, is similar to the inner truth of Scripture. The Holy of Holies, the most holy place in the Temple, is equivalent to the person of Jesus Christ. It is only when we pass through the veil into the innermost Holy of Holies that we come to meet Him face to face.

The great men who founded the United States, including George Washington, were strongly influenced by their faith in the Word of God. Washington once declared, "It is impossible to rightly govern the world without God and the Bible." Abraham Lincoln, America's most beloved president, wrote about the Bible, "Read this book for what you can accept and take the rest on faith, and you will live and die a better man."[3]

Francis Bacon, the finest scientist in England in the sixteenth century, contributed much to the scientific study of nature. Bacon wrote a pivotal book, *The Advancement of Learning,* in which he called for a study to be made of Bible prophecy to systematically show how God had fulfilled the predictions made over thousands of years. Filled with wonder at the creation of the world, Bacon wrote, "Thy creatures, O Lord, have been my books, but thy Holy Scriptures much more. I have sought thee in the courts, fields and gardens; but I have found thee, O God, in thy sanctuary, thy temples." Although he acknowledged the awesome evidence about God revealed by science and nature, he discovered that the most profound knowledge of God was found in the inspired Word of God.

Many Christians have studied the Scofield Reference Bible. However, few are aware of the spiritual motivation that encouraged C. I. Scofield to embark upon the production of a study Bible complete with cross references and study notes to help students explore the biblical text. When he was a young Christian, Scofield noted that his friend C. E. Paxson had underlined related passages and marked his Bible with notes. Scofield was initially angry at the idea that someone would deface the Bible. However, he soon realized that these markings were extremely helpful to his friend and assisted his understanding of the relationship between various passages. In later life Scofield declared that the inspiration of his friend's Bible markings led him to prepare the exhaustive study notes and research presented in the now-famous Scofield Reference Bible.[4]

The Bible is a deep well that can never be exhausted by a student of the Scriptures. Those who preach constantly from the depths of God's Word always will have something fresh and meaningful to say to their hearers.

The Seven Wonders of God's Word

We all have heard of the Seven Wonders of the World. Yet for those who will examine the evidence, the Scriptures should hold an equal fascination. The Bible manifests Seven Wonders of the Word of God.

The Wonder of Its Formation

The marvelous manner in which the Scriptures grew from the first five books of Moses to include all thirty-nine books of the Old Testament and the twenty-seven books of the New Testament in the first century of our era is one of the greatest mysteries of the ages.

The Wonder of Its Unity

The Bible is a complete library composed of sixty-six books written by forty-four different authors over a period of sixteen hundred years. The authors came from different backgrounds—including kings of Israel, warriors, shepherds, poets, a physician, and fishermen. However, the Bible is the most unified book in the world, containing a progressive revelation of the message of God without any contradictions.

The Wonder of Its Age

The Bible is the most ancient book in the world, beginning with its first section of five books written by Moses thirty-five centuries ago. What other ancient writing is read daily by hundreds of millions of people who there find answers to their most immediate problems and concerns?

The Wonder of Its Sales

The Bible is the most popular book in the world, and its continuing sales year after year are the greatest wonder in the field of book publishing. The American Bible Society printed its two billionth Bible in 1976 and presented it to President Gerald Ford. Despite the phenomenal number of Bibles that exist, it continues to outsell every other book—with several hundred million in annual sales worldwide.

The Wonder of Its Popularity

Despite the fact that the Bible was written more than two thousand years ago in an Eastern literary style, the Bible remains the most intriguing book on earth. Every year the Bible is read by more than a billion adults and young people, representing every nation and class of people.

The Wonder of Its Language

The Scriptures were written in three languages—Hebrew, Aramaic, and Greek—by forty-four writers. Most of these writers were not well educated, nor did most of them know one another. Yet the wisest men of every age have acknowledged the Bible as the world's greatest literary masterpiece.

The Wonder of Its Preservation

No other book in history has suffered more opposition, hatred, and censorship—including book burnings. Yet after thousands of years of opposition, the Bible has not only survived, it has triumphed over emperors, kings, and dictators who sought to silence its message of salvation through the blood of Jesus Christ. Those who love the Bible will never find themselves without a faithful friend, a wise counselor, and the most effectual comforter of their souls.

The Bible's Transformation of Society

Did the Bible actually change society? The answer is yes! The early Christians startled the pagan Roman world with their altruism and unselfish care for the poor, sick, and dispossessed. Despite the overwhelming wealth of the Roman Empire and the pagan empires of Egypt, Babylon, and Assyria, there is no evidence from inscriptions or archaeology that these societies ever developed hospitals, housing for the poor, or any other provision for those in great need. Early Christians, however, manifested the love of Christ by caring for the sick and the needy out of a pure altruism that shocked the jaded Romans.

As a second dramatic example, let's examine the social situation in England before the evangelical revival led by John and Charles Wesley that saved England from a moral abyss. The situation faced by England in the early 1700s was virtually the same as the current moral collapse we see in North America. Bishop George Berkeley wrote in his 1738 book *Discourse Addressed to Magistrates and Men in Authority* that the level of public morality and religion had collapsed in Britain "to a degree that has never been known in any Christian country.... Our prospect is very terrible and the symptoms grow worse from day to day." Berkeley spoke of a torrent of evil in the land "which threatens a general inundation and destruction of these realms.... The youth born and brought up in wicked times without any bias to good from early principle, or instilled opinion, when they grow ripe, must be monsters indeed. And it is to be feared that the age of monsters is not far off."

Many different writers and observers—including Daniel

Defoe, Alexander Pope, and Samuel Johnson—confirm that England was at the point of moral collapse in the early 1700s. In the previous century the Church of England had severely suppressed other Christians through strict laws, such as the Act of Conformity, forbidding Nonconformist pastors (those not endorsed by the Church of England) from teaching or preaching. Many of the greatest preachers in England were driven out of their churches for refusing to accept these laws.

When the Great Plague of 1665 killed 20 percent of the population of London, everyone who could fled the city, including most of the government leaders and leaders of the Church of England. Many of the Nonconformist pastors returned to help the dying by preaching that the only hope was found in trusting Jesus Christ. Then the apostate government passed the infamous Five Mile Act, which prohibited any of the expelled clergy from approaching within five miles of their former church. As a result of this continuing persecution, the Puritans and other nonconforming Christians were driven from their churches. More than four thousand pastors were thrown into prison. Finally, in 1714, the Schism Act prohibited anyone from teaching without a license from his bishop. The result of the suppression of the free preaching of the Word of God was the descent of England into a morass of immorality, perversion, and a widespread moral collapse.

Thomas Carlyle's verdict on this society could easily fit the condition of North America today: "Stomach well alive, soul extinct." The writer Mark Pattison wrote about the state of morals in this period as the "decay of religion, licentiousness of morals, public corruption, profaneness of language—a day of rebuke and blasphemy." As the moral code broke down, with the teaching of the gospel repressed and the crime rate rising, the ruling classes demanded severe laws to restrain criminals. The moral debasement of England can be seen in its savage laws that showed no mercy toward those who violated them.

At a time when William E. Blackstone was writing about the glory of England's "unmatched Constitution," adults and children were subject to 160 different laws that resulted in hanging. If anyone shoplifted more than one shilling, stole one sheep, harmed a tree, gathered fruit from someone's property, or snared a rabbit on someone's estate, the person could be hanged. Evangelist Charles Wesley reported in his *Journal* that he preached in one jail to fifty-two people on death row, which included a ten-year-old child. Public drunkenness was so widespread that many adults and children died as alcoholics. Millions of children and women were working in appalling conditions in factories and mines with unbelievably low wages and no safety rules. England was a moral and spiritual wasteland. The name Ichabod, meaning "the glory of the Lord hath departed," was the epitaph that should be written over this shameful century of England's history.

Yet into this cesspool God sent the only hope for England: His holy Scriptures as preached by the greatest evangelists of that age—John and Charles Wesley. In 1769 John Wesley began the Sunday school movement that ultimately flourished throughout England. The Wesley brothers' preaching brought about a spiritual revolution in England and a return to a true faith in the Word of God and its laws. John Wesley's preaching of the whole Bible transformed an immoral state into a reformed nation. As he addressed three thousand people on one occasion, he declared these words from Isaiah 61:1–2:

> The Spirit of the Lord God is upon me; because the Lord hath anointed me to preach good tidings unto the meek; he hath sent me to bind up the brokenhearted, to proclaim liberty to the captives, and the opening of the prison to them that are bound; to proclaim the acceptable year of the Lord.

The incredible spiritual energy of this renewed preaching of the gospel of Christ produced a remarkable series of Christians, including John Milton and John Bunyan. Bible-based preaching and the work of committed Christians who devoted their lives to the Bible collectively transformed the soul of that nation. Their efforts produced a passion for righteousness and freedom that became the central principle of the evangelical renewal that saved England from moral corruption. John Wesley preached, "We know no Gospel without salvation from sin.... Christianity is essentially a social religion; to turn it into a solitary religion is indeed to destroy it."[5] The revival of Christianity under the Wesleys and other great preachers produced a practical religion that transformed every aspect of their world. Wesley declared that "a doctrine to save sinning men, with no aim to transform them into crusaders against social sin, was equally unthinkable."[6]

The revival in England spread across the English-speaking world and caused innumerable souls to turn to personal faith in Jesus Christ. In the *Edinburgh Review*, Thomas Macaulay characterized "the English Bible [as] a book which, if everything else in our language should perish, would alone suffice to show the whole extent of its beauty and power."[7]

In addition to the transformed lives of individuals, the evangelical revival transformed society. Many features of modern Western society that we take for granted today resulted from the great move of God produced by the Wesleys' revival. The imprisonment of debtors and children was made illegal. Schools were opened to every child who wanted to learn. Harsh penal laws and child labor in mines and factories ended. The evangelical movement created the first hope for prosperity and self-respect that the forgotten masses of England had ever known. Finally, the return to the Bible brought about the greatest religious transformation known in history. Universal free schools, charities, and free hospitals were formed by Christians who found their motivation in following the Savior who said, "Ye shall know the truth, and the truth shall make you free" (John 8:32).

Bishop Randall Davidson declared that John Wesley was "one of the greatest Englishmen who ever lived" and added that Wesley "practically changed the outlook and even the character of the English nation." In truth, it was the return to the Bible that transformed England from a moral wasteland into a land based on the Word of God and faith in Jesus Christ. The only hope for North America is a similar spiritual revival based on a return to the unchanging Word of God.

Notes

The epigraph to this chapter is paraphrased from the writing of Professor Thomas Macaulay and based closely on his original text in the January 1828 *Edinburgh Review.*

1. It is important to note that the apostle John should have died in an attempt on his life, but God protected him.
2. Clyde F. Lytle, ed., *Leaves of Gold: An Anthology of Prayers, Memorable Phrases, Inspirational Verse, and Prose from the Best Authors of the World, Both Ancient and Modern* (Fort Worth: Brownlow, 1948).
3. Abraham Lincoln, quoted in Frank S. Mead, ed., *The Encyclopedia of Religious Quotations* (Westwood, NJ: Revell, 1965).
4. Paul Lee Tan, ed., *Encyclopedia of 7700 Illustrations* (Hong Kong: Bible Communications, 1991).
5. John Wesley, quoted in Henry Carter, *The Methodist: A Survey of the Christian "Way" in Two Centuries* (London: Epworth, 1937), 174.
6. Carter, *The Methodist,* 174.
7. Thomas Macaulay, *Edinburgh Review,* January 1828.

13

The Final Decision Is Yours

In the final analysis, the evidence presented in this book regarding the authority and inspiration of Scripture should prove to any fair-minded reader that the Bible was truly inspired by God. This fact brings us to the place where there is one basic choice that each of us must make.

For those who still reject the Bible, there are only two possibilities: either Jesus Christ is wrong or you are. The suggestion that neither side of the issue is wrong or that it doesn't really matter is untenable. An attempt to delay a decision or to ignore the necessity of making a decision means you are avoiding the real issue. Each of us must decide if we will personally accept or reject the truth about Jesus Christ that is revealed in the Word of God. Your answer to this question will determine your joy in this life and your eternal destiny in either heaven or hell.

The Bible tells us, "Believe on the Lord Jesus Christ, and thou shalt be saved, and thy house" (Acts 16:31). The clear message of the Scriptures is that our personal relationship to Jesus Christ will determine our eternal destiny—either heaven or hell. God never told us, "Believe in the Bible and you shall be saved." The demons of hell know that the Scriptures are true, but this knowledge does not save them.

The Coming Kingdom of God

The Scriptures tell us that at the end of this age there will be a generation living in the Tribulation period that will endure the greatest evil ever unleashed by Satan. The wrath of God will be poured out on unrepentant sinners during that unprecedented seven-year period. Satan will be unleashed to attempt his final rebellion against almighty God. Satan will wage a relentless campaign to establish his own kingdom throughout the earth under the rule of his personal representative, the Antichrist. However, these same Scriptures assure us that Jesus Christ will return from heaven at the moment the earth faces its final crisis, and He will defeat the armies of the Antichrist and save humanity from destruction. The Lord will defeat Satan after the terrible seven-year Tribulation, but two-thirds of humanity will have died in horrific wars, famines, and plagues during that time.

This final trial of humanity will end triumphantly with the glorious return of Christ from heaven with an army of angels and the saints of all the ages. When Christ finally defeats the evil leaders of the world, He will establish His righteous government throughout the world. The sound of gunfire will be silenced forever, the terror of torture chambers will be destroyed, the horror of starvation and plague will be removed, and the fear of violence and abuse will be lifted from the hearts of men and women. Humanity finally will experience true peace under the kingdom of the Messiah, Jesus Christ.

The Nature of God

What is the nature of God, the One who inspired the writers of the Bible? For thousands of years people in every culture and society have attempted to imagine the nature of God. They have created God in their own image or in the image of the sun, moon, stars, earth, and a hundred other objects. Regardless of their philosophical speculations about the divine intelligence that created our universe, humans will never be able to find the truth about God unless they are willing to accept God's written revelation. The Bible, from Genesis to Revelation, reveals the nature of God as a loving, holy, powerful personality who is vitally interested in the life and destiny of everyone on earth.

Years ago, philosophers assigned the name First Cause to describe the intelligent supernatural power that must have created the universe. Someone once analyzed the nature of the First Cause by comparing the nature of the First Cause, the Creator, and the nature of the universe.

The First Cause of limitless space must be infinite in extent.

The First Cause of endless time must be eternal in duration.

The First Cause of perpetual motion must be omnipotent in power.

The First Cause of unbounded variety must be omnipresent in phenomena.

The First Cause of infinite complexity must be omniscient in intelligence.

The First Cause of consciousness must be personal.

The First Cause of feeling must be emotional.

The First Cause of human will must be volitional.

The First Cause of ethics must be moral.

The First Cause of religious values must be spiritual.

The First Cause of beauty must be aesthetic.

The First Cause of righteousness must be holy.

The First Cause of justice must be just.

The First Cause of love must be loving.

The First Cause of life must be alive.

The First Cause of all things, the Creator, must be infinite, eternal, omnipotent, omnipresent, omniscient, personal, emotional, volitional, moral, spiritual, aesthetic, holy, just, loving, and alive. When we examine the nature of God as revealed throughout the Holy Scriptures, we discover that the holy nature of God is precisely as described above.

Your Final Decision

The decision you make regarding whether the Bible is the inspired Word of God is vital. It is the one decision that will affect every other area of your life. If the Bible is true, then each one of us is accountable to Jesus Christ, who will judge each of us at the end of our life. However, if the Bible is not the inspired Word of God, we can safely ignore its commands and its warnings about heaven and hell. In the absence of the Word of God, those who search for ultimate truth are like a person searching in a strange country for a hidden treasure without the assistance of a map or a guide.

After a careful examination of the evidence, any fair-minded reader can see that only a supernatural intelligence could have produced the Scriptures. The Bible contains scientific, archaeo-logical, and historical information that could not have been pro-duced by humans unless God directed them to write the actual words. However, there are many people who still refuse to acknowledge the evidence for inspiration. For them, it is not a problem of belief. Rather, it is their lack of willingness to accept information that challenges long-held assumptions. While such people can see the evidence that supports the Bible, they can't bring themselves to accept the inevitable conclusion because they would have to abandon their agnosticism. The problem is not that they can't believe the evidence; the problem is that they will not believe the evidence, no matter how powerfully the evi-dence points to the authorship of the Scriptures by God Himself.

Many who reject God and the Bible have invested so much in their declared position that they refuse to weigh the clear evi-dence. When confronted with proof that the Bible is inspired by God, they are threatened because it requires them to think seri-ously about God and their responsibility to Him. Many people have avoided thinking seriously about Jesus Christ and eternity by hiding behind their denials of the authority of the Bible. How-ever, in light of the fascinating evidence provided in this book, every one of us needs to consider the implications.

If the Bible is the Word of God, then every one of us will stand before Jesus Christ at the end of our life to answer for our sins. On that day, those who accepted Christ's payment for the debt of their sins through His sacrifice on the cross will know that their sins have been forgiven. Their destiny will be to live with God forever in heaven. However, those who rejected Christ's salvation and the hope of heaven as presented in the Scriptures will have to bear their own punishment. They will be exiled to hell forever.

The powerful evidence in this book proves the Bible is the Word of God, which provides us with a confidence that we can believe this statement of the apostle Peter: "Neither is there salvation in any other: for there is none other name under heaven given among men, whereby we must be saved" (Acts 4:12). Peter's declaration that there is no salvation without Jesus Christ runs counter to the natural human inclination to believe that all religions are equally true. Many in our society believe that if a person is sincere, God will allow that person to enter heaven. However, the Word of God declares that sincerity is not enough. If you are sincere in your faith but have chosen to place your faith in a false religion, then you are sincerely wrong.

There is only one way to reconcile ourselves to a holy God. The path to salvation is through personal repentance of our sins and placing our complete faith in Christ's sacrificial death. Every one of us has rebelled against God through our personal sins: "For all have sinned, and come short of the glory of God" (Romans 3:23). The Scriptures declare that our sinful rebellion alienates each of us from the holiness of God and prevents us from entering heaven unless our sins are forgiven. "For the wages of sin is death; but the gift of God is eternal life through Jesus Christ our Lord" (Romans 6:23). The death of Jesus Christ on the cross is the key to bringing us to a place of peace. The death of our old nature when we identify with Christ's death is the key to finding peace with God. The only way we can be filled with the grace of God is to approach Him as we would bring a container to a well: it must be empty. It is only then that God can begin to fill us with His grace and Spirit.

God can't simply ignore our sin. If we reject God and His grace, He has no choice but to reject us. God's absolute justice makes it impossible for Him to ignore our sins. God's holiness demands that death is the only acceptable payment for the "wages of sin," and those wages must be paid for His justice to be satisfied (see Romans 6:23).

If unrepentant sinners could enter heaven without repenting, their presence in the holy New Jerusalem would turn that portion of heaven into hell. If you think carefully about it, sinners who reject the forgiveness and worship of Jesus Christ would not want to live in heaven. They would despise the worship of God. The sacred nature of a holy heaven and the evil nature of sin make it impossible for God to forgive anyone's sins unless that person wholeheartedly repents and turns from his or her sins. Only then can God forgive and transform a person into a sinner who has been saved by the grace of Jesus Christ. The cleansing of our souls requires the spiritual application of the blood of Christ to our hearts.

The Way to Salvation

The gospel of John records the answers Jesus gave to Nicodemus, one of the religious leaders of Israel, who asked Him about salvation: "Ye must be born again" (3:7). Jesus explained to Nicodemus, "Whosoever believeth in him [the Son of Man, that is, Jesus Christ] should not perish, but have eternal life. For God so loved the world, that he gave his only begotten Son, that whosoever believeth in him should not perish, but have everlasting life" (verses 15–16). Every sinner stands condemned by God because of his sinful rebellion against God's commandments. Jesus said, "He that believeth on him [God's Son] is not condemned: but he that believeth not is condemned already, because he hath not believed in the name of the only begotten Son of God" (verse 18).

Your decision to accept Christ as your personal Savior is the most important decision you will ever make. It will cost you a great deal to live your life as a committed Christian. Many people will challenge your new faith. The British writer John Stuart Mill wrote about the importance of our belief in Christ: "One person with a belief is equal to ninety-nine people who only have opinions." However, the Lord Jesus Christ asks His disciples to "follow me." That decision and commitment will change your life forever. Your commitment to Christ will unleash His supernatural grace and power to transform your life into one of joy and peace beyond anything you have experienced. While the commitment to follow Christ will cost a lot, it will cost you *everything* if you are not a Christian at the moment when you die.

Jesus challenges us with these words: "For what shall it profit a man, if he shall gain the whole world, and lose his own soul?" (Mark 8:36).

If you are a Christian, I challenge you to use the evidence in this book when you witness to your friends, family members, and co-workers about your faith in Christ. The proof that the Bible is inspired by God will not convince people to place their faith in Jesus Christ. Nevertheless, the evidence proving the Bible's inspiration may remove the intellectual barriers that many people have raised against seriously considering the claims of Christ. Once they acknowledge Scripture's authority, they can begin to consider whether they want to accept Christ as their Savior.

If you have never accepted Christ as your Savior, the evidence provides proof that God inspired the writers of the Bible to record His message to humanity. The Scriptures reveal that every one of us will be judged by God as to whether we have accepted the gift of salvation and forgiveness offered by His Son, Jesus Christ. Will you accept Him as your personal Savior and find peace with God throughout eternity, or will you reject Him forever?

You have seen the evidence. The final decision is yours.

Acknowledgments

This book is a new, revised edition of the original *The Signature of God*, first published in 1996, which has sold more than five hundred thousand copies in twenty-four languages.

Many of the greatest scholars in the last two thousand years have explored the Scriptures and concluded that they are truly inspired by God. During the last few decades, I completed many research trips to the Middle East and Europe. In addition, I acquired numerous old and often rare books written by great men of God from past generations. These volumes contain tremendous archaeological, historical, and scientific evidence that confirms the inspiration and authority of the Word of God. I am greatly indebted to the work of countless Bible scholars who labored to uncover the wealth of evidence that proves the inspiration of the Scriptures. The Internet and major libraries provided invaluable assistance as I completed my research, which establishes that the Bible is the inspired Word of God.

This book is the result of forty years of research involving thousands of books, Bible commentaries, and countless hours of detailed study of the Scriptures. As this book demonstrates, our faith and hope for the future is grounded upon a strong conviction in the inspiration of the Scriptures and a confidence in the promises of Jesus Christ to return and establish His kingdom.

My parents, Lyle and Florence Jeffrey, inspired me through

their lifelong commitment to Bible study. Their profound love for Jesus Christ and the prophetic truth of the Scriptures regarding His Second Coming motivated their lifetime of ministry. Special thanks to my editorial assistant, Adrienne Jeffrey Tigchelaar, whose excellent editorial services provided invaluable assistance.

I dedicate *The Signature of God* to my loving wife, Kaye. She continues to inspire my research and writing as well as being my faithful partner in our ministry. Without her encouragement and constant assistance, this book would never have been completed. I trust that the research revealed in these pages will inform, inspire, and encourage you to personally study the Bible. If this book renews in the hearts of my readers a new love and appreciation for the Word of God, I will be well rewarded.

Dr. Grant R. Jeffrey
Toronto, Ontario
October 2009

Selected Bibliography

Aigrain, René, and Omer Englebert. *Prophecy Fulfilled: The Old Testament Realized in the New.* Translated by Lancelot C. Sheppard. New York: McKay, 1958.

Anderson, Robert. *Human Destiny.* 1887. Reprint, London: Pickering & Inglish, 1913.

Aviezer, Nathan. *In the Beginning…: Biblical Creation and Science.* Hoboken, NJ: Ktav, 1990.

Bentwich, Norman. *Fulfilment in the Promised Land, 1917–1937.* London: Soncino, 1938.

Blomberg, Craig L. *The Historical Reliability of the Gospels.* Downers Grove, IL: InterVarsity, 1987.

Blunt, J. J. *Undesigned Coincidences in the Old and New Testament.* London: John Murray, 1876.

Bright, John. *The Authority of the Old Testament.* Grand Rapids: Baker, 1967.

Cobern, Camden M. *The New Archeological Discoveries and Their Bearing upon the New Testament and upon the Life and Times of the Primitive Church.* 9th ed. London: Funk & Wagnalls, 1929.

Finegan, Jack. *Archaeological History of the Ancient Middle East.* New York: Dorsett, 1979.

Gaussen, Louis. *The Divine Inspiration of the Bible.* Translated by David D. Scott. 1841. Reprint, Grand Rapids: Kregel, 1971.

Greenblatt, Robert B. *Search the Scriptures: Modern Medicine and Biblical Personages.* 2nd ed. Philadelphia: Lippincott, 1968.

Josephus, Flavius. *Antiquities of the Jews.* Translated by William Whiston. Grand Rapids: Kregel, 1960.

Keith, Alexander. *Christian Evidences: Fulfilled Bible Prophecy.* Minneapolis: Klock & Klock, 1984.

Little, Paul E. *Know Why You Believe.* 3rd ed. Downers Grove, IL: InterVarsity, 1988.

Manniche, Lise. *An Ancient Egyptian Herbal.* London: British Museum, 1993.

Maspero, G. *History of Egypt, Chaldea, Syria, Babylonia, and Assyria.* 13 vols. London: Grolier Society, 1900–06.

McDowell, Josh. *Evidence That Demands a Verdict: Historical Evidences for the Christian Faith.* Arrowhead Springs, CA: Campus Crusade for Christ, 1972.

McMillen, S. I. *None of These Diseases.* Rev. ed. Old Tappan, NJ: Revell, 1984.

Morris, Henry M. *The Bible and Modern Science.* Chicago: Moody, 1951.

———. *The Biblical Basis for Modern Science.* Grand Rapids: Baker, 1984.

———. *Many Infallible Proofs: Practical and Useful Evidences of Christianity.* San Diego: Creation-Life, 1974.

———. *Remarkable Record of Job: The Ancient Wisdom, Scientific Accuracy, and Life-Changing Message of an Amazing Book.* Grand Rapids: Baker, 1988.

———, ed. *Scientific Creationism.* 2nd ed. El Cajon, CA: Master Books, 1985.

Petrie, W. M. Flinders. *Seventy Years in Archaeology.* New York: Holt, 1932.

Rambsel, Yacov A. *Yeshua: The Name of Jesus Revealed in the Old Testament.* Nashville, TN: Word, 1996.

Rappaport, S. *History of Egypt from 330 B.C. to the Present Time.* 3 vols. London: Grolier Society, 1904.

Rawlinson, George. *History of Herodotus.* 4 vols. London: Murray, 1875.

Richards, Lawrence O. *It Couldn't Just Happen: Faith-Building Evidences for Young People.* 1987. Reprint, Dallas: Word, 1989.

Robinson, Gershon. *The Obvious Proof.* London: CIS, 1993.

Rosner, Fred. *Medicine in the Bible and the Talmud: Selections from Classical Jewish Sources.* Hoboken, NJ: Ktav, 1995.

Rule, William Harris, and John Corbet Anderson. *Biblical Monuments.* 4 vols. Croydon: Werteimer, Lea, 1871–73.

Sayce, A. H., ed. *Records of the Past: Being English Translations of the Ancient Monuments of Egypt and Western Asia.* 6 vols. London: Bagster & Sons, 1889–93.

Siculus, Diodorus. *Library of History,* Books 1–2.34. Translated by Charles H. Oldfather. Cambridge, MA: Harvard University Press, 1993.

Smith, George Adam. *The Historical Geography of the Holy Land, Especially in Relation to the History of Israel and the Early Church.* 2nd ed. London: Hodder and Stoughton, 1894.

Stanley, Arthur Penrhyn. *Sinai and Palestine, in Connection with Their History.* London: Murray, 1905.

Stone, Michael E., ed. *The Armenian Inscriptions from the Sinai.* Cambridge, MA: Harvard University Press, 1982.

Stoner, Peter W. *Science Speaks: An Evaluation of Certain Christian Evidences.* Chicago: Moody Books, 1963.

Thompson, J. A. *The Bible and Archaeology.* Rev. ed. Grand Rapids: Eerdmans, 1972.

Unger, Merrill F. *Archaeology and the Old Testament.* Grand Rapids: Zondervan, 1954.

Varghese, Roy Abraham, ed. *The Intellectuals Speak Out About God: A Handbook for the Christian Student in a Secular Society.* Chicago: Regnery Gateway, 1984.

Vermes, Geza, ed. *The Dead Sea Scrolls in English.* 4th ed. Baltimore: Penguin Books, 1995.

———. *Discovery in the Judean Desert.* New York: Desclee, 1956.

Vos, Howard, ed. *Can I Trust the Bible?* Chicago: Moody, 1963.

Wilson, Bill, comp. *The Best of Josh McDowell: A Ready Defense.* San Bernardino, CA: Here's Life, 1990.

Wood, Percival. *Moses: The Founder of Preventative Medicine.* London: Society for Promoting Christian Knowledge, 1920.

Printed in the United States
by Baker & Taylor Publisher Services